Western Frontiersmen Series
XX

"If Edward F. Beale had been a Massachusetts man, his services to his country would have teemed the papers with his exploits, his daring and his usefulness. Still the people are neglectful of the courage, hardihood and suffering of the man who traversed this continent amid every conceivable danger from disease, the elements, and bands of ruthless savages to prepare a way for new cities and states and greater power and influence for our Republic."

The Philadelphia *Press*
October 15, 1859

Quarterdeck & Saddlehorn

The Story of Edward F. Beale

1822-1893

by Carl Briggs

and

Clyde Francis Trudell

THE ARTHUR H. CLARK COMPANY

Glendale, California

1983

Dedicated to
DELORAS H. BRIGGS
and
MARTHA C. TRUDELL

Contents

Illustrations

Preface

This account of the life of Edward Fitzgerald Beale is based entirely upon the evidence of historical records and upon reasonable deduction from that evidence. It is factual throughout. Historical references are sufficiently well described in the narrative to be identified by scholars without the need for footnotes. Newspapers and other periodicals are acknowledged in the text. All other sources are listed in the bibliography.

I have used the current spelling of certain venerable words — dispatch for despatch, as an example — and the modern designation of geographical locations and landmarks. Mohave and Mojave are used interchangeably according to government cartographic policy and common local practice: Mohave for the Arizona and Colorado River region, including the Indians of that name; Mojave for California names.

In all respects the intention throughout the story is to offer the reader clarity, comprehension and readability without sacrificing historical integrity.

My co-author, Clyde Francis Trudell, died in 1978 after more than a dozen years of dedicated search into the life and times of Edward Beale. I have been permitted to add the fruits of his labor to ongoing studies of my own covering the same era. This work is the result of our combined efforts. I hasten to emphasize that the volume at hand could not have come from my pen without the prior research of Clyde Trudell.

In his manuscript notes Mr. Trudell expressed a wish to acknowledge certain individuals and organizations for providing specific assistance: The National Archives; The National Trust for Historic Preservation; Dr. Elliott Evans, Society of California Pioneers; Irene Simpson Neasham, Wells Fargo History Room; Mrs. M. K. Swingle and Peter Evans, California Historical Society; Robert Becker and the staff, Bancroft Library; Allan Ottley, California State Library; Richard Dillon, Sutro Library; Bert Fireman, Arizona Historical Foundation; Rutherford Goodwin, Colonial Williamsburg; Jane Augusta Burch, Hitching Post Hill; Dr. W. N. Davis, California State Archives; Mrs. M. C. Merriman, Placerville; Professor Edward Ott; Sylvia Arden, San Diego Historical Society; Harlan D. Fowler; Dwight L. Clarke; Dennis M. Alward; Dennis G. Casebier; Charles St. George Pope; and Evan Randolph III.

I am no less obligated and equally grateful for the energy and good will of others. During final research and the writing phase of this work I consulted several of the individuals and institutions listed above and I wish to add my own thanks to those of Mr. Trudell. In addition, I extend my warmest gratitude to Dr. Arlen J. Hansen, University of the Pacific; Dr. Eugene K. Chamberlin, San Diego; William B. Secrest, Fresno; Lester Cole, Los Angeles; Duff Chapman, Jackson; William B. Clark, California Division of Mines and Geology; Pamela Herr, Palo Alto; Sidney Davidson Platford, Arcadia; Dr. Albert Shumate, San Francisco; and Frau Hofrat Anna Benna, Austrian National Archives, Vienna.

My special thanks for valuable aid is also extended to Earl F. Schmidt; Dr. R. Coke Wood and Dr. James Shebl and staff of the Stuart Library, University of the Pacific; staff of the Nevada State Historical Society, Reno; staff of the Huntington Library, San Marino; Marshall Fey; Ted Wurm; staff of the Steinbeck Library, Salinas; Martha R. Stewart, Utah Division of State History; Alan Wilson; William Gordon Huff; Paul Ogden; Russell Briggs; and Art Richter, Fort Tejon State Park.

Carl Briggs
Salinas, California

I

The Schooling of a Midshipman

A trim warship under a cloud of sail approached the California coast, twenty-three days out of Honolulu and racing with the wind for Monterey. Summer fog hung in a dense bank along the Pacific shore. It formed a screen several hundred feet high, grey and heavy in its bulk and black as mortal sin in its undershadow. It extended north and south as far as a seaman's weather eye could range, creating a barrier that might as well have been a stone wall between the vessel and her intended landfall in Monterey Bay. The fog would creep toward land that night, smothering the rocky points, invading the bay itself and obliterating the anchorage in the little cove at the south end.

The order came to shorten sail. The ship turned gracefully into the wind, well outside the bay. Landfall would have to wait. She'd ride out the night at sea and look for clear sailing in the morning.

Inside the bay, three fighting ships stood motionless a few hundred yards from a curved beach fronting the town of Monterey. They were anchored in a line of battle so their broadside guns could rake shore and village on one side and approaching vessels on the other. Fog to seaward provided a measure of security for the little fleet as long as the grey curtain remained closed. Eyes would look sharply to the horizon when the next morning's sun burned away the mist. Men of the sea know that a rising fog might with fatal suddenness reveal a silent enemy standing in close with gun ports open and decks cleared for action.

Mid-morning the next day, July 15, 1846, the great shroud lifted enough for the ship waiting off the coast to begin her cautious way into the wide spooned-out hollow of Monterey Bay. She ghosted past Point Pinos in the dissipating mists. Her lookout high in the yards spied the ordered masts of the three vessels in the cove. Other lookouts on those ships and ashore cried her sail at nearly the same time. Anxious moments passed, then a cheer went up. Seamen crowded the rails of the anchored ships to watch the arriving vessel.

This small fleet constituted half the United States Navy's Pacific Squadron, commanded by Commodore John Drake Sloat. Close by Sloat's flagship, the frigate USS *Savannah,* stood the sloops-of-war *Cyane* and *Levant.* The United States and Mexico were at war. Sloat had deployed his ships in battle readiness to ward off a British fleet expected to enter Monterey Bay at any moment. The British were as opposed as Mexico to the American presence in California.

The incoming ship was the USS *Congress,* a 44-gun frigate under the command of Commodore Robert Field Stockton. She rode in smartly on the long Pacific swell. Thirteen guns boomed out across the water in salute to Commodore Sloat. The thunderous reports echoed off the green, forested hills behind the town. Clouds of white smoke billowed over the bay. The *Congress* rounded under the *Savannah's* stern and came to anchor while the squadron band on the *Savannah* struck up "Hail Columbia!"

The cannon fire put to flight every gull within a mile. Their screeching added cacophonic harmony to the brassy blare of the band. The birds wheeled in intersecting circles around and between the masts of the new arrival. The sky cleared. Morning sun reflected brightly on the water. Flags fluttered in a light breeze as seamen on all four ships waved and shouted back and forth.

A young Midshipman stood near Commodore Stockton at the quarterdeck rail of the *Congress,* taking his first look at California, a land he would love, serve and call home for much of his lifetime. He was about to begin certain hazardous commissions and appointments that would directly involve him in the American conquest of California, the course of settlement in the West and the vital fashioning of his nation's destiny. His name was Edward Fitzgerald Beale. We shall come to know something of the character and purpose of this man, and of the intensity of his labors, for his was a distinguished contribution.

Edward Beale's maternal grandfather, Commodore Thomas Truxtun, was a noted American Naval hero. His father, George Nancrede Beale, served on an American warship against the British in the battle of Lake Champlain in 1814. Beale, in fact, could claim relationship through complex family ties to an illustrious succession of Naval officers and men prominent in American history. His head always seemed turned toward the sea.

He was born to George and Emily Truxtun Beale on the fourth day of February, 1822, on the family farm called Bloomingdale in the District of Columbia. His early life was stimulated by an almost continual parade of young naval officers invited to Bloomingdale by his father — cousins, friends of the family, friends of friends. His mother mended their clothes. She tidied them up and provided a home away from home until they were ordered back on duty. Ned, as his family and friends called him, heard many youthful boasts, many tales of the sea.

Ned and his older brother Truxtun enrolled at Georgetown College in 1832. Both boys dropped out in 1835 after their father's death. That was the extent of their formal institutional education. Ned spent part of his boyhood at his mother's family home in the Quaker town of Chester, Pennsylvania.

A Beale family story describes Ned once engaging in a fight with another boy on the White House grounds, where children used to play among the trees and shrubbery. It was an election year, 1828, and President John Quincy Adams sought a second term against a seasoned challenger, General Andrew Jackson. Undoubtedly reflecting the political preference of his parents, Ned defended with spirited fisticuffs the good name of Old Hickory. A tall figure dressed in a grey morning coat seized Ned by the collar and demanded the reason for such unseemly conduct.

"I was fighting for Andy-by-God Jackson," the young pugilist explained, using the appellation popular during the campaign. "This fellow called him a jackass!"

The tall man affected an expression of surprise. "Did he now? A jackass! Perhaps the likeness is not far off the mark. I am Jackson, lad, and I never forget those willing to fight for me."

Ned prevailed upon his mother in 1836 to allow him to join the Navy. He suggested that application for a Midshipman's warrant be made directly to President Jackson. His mother consented. A few days later she and Ned were ushered into Old Hickory's presence in the White House where they found him arranging personal papers to be sent down to The Hermitage upon his retirement. Emily stated the purpose of their visit. Ned reminded the President of his boyhood fight nearly eight years before. Jackson's gaunt and heavily lined features creased into a wide grin, as the story goes.

"Indeed," he chuckled. "I recall the incident well. As I recollect, you were strenuously objecting to my being called a jackass, that noble, dependable, sure-footed beast. At my farm in Tennessee I breed the fastest horses in the state and the fastest of all is my prizewinner, 'Truxtun.' I never had the honor of knowing your grandfather, son, but always held him in the highest regard and trust you will not deem it a mark of disrespect that I have seen fit to name the best horse in the state after the best seaman in the United States Navy."

Failing to find a blank sheet of paper on his desk, the President snatched up a wafer envelope on the back of which he scrawled a note to Mahlon Dickerson, his Secretary of the Navy: "Give this boy an immediate warrant."

More to do, perhaps, with Beale's future naval career was a letter from Lancaster, Pennsylvania, dated September 16, 1836. It was directed to Colonel Samuel C. Stanbaugh from U. S. Senator James Buchanan:

(I understand you are endeavoring to procure a midshipman's warrant for Edward Beale.) I wish you success in your exertions. He has many claims on the department for his appointment. Both his grandfather and father have several times perilled their lives for their country in its Naval service. Standing in the relations of friendship towards his family which I do, I feel a deep interest in his success. If, therefore, you suppose that this letter can be of any service to him with the Secretary of the Navy, you are at liberty to use it in any manner you may think proper.

We may assume both the President's note and Buchanan's letter achieved their purpose. Beale received a warrant as Midshipman dated December 14, 1836, with instructions to report to Philadelphia. There he would be received into the Navy, "providing he was fifteen years of age, stood five feet and one inch in his bare feet, and measured thirty inches around the chest." The youngster barely met these requirements but did fully comply with the further provisions that he "be able to read and write, be of robust frame, intelligent, of perfectly sound and healthy constitution, free from any physical defects or malformation and not subject to fits."

Acknowledging receipt of the warrant, Ned addressed Secretary Dickerson: "My conduct in the service will be the best evidence I can give how highly I estimate the kindness shown me in the selection you have made." The pen of the fourteen-year-old lad in writing this sophisticated letter was undoubtedly guided by his mother.

Ned reported for duty at Philadelphia on February 4, 1837, his fifteenth birthday, the minimum age for acceptance as a Midshipman. Standard regulations for uniforms had not yet been established. Recruits were obliged to furnish their own, so Ned's mother made one for him. Embellished with outsize silver buttons carefully scissored from an old uniform of Grandpa Truxtun's, the obviously homemade design earned Ned a flurry of jibes and snickers from his new comrades. He soon acquired a proper uniform, however, putting a merciful end to his embarrassment.

Prior to establishment of the United States Naval Academy at Annapolis, in 1845, Midshipmen were trained aboard "receiving ships" specifically designated as training schools. To one such ship, the USS *Independence,* young Ned Beale reported. First of the 74-gun ships-of-the-line, the *Independence* slid down the ways at Boston Navy Yard in 1814 and made her maiden cruise in 1815. When Beale boarded her for a training cruise to Europe in 1837, she had been *razeed* to a 44-gun frigate.

Our Navy followed the age-old customs of the British Navy, a harsh life for a fifteen-year-old boy. During his training period, Beale memorized Blunt's *Theory and Practice of Seamanship*. He learned gunnery, practicing at sea with the ship's cannons and ashore with wheeled artillery. He learned infantry drill; improved his marksmanship with pistol and musket; practiced with cutlass, bayonet and landing pike; and fenced, boxed, wrestled and swam. Already adept in most sports, Beale took readily to those activities.

Senior officers taught navigation, and he studied the standard text of Nathanial Bowditch, *New American Practical Navigator*. The ship's Chaplain instructed Midshipmen in moral, ethical and religious matters. Civilian schoolmasters aboard ship conducted lessons in geography, grammar, history, foreign languages and mathematics.

Beale learned that a Naval officer was expected to be more than just a capable mariner. He must prove himself a "gentleman," according to requirements set forth in 1775 by John Paul Jones. He must have a "liberal education, refined manners, punctilious courtesy and the nicest sense of personal honor." Edward Beale had all this pointedly drilled into him under a code of the strictest discipline. He grew to understand that his integrity and courage were already taken for granted or he wouldn't be there.

Following his tour to Europe aboard the *Independence*, Beale reported to the USS *Porpoise*. The Navy's primary mission at that time was to police the pirate-infested Caribbean Sea and suppress the African slave trade. Beale fell ill with "bilious fever" aboard the *Porpoise* in 1838 and went ashore at Galveston, Texas, to convalesce. It was bad enough for a sixteen-year-old lad to be ill in any "hospital" 2000 miles from home, but the hot, flat tidewater area of Texas was simply too far from the comforting green hills of Virginia and Pennsylvania. We can picture his homesickness when he swallowed his manful pride and wrote to his mother that he missed her and his sisters. Later, after recovery, Beale resumed his training in Mediterranean waters aboard the USS *Ohio,* flagship of Commodore Thomas ap Catesby Jones.

Beale took his final examinations at Philadelphia in August 1842, at the age of twenty. He received high marks and advanced to Passed Midshipman, a rank approximating that of Ensign in today's Navy.

Promoted in 1845 to Acting Sailing Master, he reported to the frigate USS *Congress,* commanded by Commodore Robert Field Stockton. It marked the beginning of a relationship of mutual respect and confidence between the two men that lasted until Stockton's death several years later.

Stockton's career established him as one of the Navy's outstanding officers. Born in Princeton, New Jersey, in 1795, he became a Midshipman at fifteen and received honorable mention for gallantry in the War of 1812. He was assigned to the USS *Spitfire* as a First Lieutenant at the age of nineteen, the youngest officer ever to hold that rank. He helped the West Indies Squadron sweep the seas of blood-thirsty pirates until not a cove in the Caribbean afforded them shelter. Stockton obtained territory in Africa in 1822 under authorization of President James Monroe for the Republic of Liberia, a colony for free American Negroes. Among the first to advocate use of steam in the U. S. Navy, Stockton's design of the USS *Princeton* made it a prototype for the numerous steam-powered vessels to follow.

Beale's duties as Acting Sailing Master aboard Stockton's ship were prescribed in Naval regulations that hadn't changed since 1802: "To inspect provisions and stores, take care of the ballast, stow the hold and spirits room, trim sails, navigate the ship and see that the log and logbook are duly kept." Advancements were slow in the peacetime Navy but responsibility and devotion to the duties of Acting Sailing Master could eventually mean promotion to Lieutenant.

Meanwhile, restless clouds of war brewed along the bluffs

above the Rio Grande. The ensuing storm engulfed Edward Beale in a most profound manner. The catalyst was a Congressional resolution on March 3, 1845, approving the annexation of Texas — this despite Mexico's threat of military force to prevent Texas statehood. Commodore Stockton was charged with carrying official word of the annexation to Sam Houston. Beale sailed with the Commodore to the Gulf of Mexico on the *Congress,* and back again to New York.

Beale again reported to the USS *Congress* on October 2, 1845, at Norfolk, Virginia. He found the ship being fitted out for a cruise to the Pacific Ocean. By then, war with Mexico seemed imminent, and perhaps war with England as well. There were longstanding irritations between England and the United States, compounded by conflicting territorial claims in Oregon. Great Britain dominated the Pacific Northwest through the long presence *in situ* of the Hudson's Bay Company. American trappers and a wave of settlers emigrating overland to Oregon threatened this domination. The boundary line between the United States and Canada stood as a major issue in the 1844 Presidential campaign. The popular slogan of the day, "Fifty-Four Forty or Fight," described a north latitude boundary designated to give Oregon to the United States. England voiced objection. She not only wanted to keep Oregon but coveted California as well. Mexico was indebted to England for some $50 million in commercial loans. England signified her willingness to cancel this debt in exchange for California.

Commodore Stockton arrived at Norfolk bearing orders to convey U. S. Commissioner Anthony Ten Eyck and U. S. Consul Judge Turrell and their families to the Sandwich Islands. The *Congress* would then join the Pacific Squadron, wherever the fleet might be. Stockton's orders called for him to relieve Commodore John Drake Sloat, who had held the station for two years and now sought retirement.

At last the *Congress* made ready for sea. With Beale aboard as Acting Sailing Master, she put out from Norfolk on October 30 and headed south toward Cape Horn and the Pacific. Some days later in the West Indies Stockton learned that a British Naval Squadron also sailed toward the Pacific. He considered this intelligence to be of prime importance to the United States and determined to get word to Washington. But how to do it? He couldn't abandon his mission by turning the *Congress* back to the States. Chances of meeting a homeward bound ship grew slimmer as they sailed on toward the south latitudes.

One morning in mid-November while still in West Indies waters, a lookout on the *Congress* sighted a vessel off the weather bow. She proved to be the merchant brig *Maria,* flying Danish colors and bound from Brazil to Antwerp. Commodore Stockton summoned Beale to his cabin and informed him he was to be put aboard the brig with dispatches for Washington. The *Maria's* captain agreed to transfer Beale to the first America-bound ship he encountered. The *Maria,* some 480 miles out of her reckoning, was all but lost anyway. The brig's Captain welcomed a navigator who could set an accurate course for Europe.

Stockton prepared dispatches for President James Knox Polk and Secretary of the Navy George Bancroft. He instructed Beale to get to Washington as best he could and then to rejoin the *Congress* in the Pacific — also as best he could.

Beale watched from the *Maria's* rail as the American frigate slipped quickly over the southern horizon, conscious, certainly, of the importance of his mission and of the great trust Commodore Stockton had placed in him.

2

A Sailor on Horseback

Midshipman Edward Beale set the merchant brig *Maria* on a proper course for the English Channel, then began a daily watch for ships heading toward the States. He maintained his watch all the way across the Atlantic but never sighted another vessel in that broad ocean. The anxious young officer may be forgiven unhappy visions, if he had any, of the Ancient Mariner, "alone, alone, all, all alone, alone on a wide wide sea!"

The *Maria* dropped Beale off at Dover, England, and he ultimately booked passage on a ship for America. He delivered Commodore Stockton's dispatches to President Polk and the Navy Department, and was told to wait for further orders.

While Beale cooled his heels in Washington, and at Chester, the likelihood of war in Texas and California continued to grow. U. S. forces under General Zachary Taylor were ordered to positions along the Rio Grande. Moreover, the prospect of war also loomed in Oregon, where Americans settled in growing numbers in a land the English considered their own. Other parts of Mexico's vast domain were about to be expropriated too. The westward migration of Mormon settlers began when church elders proclaimed: "All branches of the church shall move west of the Rocky Mountains, before the next season, by land or water. Our leaders have decided to settle on land which is in Mexican territory . . ."

Beale's ship, the USS *Congress,* reached Callao, Peru, without him and would soon join the U. S. Pacific Squadron. A British fleet — subject of the dispatches Beale carried to Washington — also moved into the Pacific to counter-balance American naval strength there.

Meanwhile, in California a well-armed United States survey party under Captain John Charles Fremont maneuvered boldly

about, giving Mexican officials a permanent case of the jitters.
When the Mexicans protested and tried to eject Fremont, American settlers in California complained loudly and took up arms.

Fremont was born in Savannah, Georgia, on January 21, 1813,
and attended Charleston College in South Carolina. He joined
the U. S. Army Corps of Topographical Engineers as a Lieutenant in 1838. His first assignment took him to St. Louis where
he joined an expedition to Minnesota and the Dakota country
under noted French scientist-mathematician Joseph Nicolas Nicollet. Fremont accompanied Nicollet again in 1839 to the upper
Missouri River, and led a survey party of his own into Iowa
Territory. He paused after that expedition long enough to
marry seventeen-year-old Jessie Benton, daughter of Senator
Thomas Hart Benton of Missouri. In 1842, he organized the
first of five major western expeditions that would involve him
deeply in the fundamental fabric of western American history.
His first western expedition took him into the northern Rockies,
the second to Oregon and California, and the third to California
again in 1845, where his presence proved to be such an irritant
to the Mexicans.

All these incidents, widely scattered and mostly unrelated —
Taylor maneuvering along the Rio Grande, settlers in Oregon,
Mormons moving beyond the Rockies, Fremont roaming at will
in California — served to push the nation closer to war. But
the westward course of America seemed inexorable. Public sentiment, enlivened by an expansionist philosophy in Washington,
sought the continental reach. Americans envisioned a United
States spanning North America from ocean to ocean. A popular
banner proclaiming "Manifest Destiny" served this purpose to
perfection. The people rallied under it as they did the Stars
and Stripes itself.

Beale, still waiting restlessly in Washington, finally received
orders from the Secretary of the Navy on March 7, 1846:

> You are permitted to take passage on the U.S. Frigate *Potomac*
> about to sail from Norfolk for Vera Cruz, thence to make your way

in the best manner you can to Mazatlan and report to Commodore
Sloat for the purpose of rejoining the Frigate *Congress.*

Should you take advantage of this permission, you will take in
charge and convey the accompanying packages to Commodores Sloat
and Stockton . . .

The very day that Secretary Bancroft issued Beale's orders,
Fremont's survey party found itself engaged in what might have
been the original "Mexican standoff" with Lieutenant Colonel
Jose Castro, military commander of the region. Fremont objected to Castro's order to get out of the territory. He and his
party barricaded themselves on top of a steep, craggy mountain
in the Gavilan Range east of Monterey. There they defiantly
raised the American flag. Castro marshalled his forces in the
village of San Juan Bautista at the foot of the mountain but
discreetly refrained from attacking the redoubt. Fremont's well-
armed band of mountain men and voyageurs bore little resem-
blance to a survey party in the usual meaning of the term.
We imagine bespectacled engineers tinkering with levels and
plumb bobs. It is entirely likely that Fremont's tough mercen-
aries would have administered a sound drubbing to Castro's
volunteer militia.

After several days of heroic posturing on both sides, Fremont
rode back down the mountain and left the area at a leisurely
pace. But the friction grated. The sparks of war glowed a little
brighter.

Beale left Washington on April 1, 1846, and took passage
from Norfolk on the *Potomac.* His destination was no longer
Vera Cruz, perhaps because of intense animosity toward Americans in Mexico. He went instead to Chagres on the East Coast
of the Panamanian Isthmus.

Pestilential Chagres, straddling the mouth of the Chagres
River, consisted of palmetto huts housing a few hundred natives.
Rising above the dense tropical foliage overhanging the south
bank were the moldering ruins of Lorenzo Castle, destroyed by
pirate Henry Morgan in 1671. A fetid stench permeated the

place and Beale lost no time in engaging boatmen to carry him up-river to Cruces, two-thirds of the way across the sixty-mile Isthmus. Beale had a naturally dark complexion, bronzed as any Spaniard after so many years at sea. With a ready command of Spanish, he experienced little difficulty making himself understood.

The alligator-infested Chagres River followed its sluggish course through tropical jungles oppressive with heat. Parrots of brilliant plumage caught his eye and colonies of monkeys chattered and scolded as the boat passed. Traveling the last third of the journey overland by mule, Beale reached Panama City, a filthy disease-ridden waterfront town eternally plagued by malaria and cholera. Its population of some eight thousand wretched souls were mostly of Spanish, Indian and Negro extraction, and every combination thereof. The city, built on a small promontory facing the sea, dated from 1519. Like Chagres, it too had been destroyed by Morgan in 1671.

Beale found new orders waiting for him at Panama City. Writing aboard the *Congress* at Callao, Peru, on April 13, 1846, Stockton commanded:

> If you receive this letter in time, you will come to this place in the Steamer *Chili* [sic] which leaves Panama on or about the 24th inst. I will wait here the arrival of that vessel.
>
> If you should not be in time for that Steamer, you will remain at Panama until the Steamer of the 24th of June and come to this place in her and here await my arrival or further orders from me.

Beale gladly engaged passage aboard the southbound *Chile*. It had been six months since he left the *Congress* to go aboard the *Maria* in the West Indies. On May 8, Beale caught up with the *Congress* and presented Commodore Stockton with the dispatches he had brought from Bancroft. The Secretary of the Navy advised Stockton that,

> It is the earnest desire of the President to pursue the policy of peace, and he is anxious that you and every part of your squadron

should be assiduously careful to avoid any act which could be construed an act of aggression. Should Mexico, however, be resolutely bent on hostilities you will be mindful to protect the persons and interests of citizens of the United States, and should you ascertain beyond a doubt that the Mexican government has declared war against us, you will employ the force under your command to the best advantage. The Mexican ports on the Pacific are said to be open and defenseless . . . you will at once blockade or occupy such ports as your force will admit.

Even as Stockton read Beale's dispatches from Washington, the battles of Palo Alto and Resaca de la Palma erupted. The spark had hit the tinder. Stockton had no way of knowing it, but flames of war flickered brightly all along the Rio Grande. In any case, Acting Sailing Master Beale was back on board; it was now time to head northward. Once Stockton completed his mission to carry Commissioner Ten Eyck and U. S. Consul Turrell to Honolulu, he would be free to seek out the Pacific Squadron. Preparations proceeded for the *Congress* to sail on the morning tide.

Thus, at the crack of dawn on May 9 the sounding of the ship's bell, which normally called for a simple changing of the watch, was followed by the shrill piping of the bosun's call summoning "All hands on deck!" The order resounded through the berthing compartments, "All hands! Tumble out!"

Below decks, "Jimmy Legs," the Master at Arms, threaded his way between the seamen's hammocks, whacking them with his cane. "Rise and shine! Come on, rouse up there! Tumble out! Lash and carry! Fore and aft!"

Breakfast was piped at six bells, but long before all had been served the drum beat "to general quarters" and all hands scurried to their posts. We can picture the main deck buzzing with disciplined, controlled activity. The various sections manned their stations, while the "topmen" scurried up the ratlines. The anchor watch manned the capstan bars. The ship "rode on the hook" with only a bow anchor holding her in position. Sailors manned the yards, each section waiting the order to drop canvas. The Sailing Master stood at the quarterdeck rail, his practiced eye watching all this activity.

"Stand by to cast off!" came the shouted command. "Break and heave the larboard anchor!"

Round and round went the anchormen in a steady tread, each man pushing his weight against a capstan bar and joining in the rhythmic singsong of the chantyman's lead, for in the old Navy, "a song was as good as ten men."

"Yo, heave ho! Heave hearty ho! Heave with a will! Heave and raise the dead! Heave and away! Yo, heave ho!" Over and over. Round and round turned the capstan winch, taking a strain on the anchor chain and slowly reeling it in. A detail at the pumps washed down the great rattling links and fed the chain into a locker below decks where it was flaked in seried coils, ready to be let out again without fouling. With a muddy, swirling eddy the anchor broke surface and swung clear. The pump crew washed it down and secured it to the bow anchor tackle. The ship rode free on the morning swell.

"Square away main yard!" the Sailing Master called out, cupping hands to mouth. "Let fall the fors'l and mains'l! Lively does it, lads! Be handy! Be handy!"

The sails snapped briefly in a luff until hauled into the breeze, and the *Congress* set off on a long reach for the Sandwich Islands.

"Farewell, Callao!" the ship's Chaplain, Walter Colton, wrote in his journal. "I have seen enough of your destitution and dirt, your pickpockets and parrots, your fish and your fleas, your brats and your buzzards."

The *Congress* enjoyed winds steady and favorable on her larboard quarter for nearly the entire journey. She rounded Diamond Head and entered the harbor at Honolulu just thirty days out of Callao. The Commissioner and Consul with their wives and children were put ashore.

During Beale's month on the open sea, President Polk declared that a state of war existed between the United States and Mexico. General Taylor moved his troops into Matamoros, across the Mexican border. Conditions worsened in California. Fremont took his brigade northward into Oregon, but started back to California again in response to official dispatches carried to him in the Klamath wilderness by a government courier, Marine Lieutenant Archibald H. Gillespie.

American settlers in California feared continuing Mexican threats to drive them out of the territory. They took matters into their own hands near Sutter's Fort and stole a herd of Castro's horses. At Fort Leavenworth, Kansas, meanwhile, Colonel Stephen Watts Kearny prepared to lead the U. S. First Dragoons cross-country to Santa Fe, New Mexico, and westward to California.

Men on the USS *Congress* watched the chartered ship *Brooklyn* move into Honolulu harbor on June 20. Beale recorded that the ship carried "a load of Mormon emigrants, at the head of whom was Sam Brannan."

The *Brooklyn* unloaded contracted cargo in Honolulu which Brannan had carried to help finance his voyage. Here was yet another force headed for California, albeit a futile one. Brannan had grand ideas about colonizing California with his 226 Mormons, even if he had to shoot a few Mexicans to do it. Stockton figured Brannan's presence might help. He knew from Mexican newspapers received in Honolulu that fighting had broken out between the United States and Mexico. Stockton authorized the sale of a supply of small arms and ammunition to Brannan, at Brannan's request — 150 muskets and fifty Allen's revolvers. Seamen transferred the material to the *Brooklyn*.

Events tumbled upon events. American settlers, flushed with victory after their successful horse raid but fearing reprisals, rebelled completely. Better to be shot as an insurgent than hanged as a horse thief. They seized the town of Sonoma, hoisted a homemade flag with a bear on it and declared California to be an independent republic.

Colonel Kearny's Army of the West departed Fort Leavenworth for Santa Fe. Brigham Young gave his blessings to recruitment of a Mormon Battalion of infantry to follow along and help out.

While the *Congress* finished taking on stores at Honolulu, Commodore Sloat waited at Mazatlan, Mexico, with the Pacific Squadron. Sloat's father, Captain John Sloat, served under General George Washington in 1791. His mother, Ruth Drake Sloat, was a direct descendent of Sir Francis Drake. Young John Drake Sloat received a Midshipman's warrant on February 12, 1800. He first served aboard the frigate USS *President* under Beale's grandfather, Commodore Thomas Truxtun. He fought in the War of 1812 as Sailing Master of the USS *United States* under Commodore Stephen Decatur. His skillful seamanship in a battle with HMS *Macedonian* was credited with maneuvering the *United States* to bring her broadsides to bear continually on the British ship. He received promotion to Lieutenant afterward upon the recommendation of Commodore Decatur.

Sloat earned his commission as Captain and Commandant of the Portsmouth Navy Yard in 1837, where he supervised construction of the USS *Portsmouth,* and rebuilding of the USS *Congress* so soundly that she was the equal in speed and maneuverability of any war vessel then afloat. Looking forward to retirement in his sixty-third year, Sloat was instead promoted to Commodore and ordered by Secretary of the Navy John Y. Mason to take command of the Pacific Squadron.

Sloat received orders from the Navy Department similar to those delivered by Beale to Stockton at Callao: If war should be declared, he was to take possession of San Francisco Bay and "blockade or occupy such other Mexican ports as your force may permit." Otherwise, Sloat was to wait. He had two 44-gun frigates, the *Savannah* and the USS *Constitution* (Old Ironsides), and four smaller sloops-of-war. The *Constitution* soon headed for home.

The British Navy's Pacific Squadron also maintained stations at Mexican ports, keeping an eye on the Americans. The brigantine HMS *Spy* rode at anchor near Sloat at Mazatlan. HMS

Collingwood, an 80-gun ship-of-the-line serving as flagship of the British Commander, Admiral Sir George F. Seymour, waited at San Blas, 100 miles down the coast. Also at San Blas were the frigate HMS *Talbot,* commanded by Sir Thomas Thompson, and the brigantine *Juno.*

Sloat received secret information early in June that hostilities had broken out between the United States and Mexico. Although still lacking confirmation of a declared war, he decided to move north to the Mexican ports on the coast of California. He hoped to do so without alarming the British, but that was hardly possible with HMS *Spy,* true to her name, watching every move.

Sloat dispatched the USS *Portsmouth* to San Francisco Bay and the sloops *Cyane* and *Levant* to Monterey. Another sloop, the USS *Warren,* remained at Mazatlan. Sloat then tried to slip out of Mazatlan with the *Savannah* in a nonchalant manner, also for Monterey. The *Spy's* Commander noted the activity, however, and departed quickly southward to warn Admiral Seymour.

Meanwhile, the USS *Congress* finished taking on stores and on June 23 left Hawaii. Acting Sailing Master Beale laid a course for Monterey, the capital of Mexican California. Stockton assumed he would find Commodore Sloat and the Pacific Squadron there. In any case, that's where the action would be. Stockton was not a man to miss out on anything, not even by loafing in an island paradise.

On July 2, 1846, while Beale and the *Congress* were between Honolulu and California, Sloat entered Monterey Bay to join the sloops *Cyane* and *Levant.* The log of the *Savannah* carried this entry: "Standing in for the anchorage of the town of Monterey. At 4 p.m. let go starboard anchor. Consul Larkin visited the ship."

United States Consul Thomas Oliver Larkin went aboard the *Savannah* to visit Sloat in his cabin because the Commodore was too ill to go ashore. In addition to his consular duties at Monterey, businessman Larkin served as a secret agent under instructions from President Polk. In that capacity, he was "to encourage the secession of California from Mexico by the voluntary act of its native inhabitants."

Larkin and Sloat huddled long into the night. Larkin advised the Commodore of conditions in California while Sloat described the notice of hostilities he had received at Mazatlan. Neither stated any knowledge of an official declaration of war. Sloat could do nothing but wait. While he did so, fighting raged in Mexico and the war had been "official" for nearly two months.

Four days later, a launch from the USS *Portsmouth* in San Francisco Bay brought news that the American settlers had captured Sonoma. Sloat decided that was close enough to being war and sent a message back with the launch to Commander John Barrien Montgomery on the *Portsmouth:*

> I have determined to hoist the flag of the United States at this place tomorrow, as I would prefer being sacrificed for doing too much than too little. If you consider you have sufficient force, or if Fremont will join you, you will hoist the flag at Yerba Buena, or at any other proper place, and take possession of the fort and that portion of the country.

On the morning of July 7, 1846, Commodore Sloat issued a general order to his crews on the three ships at Monterey:

> We are about to land on the territory of Mexico, with whom the United States is at war; to strike their flag and hoist our own . . . It is not only our duty to take California, but to preserve it afterwards as part of the United States, at all hazards.

The order restricted the conduct of the landing party, forbidding "plundering or any indignity offered to a single female, even let her standing be however low it may be."

The log of the *Savannah* recorded that at 10 a.m. on July 7, an expedition of 85 marines and 140 sailors under command of the *Cyane's* Captain William Mervine left the ships and landed at the Customs House wharf. Mervine read a proclamation and ordered the Stars and Stripes raised on the Customs House flagstaff. There was no Mexican flag to take down, and none had flown there for two months. Each of Sloat's three ships fired a salute of twenty-one guns and the squadron band paraded through the little town.

The American flag was raised by Midshipman William P. Toler, who had done so in the same place in 1842 when Commodore Thomas ap Catesby Jones prematurely "captured" California and held it for twenty-four hours before giving it back to the Mexicans. (Fifty years later, on July 7, 1896, Toler for the third and last time raised the flag at Monterey during the Golden Jubilee celebration of the conquest of California.)

Sloat's proclamation was read in both English and Spanish. A native courier carried a copy to Jose Castro, now a Mexican general, who had fled to Los Angeles:

> Although I come with a powerful force, I do not come as an enemy of Californians. On the contrary, I come as their best friend, as henceforth California will be a portion of the United States. Inhabitants not disposed to accept the high privilege of United States citizenship will have the option of leaving the country or may remain observing strict neutrality.

Sloat directed an officer with the unlikely name of Daingerfield Fauntleroy, Purser of the *Savannah,* to organize a detail of horsemen from the ship's companies and from volunteers ashore. Fauntleroy assembled a troop of thirty-five, with himself as Captain and Louis McLane, an officer on the *Levant,* as First Lieutenant. These mounted couriers established communications between Monterey, San Juan Bautista, San Jose and Yerba Buena. Sloat was thereby able to forward these orders overland to Commander Montgomery at San Francisco Bay:

> If you have sufficient force, or if Fremont will join you, take possession of Yerba Buena, Sonoma, Bodega and Sutter's Fort. I wish very much to see Captain Fremont that we may understand each other.

He enclosed copies of his proclamation and requested that a similar one in English and Spanish be posted wherever the flag was raised.

Commander Montgomery dispatched Lieutenant Joseph Warren Revere of the *Portsmouth* (grandson of Revolutionary War patriot Paul Revere) to Sonoma and forwarded flags to Bodega and Sutter's Fort. Montgomery informed Sloat on July 9,

> . . . I landed (at Yerba Buena) this morning with seventy men, including marines, and . . . hoisted our flag in front of the Custom House in the public square with a salute of twenty-one guns from the ship, followed by three hearty cheers on shore and on board . . .
>
> I then addressed a few words to the assembled people, after which your excellent proclamation was read in both languages, and posted upon the flagstaff . . .

Lieutenant Revere returned to the *Portsmouth* on July 11 and reported to Montgomery:

> . . . I landed at the town of Sonoma . . . on the 9th inst. Having caused the troops of the garrison and the inhabitants of the place to be summoned to the public square, I read the proclamation of Commodore Sloat to them, and then hoisted the flag of the United States upon the staff in front of the barracks . . .

Conforming with Sloat's directive, Commander Montgomery sent a launch up the Sacramento River with a message for Captain Fremont at Sutter's Fort:

> Last evening I was officially notified of the existence of war between the United States and the Central government of Mexico, and have this morning taken formal possession of this place and hoisted our flag in the town. Commodore Sloat, who took possession of Monterey on the 7th instant, has directed me to notify you of this change in the political condition of California and to request your presence in Monterey, with a view to future arrangements and cooperation at as early a period as possible . . .

Fremont wrote in his memoirs, "At dawn of the 11th we ran up the flag of the United States amid general rejoicing, and fired a national salute of twenty-one guns." Fremont formed his battalion, leaving Edward Kern in command at Sutter's Fort, and rode south to report to Commodore Sloat at Monterey.

And so it was that the USS *Congress* laid doggo for a night outside the coastal fog bank and sailed dramatically into Monterey Bay on the morning of July 15, 1846.

Chaplain Walter Colton noted on the morning of the 16th that the *Cyane* warped out of her berth and the *Congress* warped into it. "Our ships are now moored in a line, command the anchorage and present a very warlike appearance."

If Sloat felt nervous about raising the flag over Mexican territory without specific orders from Washington, a sight which unfolded on Monterey Bay that same afternoon surely did not put him at ease. Chaplain Colton described it:

> This afternoon, a large ship was discovered rounding Point Piños. She entered the harbor under a cloud of canvas, and proved to be the *Collingwood,* bearing the broad pennant of Admiral Seymour. She came to anchor outside the *Congress* and *Savannah.* Our band greeted her with "God Save the Queen," which she returned with "Hail Columbia!" She is an 80-gun ship, and looks majestic on the wave. The Admiral was greatly surprised to find Monterey in possession of the Americans.

Seymour anchored the *Collingwood* within pistol shot of the *Savannah* and received permission to come aboard the American vessel. Sloat later recorded: "We were ready for action. The decks were cleared, the gunners stood by loaded cannon. We did everything but show our teeth — run the guns out the portholes."

The experienced eye of Admiral Seymour observed these preparations and he remarked that Sloat appeared about to give his crew some gunnery practice. Sloat pointed to the American flag flying on shore and admitted, "It might take some practice to keep it there."

Seymour was curious. "What would you have done had there been the flag of another nationality here upon your arrival, guarded by a ship-of-the-line?"

Without hesitation, Sloat replied, "I would have gotten in at least one broadside, perhaps gone to the the bottom, and left my government to settle the matter."

The question was moot. HMS *Collingwood* in all her glory was no match for Sloat's line of four American warships, and no one knew that better than Admiral Seymour. Sloat later reported to the Secretary of the Navy:

> The visit of the Admiral was very serviceable to our cause in California, as the inhabitants fully believed he would take part with them and that we would be obliged to abandon our conquest, but when they saw the friendly intercourse between us and found he could not interfere in their behalf, they abandoned all hope of ever seeing the Mexican flag fly in California again.

Sloat had less than complete confidence in Daingerfield Fauntleroy's *Californio* couriers, for he instructed Montgomery, "Send me a courier every week, but do not pay him until he brings you a receipt from me."

At San Jose, fresh horses were provided by Tom Fallon, Captain of the San Jose Volunteers, who on the 12th wrote Montgomery for permission to raise the flag and was advised, "By all means, hoist the flag if you have sufficient force to maintain it there. Once raised, it is not to be hauled down."

Fauntleroy received orders to take possession of San Juan Bautista. He arrived there on July 17 and found Captain Fremont already in command of the town. Fauntleroy escorted Fremont and his party through the Gavilan hills and down the broad Salinas Valley. The procession came into view at Monterey on July 19. Lieutenant Frederick Walpole of HMS *Collingwood* described it:

> A vast cloud of dust appeared first, and thence in a long file emerged this wild party. Fremont rode ahead, a spare, active looking man. He was dressed in blue blouse and leggings and wore a felt hat. After him came five Delaware Indians who were his bodyguard.

Behind the Indians came Lieutenant Gillespie and scouts Kit Carson, Joseph Walker and Alexis Godey. In a column of twos rode men in buckskins with rifles slung over saddle pommels, knives and pistols tucked in belts. Tanned dark as Indians, heavily bearded and with hair streaming from under skin caps and broad-brimmed hats, they presented the savage appearance of a force whose right of passage few would hazard to challenge.

Fremont's column moved rather grandly through town and made camp in a grove of trees at the upper end, away from the beach. Sloat, still sick and confined to his cabin, summoned Fremont aboard the *Savannah*. Lieutenant Gillespie accompanied Fremont and described the confrontation:

> Commodore Sloat manifested a feeling of dissatisfaction that Captain Fremont and myself had not reported ourselves and the forces under our command to him, and wanted to know by what authority we were acting. Captain Fremont replied that he had acted upon his own authority. Commodore Sloat then expressed much surprise and distress and said he had acted on the faith of our operations in the north!

Commodore Sloat had also acted on his own authority, but apparently suffered misgivings. Edward Beale's impression seems to substantiate Sloat's self-doubts:

> When we arrived at Monterey, we found that Commodore Sloat had anticipated the Mexican War and had already hoisted the American flag and took possession of the town. Almost immediately he left for Washington in order that he might defend his action which, if premature, would occasion or submit him to censure of the authorities.

Fremont had no such fear. He offered Sloat the cooperation the Commodore had requested through Montgomery and was prepared to march his battalion south to take Santa Barbara, Los Angeles and San Diego. He would defeat Castro or drive him out of the country. Sloat, however, had no intention of provoking or engaging in hostilities. He had been assured that Castro could muster only a hundred poorly armed men and would submit docilely once the squadron secured the southern ports.

Fremont possessed contrary intelligence. Castro had at least 400 mounted and well armed men prepared to contest every foot of southern soil, and was in no mood to submit "docilely." With a war apparently shaping up, Sloat prepared to close up shop and head for home.

At his camp above town, Fremont entertained officers from the American and British warships with shooting matches. Avowing that the plains of Tartary had never seen a wilder band, Lieutenant Walpole commented:

> Here were true trappers, the class that produced the heroes of Fennimore Cooper's best works . . . (Fremont) has one or two with him who enjoy a high reputation on the prairies. Kit Carson is as well known there as the Duke (of Wellington) is in Europe.

There at the camp on the edge of Monterey, Beale and Fremont had their first encounter. Fremont described it in his memoirs:

> I first met Edward Beale in Monterey in July of 1846. At our meeting commenced intervals of agreeable companionship on interesting occasions that resulted in a family relationship which has continued for forty years.

Beale and his shipmates had their turn to play host on the Twenty-second when Fremont and his men went aboard the USS *Congress,* leaving Chaplain Colton with a vivid impression:

> Captain Fremont's band of riflemen visited our ship today and lunched with us. Many of them are trappers from the interior wilds who have neven seen a man-of-war before. They looked at our frowning battery with a wonder for which their trap dialect had no expression. The Indians connected with the body wanted to know how such an immense mass could be put on the trail. We pointed to our sails, clewed to the yards; they shook their heads in incredulity. They seemed to think there must be some invisible monster in the hold, whose terrific energies caused the ship to go . . . The article which seemed to interest them most was the rifle of Commodore Stockton; they handled it with that yearning fondness which a mother feels clasping her first-born.

On July 23, eight days after the *Congress* arrived from Honolulu, Sloat turned over command of the Pacific Squadron "and operations ashore" to Commodore Stockton. He transferred his gear to the sloop *Levant* and appointed Captain Mervine of the *Cyane* to be commander of the *Savannah*. Sloat departed on the *Levant* on July 29, never having set foot ashore at Monterey. He wrote to Secretary of the Navy Bancroft from Mazatlan that ill health prevented attention to his duties but at the time of his departure, "the United States were in quiet possession of all Alta California north of Santa Barbara."

When Mervine took over the *Savannah,* Commander Samuel Francis Dupont, Executive Officer of the *Congress,* was advanced to Captain and given command of the *Cyane*. Fremont proposed that his battalion be taken by ship to San Diego, where he could secure horses and drive the Mexicans from Los Angeles. Captain Dupont received instructions from Stockton to carry out that mission with the *Cyane*.

Stockton was the very antithesis of the aged and ailing Sloat. In excellent health and spirits at fifty-three, Stockton and the thirty-three-year-old Fremont found themselves kindred souls. Hesitancy and indecision were traits unknown to them. Stockton's first order of business after taking command of the squadron was to muster Fremont's mixed party of trappers, Indians, voyageurs and settlers into the "Naval Battalion of Mounted California Volunteer Riflemen." The troop had the military organization of a Marine Corp battalion. Stockton commissioned Fremont Lieutenant Colonel in command.

Stockton outlined his grand strategy. Once Fremont had captured San Diego, he and his battalion would ride north. Stockton would sail to San Pedro with the *Congress* and lead a landing party inland. The two forces would join for the assault on Los Angeles. When all California ports were in American hands, Stockton would take the Pacific Squadron south, blockade the Mexican ports, organize his ship's companies into an army and march across Mexico to capture Mexico City. Fremont was to remain in California as Military Governor until Washington decided otherwise.

Stockton's sailors had little aptitude for such land operations but "Old Bobby," as his men called him, saw no reason why they could not be trained into an "army of horse and foot." For the next two weeks, the marines drilled four companies of "jacks" as infantrymen. Carriages and wheels were made by ship's carpenters for guns to be landed at San Pedro, and gunners assigned to handle them. Daingerfield Fauntleroy's troop continued its patrolling.

Another troop was formed to act as mounted riflemen and Stockton appointed Edward Beale to command these carbineers. Beale's father had taught him to ride. He loved horses and jumped at the chance to be a leader of "cavalry." Navy garb wasn't made for hours in the saddle, however, and Beale instructed his men to reinforce their britches with cowhide. His shipmates dubbed the troop the "leather-ass dragoons."

Fauntleroy had most of the available leather harness, and Fremont prepared to take his own battalion's saddles and tack on the *Cyane,* so the carbineers spent a good part of their time braiding bridles and reins from rope. All this material went aboard the *Congress.* Beale planned to acquire horses for his troop after they landed at San Pedro.

In later years, Beale expressed a high opinion of Commodore Stockton in an account to Hubert Howe Bancroft:

> Being intimately associated with him, or at least as much so as a subordinate of a very low rank could be with his distinguished position, I had constant opportunities of hearing him discuss familiarly the necessities of the situation. He proposed to . . . march into an unknown country to fight such battles as might be necessary and to conquer that portion of California in its most densely populated portion. He prepared at once for that enterprise which, considering the slender means placed at his disposal, should rank with the greatest enterprises ever proposed by a maritime commander . . . He asked no aid from anyone.

This last statement was only partly true. Companies of volunteers were formed at each *pueblo,* and Stockton had taken Fremont's battalion into the Naval service to assist him.

Once final plans were drawn, Fremont received orders from Stockton, written aboard the *Congress:*

> You will please embark on the USS *Cyane* with the detachment of troops under your command on Saturday afternoon. The ship at daylight on Sunday morning will sail for San Diego, where you will disembark your troops and procure horses for them, and will make every necessary preparation to march through the country at a moment's notice from me . . . The object of this movement is to take, or get between the Colorado and General Castro. I will leave Monday on this ship to San Pedro so as to arrive there about the time you may be expected to have arrived at San Diego.

While this flurry of activity developed at Monterey, Sam Brannan and his 226 Mormon followers sailed through the Golden Gate into San Francisco Bay on the leaky old *Brooklyn.* Brannan's little army of Saints was all primed to conquer California for the greater glory of . . . well, maybe for the greater glory of Sam Brannan. The date was July 31, 1846, and the first sight he beheld when the *Brooklyn* rounded into Yerba Buena Cove was the adobe Customs House over which flew the Stars and Stripes. Sam Brannan was too late.

3

The Californios

Alexander Freiherr von Humboldt expressed an opinion in the early 1800's that Spain had strengthened her far-flung New World empire to the point where she could look forward to perhaps a century of security — barring some kind of outside interference. He noted that outside difficulty might come from Napoleon, and it did.

This interference — the Peninsular War, which got underway in 1807 — prevented Spain from giving proper attention to remote outposts like Alta California. Problems resulting from neglect devolved upon the newly established Republic of Mexico after 1822. Internal political stresses in the Mexican central government served to perpetuate the neglect of California. Local government in that province suffered its own weakening quarrels and upheavals. Many Californios came more and more to consider themselves independent of the central government. Such disorders did nothing to prepare California to resist the growing and alarming influx of American adventurers and settlers after 1840.

Mexican opposition to American encroachment in what is now northern California never amounted to much and disappeared altogether as soon as the 1846 conquest got underway. But southern California — closer to Mexico, more firmly established, less "Americanized" — did not give in so easily.

General Jose Castro fled to Southern California when the Americans took up arms in the north. Commodore Stockton expected but mild resistance to his amphibious exercise in the south and got none at all — for awhile. Fremont and 150 crack riflemen departed Monterey on the USS *Cyane* on July 24. The sloop battled stormy seas for five days before finally standing in for the peaceful harbor of San Diego.

The landing party went ashore at the old hide warehouses on the *playa* and marched the several miles into town. Fremont found that most of the young men of San Diego had joined Castro. Those remaining were either American settlers or Californios friendly to the American cause. Fremont enlisted their aid in securing horses for his battalion.

San Diego had changed but little from the "small settlement of about forty brown looking huts" visited by Richard Henry Dana in 1835. A couple of newly whitewashed casas improved appearances, notably the one belonging to Juan Bandini. Battlements of the old presidio on the hill above town had long since disappeared.

Edward Beale's carbineers and the rest of the sailors-turned-soldiers were transported with their cannons and supplies to San Pedro on the *Congress*. Stockton set the various companies to marching and drilling again, writing that the trek to Los Angeles would be "a longer march than has ever been made in the interior of a country by sailors after an enemy." That might have been true, but the Commodore and his men were destined to make a far longer march before finally winning California.

Fremont's mounted battalion moved north from San Diego and joined with Stockton's force on the flat, sandy plains south of Los Angeles. There they learned that Governor Pio Pico and General Castro had fled inland to the San Gabriel Mountains, their troops scattered and demoralized.

Captain Jose Maria Flores and other Mexican officers deserted Castro and surrendered to Stockton. They were paroled on their oath they would return to their homes, keep the peace and not bear arms again.

Approaching the outskirts of Los Angeles, Stockton called up the color guard and the band, and the little American army affected a bit of a flourish as it marched into *El Pueblo de Nuestra Senora la Reina de los Angeles de Porciuncula.*

"We marched through the streets unopposed," Fremont wrote Senator Benton, "more like a parade of Home Guards than an enemy taking possession of a conquered town." Had he said "abandoned town," his report would have been more accurate but perhaps less colorful. Stockton himself noted in his report to Secretary Bancroft,

> I entered the famous City of Angels . . . and took unmolested possession. The flag of the United States is flying at every commanding position and California is in undisputed possession of the United States. Thus, in less than a month after I assumed command of the United States forces in California, we have chased the Mexican Army more than 300 miles along the coast, pursued them thirty miles in the interior of their own country, routed and dispersed them, secured the territory of the United States, ended the war, restored peace and harmony among the people, and put a civil government into successful operation.

Stockton wanted Secretary Bancroft to learn of his accomplishments without delay, although this boastful description is largely fanciful optimism. Stockton prevailed upon Fremont to release his best scout, Kit Carson, as the bearer of these glad, if premature, tidings.

Christopher Carson was born in Madison County, Kentucky, on December 24, 1809. He left home at seventeen and joined a party of Santa Fe traders. In 1829, he traveled overland to California with Ewing Young, and later became a trapper in the Rockies. Sir William Drummond Stewart, a Scottish adventurer traveling with the fur brigades, met Carson on the Green River and his description is as accurate as any, if the last sentence not be taken too literally:

> Carson's stature is short. He stands no more than five and one-half feet tall, his weight ten stone (140 pounds), all sinew and muscle. He shaves his face, his hair is shaggy. It was his habit, he said, to drink nothing but water.

Carson, like Beale and Fremont, made up for lack of height and heft with more than average physical strength, fearlessness and endurance.

Charles Lewis Camp in *Kit Carson in California* had this to say about the scout:

Kit Carson was a man of great energy and decision of character, alert, poised, calm in danger, and among the keenest, shrewdest and bravest of experienced frontiersmen . . . Yet his appearance was unheroic enough — short and stocky, grey-eyed, blond-haired and bowlegged. He had, however, those qualities of modesty, sobriety and strict veracity not proverbially common among the trappers of his day . . . Those who knew him well — General Sherman, General Rusling, General Beale, General Fremont, Mrs. Fremont, Colonel Peters and a host of other friends — respected, honored and loved him.

An impatient Kit Carson departed Los Angeles for the Colorado River with an escort of fifteen men. His route to Washington would take him through Santa Fe, close to his home at Taos. He looked forward to at least a brief visit with his wife and family before continuing east. Carson carried Stockton's report and letters from Fremont to Jessie Fremont and her father, Senator Benton.

Archibald Gillespie, now a Major in Stockton's Naval battalion of volunteers, remained with a garrison of fifty men to hold Los Angeles. Stockton sailed with Beale's carbineers and the sailor army to Monterey on the *Congress*. Fremont returned to Sonoma as Commander of the Northern District, with the promise of becoming Military Governor of California when Stockton departed for southern waters.

Stockton and Beale continued northward from Monterey to Yerba Buena with the *Congress* and *Savannah* to take on supplies for the move south into Mexico. He ordered elections held in the six former Mexican districts of California to choose alcaldes, a combination of mayor and justice of the peace, "in accordance with the former laws and usages of the Mexican government until Washington should direct otherwise."

As Commander of the Southern District, Gillespie imposed military law at Los Angeles, the only law with which he was familiar. He established a curfew and prohibited assemblies or the bearing of arms, much stricter rules than an alcalde would proclaim. Beale later commented on Gillespie's position:

It was an unfortunate thing that he did so, and led to after troubles. Gillespie made annoying orders, such as the Mexican population were unused to, instead of conciliating them with kindness and by allowing them all the freedom they had been accustomed to.

From the San Gabriel Mountains, Jose Castro and Pio Pico had continued retreating all the way to Sonora. The "peace and harmony among the people" under American rule didn't last long, however. Captain Jose Maria Flores violated his parole and gathered together a couple of hundred armed men. (The actual number has never been determined.) He placed Los Angeles under siege on September 25, 1846, and forced Gillespie with his small garrison to retire to San Pedro. Flores declared all California to be free and independent from American rule. He proclaimed himself Governor and Commandante General.

At Yerba Buena, Stockton remained ignorant of the turn of affairs in the south only as long as it took a superb horseman to ride the 500 miles. Beale wrote that Stockton had called him to his cabin on the *Congress:*

> He thought it important there should be a governor agreeable to the people at San Jose and for that purpose intended me. Before I could receive his written instructions the surprising intelligence reached him of a rising at Los Angeles of the Mexican people and the fact that Gillespie had been forced to retreat to San Diego. All we had done in the previous campaign had been undone!

This disturbing report reached Stockton by the courier John Brown, known as "Juan Flaco" to the Mexicans. He made one of the most remarkable horseback rides in American history. Brown was one of the volunteers left at Los Angeles. As Gillespie retreated to San Pedro, Brown slipped through the Mexican lines and rode furiously to Yerba Buena. He covered almost 500 miles in five days.

Beale wrote that his commander "was not a man to cry over spilt milk, but said the next time he would make it stronger and begin work again from San Diego." Stockton ordered Captain

Mervine to take the *Savannah* to Gillespie's relief at San Pedro.
Beale's instructions for San Jose were cancelled. Instead, Stockton ordered him to find Fremont, who was somewhere in Northern California, advise him of the rebellion in the south and
convey instructions to bring his battalion to San Francisco. Small
boats from the *Congress* were assigned to Beale and he set off
on his search for Fremont. Beale found him at Sonoma, and
Fremont noted in his memoirs that he was

> . . . ordered to come forthwith to San Francisco with all the men
> and saddles I could obtain. Beale was a real midshipman of the old
> type, happy and spilling over with good spirits as mostly midshipmen
> are used to be when away from the restraints of the ship. The delta
> of the San Joaquin and Sacramento rivers and the bay and its sloughs
> at that time were not familiar to seagoing men or, indeed, men of
> any kind. Of his navigation through the *tulares* in search of me I will
> let Beale speak for himself.

Beale put his recollections into a letter written at Fremont's
request in 1872:

> I remember the lovely spring-like morning. It was autumn but
> ought to have been spring because I was so happy when ordered to
> command a squadron of boats and go find Fremont . . . Wide and
> beautiful before us was the splendid and lovely bay. We looked
> curiously at Red Rock, passed *La Isla de las Yeguas* (Mare Island)
> and met the furious tide of Carquinez Straits. My remembrance is it
> steered us!

Beale recalled camping for the night and next morning looking
out over a "vast ocean of tules and toward where the Sacramento
and San Joaquin came together in the great *mere* of that wonder-
ful delta." Beale said they discovered a man on horseback.

> . . . whereupon we prepared to give him a broadside, and were
> already owners in fancy of a horse and saddle when to our disgust
> he spoke English and proved to be Jake Snyder of Fremont's battalion
> . . . I went with him to Sonoma, two on one horse, I holding onto
> the taffrail when at a gallop! The town was all ablaze. Old Ide was
> there, and Cosgrove, and Snyder and Hensley and Bidwell and Gib-
> son and a lot of others. The next day we all went to the boats and

set sail for the bay again . . . Fremont being naturally in the fastest boat with me, we outsailed the fleet and at nightfall hauled up on an island . . .

Next day, Beale delivered Fremont to the *Congress*. This experience cemented a friendship between Beale and Fremont that endured throughout their lives.

Stockton ordered Fremont to procure horses and ride to Southern California with his battalion, recruiting as he went. Stockton made ready to sail for San Diego. From there his battalion of sailors would march north. The two battalions would meet at Los Angeles and drive out General Flores, who they learned had been joined by Governor Pio Pico's brother, General Andres Pico. Fremont left for the long 500-mile march south with a large herd of cattle, adding volunteers along the way until his battalion strength reached 400.

Meanwhile, the *Savannah* sailed for San Pedro, arriving there on October 7. Lieutenant Marius Duvall gave a good account of the proceedings: "Captain Archibald Gillespie came aboard and reported he had evacuated the *Pueblo de Los Angeles* after having spiked his guns, on account of the overpowering force of the enemy." Captain Mervine then decided to retake Los Angeles on his own. Without waiting for Stockton, he landed 299 men on October 9, picked up Gillespie's volunteers and started back toward the pueblo. At Rancho Dominguez, some miles short of his objective, a party of 120 mounted Mexicans under Captain Jose Antonio Carillo blocked Mervine's way — hardly an "overpowering force." Lieutenant Duvall recorded the incident:

> The enemy appeared before us mounted on fine horses, each man armed with a lance and carbine, having also a four-pounder field piece. We made frequent charges driving them before us but owing to the rapidity with which they could carry off the gun using *lassos,* enabled them to choose their own distance entirely out of range of our muskets, content to let the gun do their fighting. Finding it impossible to capture the gun, the retreat was sounded, for to continue the march would be sacrificing a number of lives to no purpose . . .

Mervine buried six of his dead near the mouth of San Pedro Bay. He carried his wounded back to the *Savannah* and set sail with Gillespie and the volunteers for San Diego. There he found that the anti-American insurrection had spread to San Diego. The garrison of volunteers left in charge by Fremont had been driven from the town.

While Mervine retreated from Rancho Dominguez and Beale prepared his carbineers to sail on the *Congress,* Kit Carson's courier party made its way eastward beyond the headwaters of the Gila River to the banks of the Rio Grande in New Mexico. They turned upstream and rode steadily northward toward Socorro and Albuquerque. On October 6, Carson halted his men to observe a ragged dust cloud on the horizon. Dust clouds in that country were not uncommon, but an experienced frontiersman proceeded with considerable caution if he knew the disturbance was caused by a large band of men on horseback. No doubt, the party paused at some vantage point to check their firearms and watched with all senses alert.

Emerging out of the dust cloud, to the certain surprise of Carson's men, moved a column of some 300 U. S. Dragoons. It was the Army of the West. At the head of the column rode Stephen Watts Kearny wearing the new gold stars of a Brigadier General. Along side Kearny, or probably out in front, rode his scout Thomas Fitzpatrick and another oldtimer, Antoine Robidoux — men easily recognized by Carson. They had all trapped beaver in the Rockies during the days when everything west of St. Louis was unknown and hostile frontier. Fitzpatrick, usually called Broken Hand, had been Carson's friend since 1831.

Their meeting followed the traditional pattern: Carson's little band charged down on the column with bloodcurdling screams, for all the world like an attack by savage Indians.

After initial greetings, formal and informal, the column moved down the river a few miles and made camp in a grove of cottonwoods. There Carson learned that the Mexican Army in New Mexico had retreated southward after the outbreak of war.

The Army of the West had taken Santa Fe on August 18 without opposition. Kearny placed Carson's friend Charles Bent in charge as Governor of the occupied territory and departed westward to conquer California.

While Carson, Fitzpatrick and Robidoux hunkered down to discuss old times and new wars, Kearny carefully read Commodor Stockton's report describing the end of hostilities in California with "peace and harmony restored among the people." Carson, of course, knew nothing about the Southern California uprising.

Kearny had already split his forces, sending some of his troops into Mexico under Colonel Alexander W. Doniphan. Now he decided to split his army once again and explained his action in a dispatch to Washington:

> I received an express from Commodore Stockton and Lieutenant Colonel Fremont reporting that all of California was in possession of the Americans; the American flag was flying from every important position in the territory. The war was ended. In consequence of this information, I directed that 200 dragoons under Major Sumner should remain in New Mexico and that the other 100 with two mountain howitzers under Captain Moore should accompany me as a guard to California.

All was not peaceful in California, as we know, nor was it so in New Mexico. Soon after Kearny left Santa Fe a bloody uprising at Taos resulted in the murder of Governor Bent. Before the revolt finally subsided, scores of the insurgents and twenty-five of the American force lay dead.

Over Kit Carson's objections, Kearny insisted the scout turn around and guide him and his dragoons to California. Kearny ordered Fitzpatrick to carry Stockton's report and Fremont's letters on to Washington.

By late October Fremont had advanced his party to San Juan Bautista, south of San Jose. The force now numbered over 400 mounted riflemen and a score of Indians. Two field pieces arrived from Monterey in charge of Lieutenant Louis McLane of the

USS *Levant*. One of Daingerfield Fauntleroy's couriers brought Fremont a packet from Consul Larkin containing letters from Jessie and Senator Benton. Jessie's letter told him that President Polk had promoted him to Lieutenant Colonel. "So your merit has advanced you in eight years from an unknown second lieutenant to the most talked of and admired man in the army!" she wrote. It is doubtful the Army "regulars" shared Jessie's admiration, but the Naval battalion rank bestowed by Stockton was now official in the Army too. He would henceforth be, in truth, Colonel Fremont.

He got as far south as San Luis Obispo when he heard of Mervine's defeat at San Pedro. The Californios again controlled all the country from Santa Barbara to San Diego. The horses and cattle that Fremont had expected to procure from ranchos en route were driven off by their owners and hidden in the hills. Consuming thirteen beeves a day, Fremont's men quickly used up their herd and Fremont had to put them on half rations. Moreover, it had been a dry year. The horses and mules were exhausted from lack of forage and water. He turned back reluctantly, sending word to Stockton of his change in plans. Back at San Juan Bautista, Fremont's men rounded up a herd of 100 head of cattle and 500 horses. On December 3 the long march down Salinas Valley began again.

Once more Stockton sailed south on the *Congress* with Beale's carbineers and the sailor army, bound for San Diego. The Californios who had routed the American garrison lacked organization and were themselves soon routed. A last token stand taken by a few Mexicans on Presidio Hill soon waned and San Diego "fell" for a second time. Stockton put the sailors and marines to drilling again for battles yet to be waged. The Commodore ordered twelve guns mounted on the hill in embrasures between casks filled with dirt. "Bobby's Boys" dubbed it Fort Stockton. Detailed as a cavalry officer, Beale switched once again from quarterdeck to saddlehorn. He rounded up cattle, horses and mules wherever he could find them. He experienced a flurry of excitement on at least one occasion. Beale later wrote:

> This [assignment] gave me every opportunity of acquiring knowledge of the country and people, in which I was aided by a tolerably good knowledge of Spanish. In one of these excursions, having with us several hundred head of cattle, we were attacked by the Mexicans and rather roughly handled. We nevertheless succeeded in beating them and carrying in the valuable loot we had collected.

His foraging expedition, according to Stockton's report, drove in ninety horses and 200 head of cattle.

Gillespie assumed command of the marines. The volunteer garrison returned to town and a good portion of the *Savannah's* crew joined the ranks. Indian scouts reported that General Andres Pico had stationed himself at Rancho San Bernardo with fifty men. Stockton ordered Gillespie to attack and destroy this camp.

Meanwhile Californio Rafael Machado deserted Pico. He told Stockton the Mexicans had been reinforced by an additional hundred men. Matters were delayed while Gillespie's party was similarly increased. Before Gillespie could march on Pico's force, however, there appeared one Edward Stokes bearing a letter addressed to Commodore Stockton. It carried such startling news that all plans were immediately cancelled.

4

At San Pasqual

Commodore Stockton had accepted an offer of hospitality
from Juan Bandini and established his headquarters in the Bandini's San Diego home, the biggest house in town. Stockton
savored his role of Commander and Military Governor. Not
all his time was devoted to matters of war, either, and Casa
Bandini became the social center of the community. Stockton
and his officers enjoyed frequent dancing parties, with daughters
of the Bandinis and their friends acting as hostesses. The squadron band often provided the music.

It was in the midst of one such fandango that rancher Edward
Stokes suddenly appeared and handed Stockton a letter dated
December 2, 1846. The letter originated at "Headquarters,
Army of the West, Camp at Warner's." It bore the signature
of "S. W. Kearny, Brigadier General, U.S.A."

I, this afternoon reached here (Warner's Ranch, forty-six miles
northeast of San Diego), escorted by a party of First Regiment Dragoons. I come by orders of the President of the United States. We
left Santa Fe on the 25th of September, having taken possession of
New Mexico, annexed it to the United States, established a civil
government in that territory and secured order, peace and quietness
there. If you can send a party to open communications with us, on
the route to this place, and to inform us of the state of affairs in
California, I wish you would do so, and as quickly as possible. Your
express by Mr. Carson was met on the Del Norte [Rio Grande],
and your mail must have reached Washington at least ten days since.
You might use the bearer, Mr. Stokes, to conduct your party to this
place. The fear of this letter falling into Mexican hands prevents
me from writing more.

The news stunned Stockton. He had no knowledge of Kearny's
approach or the size of his "party of First Dragoons." What-

ever its size, it would be a welcome addition to his Battalion of
Sailors. He changed Gillespie's orders, instructing him to go to
Kearny's support with a detachment of mounted riflemen and
a field piece. He wrote to Kearny:

> Captain Gillespie is well informed in relation to the present state
> of things in California, and will give you all the needed information.
> I have this evening received information, by a deserter from the rebel
> camp, of the arrival of an additional force in this neighborhood of
> 100 men, which makes their number about 150. I send with Captain
> Gillespie, as a guide, the deserter that you may make inquiries of
> him, and if you see fit, endeavor to surprise them.

Stockton signed himself, "Commander-in-Chief and Governor
of the Territory of California," so there would be no doubt
in the General's mind with whom he was dealing.

Edward Beale and James M. Duncan were ordered to accompany Gillespie with some of Beale's carbineers and a brass four-
pounder. Guided by the deserter, Rafael Machado, Gillespie,
Beale and thirty-eight men, some of them local volunteers, made
their way up the valley past Mission San Diego de Alcala. They
could expect to fall in with Kearny some forty miles northeast
of San Diego. Also under Gillespie's command were two of
Fremont's men, scout Alexander Godey, who scrawled his name
"Alexis," the extent of his literacy, and a Delaware Indian.

A two-day forced march in cold, steady rain brought Gillespie's small party to Kearny's camp. There Beale expressed surprise to find Kit Carson, whom he had last seen at Los Angeles
departing overland for Washington. From Carson, Beale learned
details of the Army of the West. Kearny's orders from President
Polk were to secure New Mexico and then proceed on to California where, "Should you conquer and take possession of California, you will establish a civil government."

The President seemed unaware that the Secretaries of the
State and Naval departments had issued virtually identical
orders to both Sloat and Stockton, a complication which eventually led to monumental squabbling among General Kearny, Commodore Stockton and Colonel Fremont.

Kearny's sad little army consisted of exhausted men and half-starved mules and horses. It rained steadily on the Army of the West since leaving Warner's Ranch. They were mentally fatigued as well as physically worn down, cold and sick. Beale noted their pitiful condition. He told General Kearny that by the right-hand road he would meet the Mexicans ready to dispute his way. By the left-hand road he would get to San Diego without opposition. Beale strongly advised avoiding the enemy, who was well armed and superbly mounted. Carson and Gillespie, however, had a low opinion of the Mexican's desire or ability to fight. And Gillespie, still smarting from his ouster at Los Angeles, hankered for revenge. Kearny ignored Beale's advice and decided to take the right-hand road. Rather than avoid General Andres Pico, he would seek him out. Carson later said Kearny chose to press the attack with an eye to capturing Pico's horses.

Kearny learned from Stokes that Pico had moved his force to San Pasqual, a small Indian rancheria nearby — on the right-hand road. Despite the depleted condition of his command — and probably a bit strung out from fatigue himself — Kearny resolved, with the help of Gillespie's men, to attack Pico's camp. On the night of December 5, he ordered Lieutenant Thomas C. Hammond to reconnoiter the area with a patrol of ten men guided by Rafael Machado. Hammond returned at 2 a.m. to report that his party had discovered the enemy camp, and had in turn been discovered but not pursued. Army surgeon John Strother Griffin wrote in his journal that notwithstanding the Mexican's knowledge of their presence, "General Kearny still naively expected to surprise the enemy."

San Pasqual was situated in an area of rolling foothills rising gradually from the sea toward the Santa Rosa Mountains, which are the northern end of the Peninsular Ranges of Baja California. The hills are mostly rough, rocky ridges cut by canyons which open into frequent small, flat valleys of sandy soil and semi-desert vegetation. The little collection of hovels called San Pasqual squatted in one such valley some thirty miles north of

San Diego. It was hardly an auspicious location for battle, and certainly not a convenient one. But the places where men die are seldom auspicious and never convenient. For twenty-one Americans it was scruffy country with nothing more to recommend it than plenty of sand to soak up their blood.

The Army of the West moved out at dawn on December 6. First in line of march rode Captain Abraham Robinson Johnston with an advance guard of twelve men. General Kearny followed closely with a small group consisting of Lieutenant William Hemsley Emory of the Topographical Engineers and Lieutenant William Horace Warner with five men of their survey party. It isn't clear why a survey party rode in such a vital forward position. Nothing else about the engagement makes good sense either. Next rode Captain Benjamin D. Moore and Lieutenant Hammond with fifty dragoons, then Gillespie with the troop from San Diego.

Edward Beale and Lieutenant Davidson followed with the three pieces of artillery. Major Thomas Swords brought up the rear guard with the baggage train of pack-mules. The advance on the Mexican position straggled out for half a mile. Captain Henry Smith Turner rode back and forth along the line attempting to close up the gaps between units. Constant rain had dampened the powder in their carbines but it occurred to no one to order the weapons recharged.

From a hillside above the Indian village, Johnston's advance party observed Pico's men moving about in the morning drizzle. Kearny came up and without waiting for the main body of his troops ordered Johnston to charge the camp. It isn't known how Johnston reacted to this command, but it must have come as a shock. We can only assume he would have been much more comfortable with the full force of dragoons at his back and not leading an attack with just his small advance guard and Emory's surveyors. But off he rode, dutifully leading his group in a scrambling charge down the hill.

Pico's men were not professional soldiers. Indeed, they were nothing more than a pickup force of militia rangers, California vaqueros armed with long lances. They were all expert horsemen, but at a disadvantage fighting on foot. Yet, seeing only a small force charging down upon them, they stood their ground. They fired what weapons they had and prepared to receive the gringos on their lances.

The brave Captain Abraham Johnston fell almost immediately with a bullet through his forehead. His death brought the charge to a halt and allowed the Californios time to run for their horses. Kearny now decided to wait for Moore, Hammond and the fifty dragoons to come up. The Californios mounted and drew off rapidly down the little valley in apparent disarray. The dragoons followed in a wild charge, tearing down the hill and through the village as fast as they could spur their jaded mounts.

When Pico reached a fork in the valley road, he took half his men on ahead, while the remainder under Captain Juan B. Moreno took the fork. The Americans dashed after Pico. Moreno circled back and charged their rear. Pico suddenly wheeled his lancers around to charge their front. The dragoons found themselves in a classic trap. They were surrounded by Californios. Their sabers proved a poor match for the long lances. The butchery was terrible but brief. The Americans were unhorsed and lanced repeatedly as they lay on the ground.

Captain Moore died during hand-to-hand combat with General Pico. Moore's sword broke at the hilt in parrying the General's thrust. Two Californios, Jose Antonio Serrano and Leandro Osuna, rushed in and killed Moore with their lances.

Gillespie's skill as a swordsman proved of no avail as the lance of Dolores Higuera pierced his chest. The shaft caught him a glancing blow and knocked out two of his front teeth. Thrown from his mount, Gillespie feigned death while Higuera made off with his horse.

Kit Carson rode in the van of Hammond's charge when his horse fell. The stock of his rifle broke off and he lay on the ground as the entire troop of dragoons galloped over him. He was miraculously unhurt. The fall, in fact, may have saved Carson's life. Of Hammond's troop of fifty, thirty were either killed or wounded. Before Carson could remount and get back into the fight, the action was over. General Kearny received two lance wounds but managed to retain his seat until Beale, Davidson and Henry Baker came up with the artillery.

Before Baker could bring his howitzer to bear, Gabriel Garcia delivered a fatal thrust with his lance. Francisco Lara attempted to run off Beale's little four-pounder. Beale coolly stood his ground. He seems to have been one of the few Americans to keep his powder dry, for one shot from his pistol brought the Mexican down with a shattered leg.

The Californios beat a hasty retreat when they saw the American rear guard advancing. The mules hauling Baker's howitzer became frightened in the noise and confusion and plunged wildly after the retreating enemy. The lancers made off with the gun as a prize. Major Swords came up with the rear guard and collected the dead and wounded, all of whom had been lanced repeatedly. Kearny's wounds were painful enough for him to turn over command to Captain Turner.

A shot killed Pablo Vejar's horse. Vejar and Francisco Lara, the man Beale dropped with his pistol, were taken prisoner. Philip Crossthwaite, one of the San Diego volunteers, took charge of the captives. It was all he could do to keep Fremont's Delaware scout from scalping them.

The battered force made camp on an elevated position, defendable but without water. Beale's howitzer kept the lancers out of range.

Pico sent a messenger to Flores at Los Angeles reporting eleven of his men slightly wounded and asked for reinforcements to wipe out *los gringos,* whose position was so precarious they had no chance to escape. Many of the Americans' horses were killed. They were out of food and water. The ground was so covered with rocks and cactus it was difficult to find places where the wounded could be stretched out in any comfort.

Dr. Griffin spent the remainder of December 6 dressing wounds. Among the dead he listed captains Johnston and Moore, Lieutenant Hammond and sixteen others. He listed Edward

Beale among the wounded, along with General Kearny, Captain Gillespie, Captain Gibson of the San Diego volunteers, guide Antoine Robidoux, Lieutenant Warner of the Engineers, Sergeant Cox, privates Kennedy and Streeter, and ten other dragoons. Within a few days, Cox and Kennedy died of their wounds, thus revising the list to twenty-one dead and sixteen wounded.

Beale's injury was apparently slight for he never mentions it in his writing. Accounts of General Pico's losses vary. Kearny maintained in his official report that the number of dead and wounded "must have been considerable." Judge Benjamin Hayes and William Heath Davis, residents of San Diego who knew most of Pico's men personally, swore that Pico did not lose a single man. Pico's report to General Flores that he had eleven slightly wounded is generally accepted as correct if we discount Beale's victim, Lara, whose shattered leg had to be amputated later at Los Angeles.

The American dead were buried at night, Lieutenant Emory mourning,

> Thus were put to rest together and forever a band of brave and heroic men. The long march of 2,000 miles had brought our little command, both officers and men, to know each other well. Community of hardships, dangers and privations had produced relations of mutual regard which caused their loss to sink deeply in our memories.

Beale suggested that wheeled carretas be sent for at San Diego to transport the wounded. Acting on Beale's suggestion, Captain Turner sent Alex Godey and Thomas Burgess to carry a letter through the Mexican lines to Commodore Stockton:

> Headquarters, Camp near San Pasqual. At early dawn this morning General Kearny with a detachment of United States Dragoons and Captain Gillespie's company of mounted riflemen had an engagement with a very considerable Mexican force near this camp. We have about eighteen killed and fourteen or fifteen wounded, several so severely that it may be impracticable to move them for several days. I have to suggest to you the propriety of dispatching, without delay, a considerable force to meet us on the road to San Diego. We

are without provisions . . . General Kearny is among the wounded, but it is hoped not dangerously; Captains Moore and Johnston, First Dragoons, killed; Lieutenant Hammond, First Dragoons, dangerously wounded.

Even as Turner wrote, Hammond lay dying and some of the other wounded were in critical condition. Godey and Burgess rode all night. They succeeded in evading the enemy and reached San Diego the morning of the Seventh. While returning with Stockton's reply, both men were taken prisoner by Pico's lancers. Godey hid Stockton's written message in an oak tree before he was captured. (One of Bandini's vaqueros found it years later.) It was perhaps just as well the besieged camp never received the message. Addressed to "H. S. Turner, Captain, U.S.A., Cmdg. at Camp near San Pasqual," it read:

Your letter by Lieutenant Godey communicating to me the sad intelligence of the fight which took place yesterday at early dawn, reached me last night, and I would have instantly sent a detachment to aid you but unfortunately every horse that could travel had been sent with the riflemen, and left us without any means to transport our artillery. We have not an animal in the garrison that can go two leagues, besides we have no conveyance or means of any kind to transport the wounded . . .

While the men on the hill waited in misery through the long night, Carson and three of his mountain men — Peterson, Londeau and Perrot — made up *travois* drags to be drawn by the remaining mules for transporting the wounded. The command made ready to move out at first light. Emory wrote:

Day dawned on the most tattered and ill-fed detachment of men that ever the United States mustered under her colors. Our provisions were exhausted, our horses dead, our mules on their last legs, and our men now reduced to a third of their number, ragged, worn down by fatigue and emaciated.

But move out they did. As the straggling column advanced, the lancers retired, always safely out of range. By mid-afternoon of the seventh, the plodding men reached Rancho San Bernardo and feasted on the owner's chickens. A small hill with a steam at its base offered a fair camping spot. The Americans successfully routed some of Pico's men from its slopes. The enemy took up a position controlling the stream, however, and Kearny found himself again under siege.

A lancer approached the camp at daylight under a flag of truce. He carried a proposal from General Pico for an exchange of prisoners — Godey and Burgess for Lara and Vejar. Lara preferred to remain under Crossthwaite's care. Kearny sent Emory to make the exchange with only Vejar, for whom Emory was given Burgess. The return of Burgess was disappointing, for he knew nothing of the contents of the letter from Stockton.

In a lengthy oration before Congress crediting Edward Beale with the exchange of prisoners, Senator Benton gave an entirely different version:

> The flag of truce carried a proposition to exchange prisoners but Kearny was alarmed at it and saw nothing in it but a trick and lure to perfidy. He was afraid to meet the flag, and none would venture to go. There was a lad present, his name Beale, who volunteered to go. Great was the alarm at his departure. The little river San Bernardo was crossed at a plunging gallop. Thus he set out, protected by a flag and followed by anxious eyes and palpitating hearts. Approaching a picket-guard, his mission was made known for Beale spoke Spanish. Kearny had but one Californian, sole fruit of the victory at San Pasqual . . .

Benton had obviously not read Emory's account of the exchange, nor artist John Mix Stanley's. As Stanley remembered it the truce originated with the American camp: "A white flag was sent to Senor Pico, the Californian commandant, and an exchange of prisoners effected." Beale was hardly a "lad," but within a month of his twenty-fifth birthday. Each side had two prisoners, not one. Beale by the widest stretch of the imagination would not have described the disaster as a "victory."

It became apparent from Pico's failure to attack that he intended to starve the Americans into submission. Any attempt to break through the Californio lines would surely result in death, but Kearny saw no alternative. His men were determined to die fighting rather than surrender. He decided to hold out for one more day and make a last attempt to get word through to Stockton.

Again Senator Benton lectured Congress:

> To send another express to Stockton seemed hopeless, the distance and dangers were so great. Besides, who would venture to go, seeing the fate of Godey? It was a moment to find a hero, and one presented himself. It was again the lad Beale. Asked whom he would have as his companions, "Carson and my Indian servant," was the reply. Carson has since told me that Beale volunteered first.

In his memoirs, however, Carson said he volunteered first and Beale agreed to go with him. Beale, of course, had no "Indian servant." The Indian was Fremont's Delaware scout who had been with Godey and the San Diego volunteers. In still another version, William E. Smythe identified the Indian as Panto, alcalde of the San Pasqual rancheria.

Nevertheless, Beale, Carson and the Indian started the night of the Eighth on their hazardous thirty-mile venture, barefooted and crawling part of the way to avoid alarming the Californio sentinels. They stayed together for awhile, then separated to increase the chances of at least one getting through. The Indian made it in first on the afternoon of the Ninth. He had barely reported to Stockton when Beale was brought in, closely followed by Carson, both completely exhausted. They lost their shoes and their feet were badly torn and bleeding from rocks and cactus thorns.

As they were being cared for, the USS *Portsmouth* sailed into San Diego harbor from San Francisco. Seaman Joseph Downey recorded what happened:

> By 5 p.m. we were anchored in the harbor. Fighting Bob [Stockton] sent an order down for the Old Man [Commander Montgomery] to land and dispatch forthwith to town 150 men, with a due complement of officers, and come himself prepared to assume command of the governorship of the town. In a very few minutes the crew was on deck, muskets, carbines, pistols, pikes and ammunition strewed all

over the quarterdeck and the men formed into different companies. Every officer fore and aft was to go, save the gunner and Lieutenant Misroon. We were ordered into line and off we started at a dog trot to the quarters of Commodore Stockton where we were ordered to procure marching rations as we were to march in an hour to relieve the command of General Kearny.

Stockton ordered the relief to start at once. Somehow, he managed to scare up horses and wagons to carry provisions. Under command of Lieutenant Andrew F. V. Gray of the *Congress,* 180 jack-tars and marines with two howitzers marched all night of the Ninth. They laid over the next day to avoid discovery by the Californios and continued their march the next night.

At Kearny's camp, the hours of the Ninth dragged slowly. Dr. Griffin noted, "We are reduced to mule meat." Sergeant John Cox died and was buried on the hill. The weather remained cold and Emory feared for the life of the old mountain man, Antoine Robidoux, who had been severely lanced:

> The loss of blood from his wounds, added to the coldness of the night, made me think he would never see daylight. I found my cook heating a cup of coffee and one of the most agreeable little offices performed in my life was to pour this precious draft into the waning body of Robidoux. His warmth returned, with hopes of life. In gratitude he gave me half a cake made of brown flour, black with dirt. I ate more than half of it when several of the most loathsome insects were exposed to my view. My hunger overcame my fastidiousness, and the *morceau* did not appear particularly disgusting.

Robidoux, nearly as well known and highly regarded in the fur trade as Kit Carson, entered New Mexico in the early 1820's. Like Carson, he made his home there and distinguished himself as a trapper, trader, legitimate businessman and, in 1830, president of the Santa Fe *Junta del Ayuntamiento,* or town council. Robidoux built and operated the first trading post west of the Continental Divide in the Rockies, called Fort Uncompahgre in what is now southwestern Colorado. He later constructed Fort Uintah, usually called "Fort Wintey," south of the Uintah

Mountains, and perhaps a third outpost somewhere in that wilderness. The Ute Indians destroyed his "forts" in the mid-1840's. Like so many old trappers, Robidoux turned to earning his living as a scout, guide and interpreter.

They butchered another mule on the hill next day. Dr. Griffin reported that most of the wounded showed improvement. When night fell with no sign of the prayed-for relief, Kearny felt they must move off the hill at daylight. The wounded were lashed to the *travois*. Early in the morning of the Eleventh, the men heard the creaking of wheels. Lieutenant Gray and his men climbed "Mule Hill" in the first light of dawn, where they were greeted with whoops of joy. The relief column distributed food while the wounded were made comfortable in the wagons. The enemy had disappeared from sight. They broke camp and by late afternoon the combined forces reached Rancho los Penasquitos, where all hands feasted on Francisco Alvarado's turkeys, chickens and wine.

When the company reached San Diego on the afternoon of the Twelfth, the wounded were distributed among the homes of San Diego families to be treated by Dr. Griffin and *Cyane* surgeons Charles D. Maxwell and Lewis B. Hunter. Private Joseph B. Kennedy died on December 21. The bodies of all the dead were later recovered from their hasty burial places and interred in the American Cemetery in San Diego. Their remains were ultimately reinterred in a grave at the United States Military Cemetery at Fort Rosecrans, San Diego.

Kit Carson stated in his memoirs years later that "Lieutenant Beale was sent aboard the *Congress,* deranged from the fatigue of the service he performed and did not recover for two years." Carson overstates Beale's condition. Although Beale recovered his strength slowly, he had sufficiently recuperated by the end of December to take part in the march on Los Angeles. A month after that he and Carson left San Diego overland for Washington.

With his long march to the Pacific ended, General Kearny found that San Diego and all of California north of Santa Barbara were in American hands. Only Los Angeles and its immediate environs were still under control of the Californios. Stockton had already established a civil government with himself as Military Governor of California, a post he explained to Kearny had been promised by Stockton to Fremont. Kearny made no objection at the time.

Neither the Mormon Battalion, on its way by land, nor Stevenson's Regiment of New York Volunteers, on its way by sea, had yet arrived in California. Kearny had but fifty-seven able-bodied dragoons. In contrast, Stockton commanded 700 sailors and marines, Fremont's Naval battalion of 400 or more, and some scattered northern volunteers. Nevertheless, Stockton offered overall command to Kearny, who refused it until his own army forces arrived. Preparations for the move on Los Angeles proceeded with Stockton retaining his position as Commander-in-Chief.

Kearny's first report to the Adjutant General from San Diego, dated December 12, 1846, described his operations up to December 5 and his meeting with Gillespie's initial relief column from San Diego. Kearny claimed Gillespie told him he "would have to contend with an enemy of 600 or 700 in arms." But Gillespie knew about only the 150 lancers under Andres Pico which had been reported by Rafael Machado.

In a second report, Kearny gave his version of the battle on the Sixth. It is filled with distortions. "As the day dawned, we approached the enemy at San Pasqual, who was already in the saddle." In fact, the lancers were afoot when Kearny first approached their camp. "Captain Johnston made a furious charge upon them supported by the dragoons." Actually, Johnston's charge was made by his small party with no support at all from the dragoons. "After which the enemy gave way, having kept up from the beginning a continued fire upon us." If this was true, the Californios must have been uncommonly poor marksmen for only the body of Captain Johnston and one other showed gunshot wounds. Kearny continued:

Upon retreat of the enemy, Captain Moore led off rapidly in pursuit, accompanied by the dragoons on their horses and followed slowly by others on their tired mules. After retreating about half a mile the enemy, well mounted and among the best horsemen in the world, rallied their whole force, charged with the lances and on account of their greatly superior numbers but few of us in front remained untouched. We again drove them and they fled from the field, which we occupied and camped upon.

Kearny does not mention Beale and Baker bringing up the artillery that actually occasioned the enemy's retreat. Neither does Kearny reveal that the enemy withdrew as a ruse to lure his troops into an ambush. His report continues:

> The enemy proved to be a party of 160 Californians under Andres Pico and the number of their dead and wounded must have been considerable. They carried off all but six.

If they did leave six behind, it is a curious matter. There were no Mexican dead. Kearny took but two prisoners, Vejar and Lara. Furthermore, Kearny reported the loss of Captain Johnston and "sixteen men killed, six officers and eleven men wounded," contending that,

> The great number of our killed and wounded proves that our officers and men have fully sustained the high character and reputation of our troops, and the victory thus gained over more than double our force may assist in forming the wreath of our national glory.

The courage of Kearny and his men is not to be questioned, but it is difficult to view the battle as a victory. Although Kearny initially gives Pico's strength as 160, approximately the size of his own, in the next paragraph he says that the enemy is "double our force." He singles out Captain Turner and Lieutenant Emory for "gallantry and good conduct in the field," but to his shame Kearny never once mentions Edward Beale, Kit Carson or the Delaware Indian. It was they who brought the relief that saved what was left of Kearny's command.

These excerpts from Kearny's reports register the general tenor of his attempts to portray San Pasqual as a great victory. He even prevailed upon his officers to adopt his own version of the affair. Captain Turner left no official account of the battle in his journal, but he briefly summarized it in a letter to his wife dated December 21. Writing from San Diego, he counted the enemy as "quadruple our strength." Turner also made no mention of Beale or Carson and only casual reference to "the reinforcements sent out by Commodore Stockton, who having heard of our fight very wisely considered that such assistance would be acceptable to us." Neither did he mention that Stockton's assistance came in response to his own appeal for relief.

In contrast, Kearny expressed his gratitude to Stockton in his report: "I offer my thanks to Commodore Stockton and all of his gallant command for the very many kind attentions we have received and continue to receive from them."

Turner, however, did not share his superior's opinion. Turner's complaints about his benefactor's conduct are made explicit in another letter to his wife:

> We have had a great deal to contend with since our arrival, in the discourteous conduct of Commodore Stockton. He is doing his utmost to undermine us at home by conniving at the reports for publication of our battle at San Pasqual. Several of his satellites, the loathsome sycophants he has kept about him, have been preparing them.

These references must have been to Beale, Gillespie and Carson, for what others would be reporting to Stockton accounts at variance with Kearny's and Turner's version?

Edward Beale received this testimonial on December 21 from a group of his shipmates:

> Dear Beale,
>
> We your friends and brother officers have ordered from England a pair of epaulettes and sword to be presented to you by the hands of Lieutenant Tilghman, in testimony of our admiration of your gallant conduct in the bold and hazardous enterprise of leaving General Kearny's encampment, after the Battles of San Pasqual and San Bernardo of the 6th of December, 1846, for the purpose of bringing information to the garrison of San Diego and obtaining relief for the suffering troops. Your bravery in the field of action and cool determination in the service above merits our warm applause and we con-

gratulate you on the opportunity of distinction which you so hand-
somely improved . . . Hoping that the President of the United States
will not overlook your merit and that you may speedily wear the
epaulettes and sword as the mark of your legitimate rank, we remain,
yours faithfully.

Twenty of Beale's fellow officers of the Pacific Squadron signed
the presentation. In time, the sword and epaulettes intended for
the rank of Lieutenant arrived from England. Commodore Stockton advanced Beale immediately from Passed Midshipman to
Acting Lieutenant, although the promotion did not receive
official confirmation until August 3, 1850.

Agonizing over the Battle of San Pasqual didn't occupy the
Americans for long. The enemy remained in the larger field,
and the field had yet to be taken.

5

California Conquered

Preparations were advanced at San Diego for the march on Los Angeles. The sailor army and Kearny's men drilled, exercised the artillery and fired at targets. The whole command paraded each afternoon under the direction of General Kearny, who had recovered enough from his wounds to return to active duty. Seaman Joseph Downey of the *Portsmouth* watched with interest:

> [The men were] instructed in the mysteries of having no eyes but for the commander, and no ears to hear naught but the commands. They were taught to march and countermarch, wheel by platoons and battalion, and form a hollow square to receive a charge of cavalry. They were drilled to charge, and such a hurrah accompanied this movement would have scared the Californians, if nothing else!

Commodore Stockton wrote Secretary Bancroft that one hundred more horses would enable him to mount some of his own men, "and before long I expect to be General of Dragoons as well as Commodore-Governor and Commander-in-Chief!" Downey tells, tongue-in-cheek, why this never came about:

> During the drilling period the idea popped into the brain of the Commodore. He would form a corps of horse marines, a body often talked about but never seen. Long marines got short horses and short marines long horses. Those were good riders got gentle horses and those who had never mounted a horse got the wildest of the lot. Every man equipped himself with the enormous spurs worn in this country and awaited the command to mount. No sooner mounted than a number were dismounted, some came over the head and some over the stern of the horse. Horses ran away with and without riders and marines were strewed from one end of town to the other. I shall say no more about this but to say this scheme did not work!

Edward Beale with his mounted troops again collected horses, mules and cattle. Teams were assigned and provisions and ammunition loaded. Five cannons were mounted on wheels. General Kearny seemed determined to wipe out the memory of San Pasqual, the sailors equally determined to avenge the double loss of Los Angeles under Gillespie and Mervine. They all knew that the Mormon Battalion and Stevenson's Regiment were on the way, and they deemed it necessary to defeat the enemy before the soldiers arrived to deprive them of the glory.

Stockton, as Commander-in-Chief, appointed Lieutenant Stephen C. Rowan of the *Savannah* Troop Commander of the sailor army. Kearny objected. He said that he should be in command. "I immediately sent for Lieutenant Rowan," Stockton put into the record, "assembled the officers, and stated to them that General Kearny had volunteered to take command of the troops, but that I retained my own position as Commander-in-Chief." Stockton did not state in the record whether Kearny was present to witness this statement. The General continued to address the Commodore in communications as "Governor of California and Commanding United States Forces," so Stockton had no reason to think he was regarded as anything else. This complex division of authority seems typical of the muddled war picture in California. Kearny commanded the troops, but Stockton commanded Kearny.

Stockton selected as aides-de-camp Lieutenant Andrew F. V. Gray, leader of the relief expedition to Mule Hill, and Captain Miguel Pedrorena of the San Diego Volunteers. Edward Beale received orders to lead one company of mounted carbineers, James M. Duncan a second company. Richard L. Tilghman, a lieutenant from the *Congress,* commanded the artillery. His cannoneers carried pikes and pistols. Lieutenant John W. Livingston of the *Congress* captained the 100 marines. Gillespie continued to command the mounted San Diego Volunteers, who were assigned as skirmishers and were enviously called by Downey the "twenty-five dollar men" — twice his monthly salary. Kit Carson and a squad of his mountain men rode ahead as scouts.

General Kearny appointed Lieutenant Emory to be his aide. The fifty-seven dragoons proceeded on foot, exchanging for pikes the long cavalry sabres which had proven so ineffective at San Pasqual. Captain Turner, Lieutenant Warner and Dr. Griffin marched with the dragoons. Captain Santiago E. Arguello of the San Diego Volunteers managed a group of vaqueros engaged to herd the cattle. Lieutenant George Minor of the *Savannah* took charge of the wagon train bringing up the rear. Major Swords had been sent to the Sandwich Islands. The balance of 300 sailors formed five companies of musketeers.

Stockton's Battalion of Sailors now mustered a complement of 600 fighting men. Each company was assigned the place it would hold in the line of march. Their route was El Camino Real, a 100-mile road connecting the Missions of San Diego de Alcala, San Luis Rey de Francia, San Juan Capistrano and San Gabriel Arcangel near Los Angeles. Seventy-eight years of constant use had worn the old trail into a well marked thoroughfare requiring no guides.

The *Cyane* arrived at San Diego on December 27 and contributed her share of seamen to Stockton's growing army. The next day, companies were assigned baggage wagons and received provisions for seven days at one half ration per day. The battalion assembled on the Twenty-ninth in the San Diego plaza in full marching order, "every man with light heart and heavy knapsack," quipped Downey:

> The artillery, baggage, provision and ammunition cars [were] in their proper places, the *vaqueros* hallooing at the top of their voices to keep the cattle in order. It was a splendid and heartwarming sight to see these brave men who had in a manner unsexed themselves and become what a sailor hates most – soldiers! No man less acquainted with the *minutae* of a sailor's character than Stockton could ever have done it.

Rudyard Kipling would have loved this moment, the true embodiment of, " 'E's a kind of giddy harumfrodite, soldier an' sailor too!"

Stockton, Kearny, the San Diego volunteers, Beale's and Duncan's carbineers, Carson's scouts and Arguello's vaqueros were the only mounted elements. Stockton gave the order and the Battalion of Sailors moved out afoot. The men from the *Cyane* had but two days of drill and stumbled along in the ranks, footsore in the first three miles.

After a tedious five-day march to Mission San Luis Rey, a distance no greater than forty miles, the men rested among the ruins on January 3 and 4, 1847, and, according to Downey,

> . . . put to use a quantity of good old wine, and amuse themselves by leaving as mementos the names and effigies of our separate ships, done in charcoal upon the whitewashed walls.

Later that year, men of the Mormon Battalion gave the walls a new coat of whitewash and, to posterity's loss, covered up the sailors' art.

The battalion plodded onward to Mission San Juan Capistrano, sixty-five miles from San Diego, where Downey wrote:

> A goodly quantity of Californians and Indians gawked at the arrival of this long train of men and wagons. Fond of pomp, the Commodore ordered up the band and we marched past in all the pride of a military display. The gazers returned to that height of California comfort, a cigar and a dish of frijoles, and never troubled themselves further with the march of an enemy through their country.

The battalion approached the San Gabriel River (at what is now the Montebello area of Los Angeles) on January 7, 1847, where, true to his threat, Flores awaited them. The marchers saw a troop of thirty horsemen on a small hill. The sun shone bright as silver on their lance tips, the shafts decorated with red flags and ribbons. Before they had come within gunshot range, however, the troop galloped off and disappeared over the hill. Unintimidated, the battalion continued up the rise and made camp.

Jose Maria Flores, despite his title of General, had never commanded regularly trained professional soldiers — nor did he have any to command now. On the other hand, all of the Americans with the exception of the San Diego volunteers and a handful of mountain men and scouts were trained military men accustomed to strict discipline. The vaqueros under Flores were well fed and rested, however, and they rode fresh mounts.

Downey described the final preparations for battle:

> At early dawn the bugle blew, calling us to duty. When we got in line the "Old Soldier" [Kearny] bade us recollect that we were to cross the *Rio San Gabriel,* saying, "The Commodore has given me sole charge of you jacks. We have to cross the river and whip the enemy and we will do it if you jacks obey implicitly the orders given you. Let every man conduct himself so that the 8th of January, 1847, may be placed in the calendar of fame alongside January 8, 1815, when General Andy Jackson whipped the British at New Orleans."

Stockton also had to speak his piece, and pledged, "If I live and the enemy will fight, I will give San Gabriel a name in history along with that of the Bridge of Lodi." At the conclusion of their orations, the Old Soldier and Fighting Bob were given three cheers and the battalion moved forward in two columns with the dragoons in front and three pieces of artillery in the rear. The rear guard marched with the remaining two cannons, forming a rectangle in the center of which were the wagons, cattle and mules. Downey recalled:

> As we drew near the river, on the opposite bank rose a small hill on which Flores and his horsemen were in plain view, at least 600 or 700 men, all mounted, their lances glittering in the sun. We were in the dark as to whether they had any artillery, but the first shot set all doubt to rest. It fell so short it caused a laugh of derision and the second flew clear over our heads, and again the laugh went around . . . The dragoons were first to ford the river, looking back to find our artillery stuck in the quicksands. Fighting Bob's dander was up. Off he comes from his horse and seizes the drag ropes. "Now men, pull for your lives," says he, "don't for the love of God lose these guns!" Each man seizes hold with a will and, with a cheer, over they go, while the water is ploughed in all directions with discharges of grape, which flew like hail around them. The guns were crossed, the Commodore taking charge of them himself, and in less than three discharges a loud cheer announced he had capsized one of their guns.

The main body were steadily advancing, the Old Soldier, gathering his pistol in one hand and riding whip in the other, got off the animal and reached the bank at the head of the column. Above the din of battle could be heard his voice, "Steady my lads, steady. Keep perfectly cool you jacks, don't hurry yourselves." All this time the artillery were banging away at each other and in the midst of all stood Fighting Bob with telescope in hand, sighting first this gun and then that, his face glowing with animation . . . When the last were across we were ordered to form to repel a charge of cavalry.

As they had been drilled so many times, each front rank man dropped to one knee and placed his bayonetted musket or pike butt firmly on the ground at a forty-five degree angle, presenting a wall of bare steel to the onrushing lancers. In the rear file, each man cocked his musket and drew a bead on a target. Down came the enemy at full gallop, red sashes streaming and bright lances gleaming.

The determined Americans stood firm in the face of this cavalry charge — these sailors from eastern seaboard towns, soldiers from heartland farms and villages, trappers and frontiersmen more accustomed perhaps to the skulking of Indians in the silent forest, Californians bravely facing eternity on the deadly lances of their own neighbors. Uncommon fortitude is needed to stand calmly in the face of such an onslaught, but stand they did. Uncommon courage is needed, as well, to charge with lances upon a larger army. The Californios were simply outgunned from the beginning, but charge they did. When General Kearny shouted "Fire!" a sheet of flame met the oncoming lancers. Men and horses went down. Others shied and turned and stumbled. With their line shattered, and perhaps their nerve as well, the lancers wheeled and raced for the hill.

The enemy force reformed and bravely attempted the same assault again and again, each time to be met and repulsed by that wall of steel and lead. It was a far different scene than the forlorn fiasco at San Pasqual. As the Californios disappeared over the hill for the third time, General Kearny rushed to the front and waved his sword. "Up, jacks! Up and at them! Charge! Charge and take the hill!"

With fixed bayonets and pikes, the men did indeed scramble up the hill. Kearny and Stockton led all the way. When they gained the crest the enemy was nowhere to be seen.

The Americans made camp on the hill and remained unmolested during the night. At dawn, the battalion resumed its march in the same order as the previous day. They reached an area called *Canada de Los Alises,* or The Mesa (now deep in south-central Los Angeles). The enemy appeared and challenged their advance. The battalion of sailor-musketeers and Beale's and Duncan's carbineers again formed a square to repel cavalry. With a great shout the enemy horsemen came bravely down upon them. Stockton's men poured volleys into them, causing many to reel in their saddles. None fell, for the men were strapped on their horses this time. After a final charge, the lancers galloped off to the shelter of a ravine, leaving the Americans masters of the field. "Kit Carson," Downey wrote, "was the coolest of all. Wherever the Mexicans were nearest, there was Kit. Every time he fired he brought down his man, and then would go on loading coolly, as if he were shooting ducks for amusement!"

Yes, Carson by all means cool and capable, as we might view him for a moment through Downey's eyes. Carson had survived and excelled in a time and in a land whose everyday hazards made a mere charge of cavalry seem frivolous by comparison. Shooting ducks, indeed. One can imagine a twinkle in his grey eyes as he mentally compares this Californio militia to a businesslike war party of, say, Blackfoot or Comanche Indians. Load and fire. Smoothly and methodically. Load and fire. No hurry here. Load and fire. Six hundred men and five cannons around him, a regular damned army! Load and fire. Pick a target, sight calmly, squeeze the trigger. Feel the long barrelled rifle kick hard against his shoulder. A be-ribboned lance falls to the ground a hundred yards away and a rider slumps forward on the mane of a frightened, wheeling horse. Load and fire . . .

Historic assessments of these two incidents — the battles of San Gabriel River and The Mesa — remain uncertain. Downey describes a pitched battle at both places, but Kit Carson related years later that only the artillery exchanged volleys. We are somewhat reminded of Marechal Bosquet's remark on the Charge of the Light Brigade in 1854. "It is magnificent, but it is not war." Carson seemed not to consider them battles at all, but Carson's memory faded in his later years. The casualties must be considered. Surely, to those who fell on the field of battle it was very definitely a war. The truth then, relying on primary sources, lies somewhere between Downey's colorful account and Carson's deferential modesty. It continues to resist exposition.

That night, after the incident at The Mesa, Stockton's army made camp for the last time. When the battalion reached Los Angeles the next morning, Downey observed that

> The town was deserted and as we entered, the enemy retired. Behold us then, gentle reader, a battalion of sea boys, the Stars and Stripes waving over us and our band playing away for dear life while every tar shoulders his musket and steps out as if he had been for forty years a soldier.

To keep the town was the next problem. The sailors were needed back on their ships, and Gillespie's earlier experience indicated it took more than a few volunteers to hold the place. Colonel Fremont, whose battalion had been expected to co-operate in the conquest, was nowhere in sight. To complicate matters, the sailors discovered — as sailors are wont to do — large quantities of aguardiente, a fiery Mexican brandy. Their condition, if Downey's recollections were accurate, was such that Flores could have retaken Los Angeles with a corporal's guard:

> From quarters to quarters, you would see drunken men on all sides. The guardhouse was full, the very guard was drunk. The officers had all imbibed, save only the old General and the Commodore. I do not

think there were many who could have told how many beans it took to make five! Plenty of men never drew a sober breath, yet if chance had offered, between *aguardiente* and natural courage they would have faced a battery of 500 pieces backed by 10,000 cavalry!

It can be assumed that Edward Beale, never known as a teetotaler, joined with his friends in these celebratory activities. While their men roistered, Kearny and Stockton waited for Fremont. On January 12, Kearny drafted his report to the Adjutant General:

> At the request of Commodore R. F. Stockton, who in September last assumed the title of Governor of California, I consented to take command of an expedition to this place, the capital of the country. Commodore Stockton accompanied us.

Surely he never showed this report to Stockton, who himself was busily advising the Secretary of the Navy that he had marched from San Diego with 600 fighting men "aided by General Kearny with a detachment of sixty men." He made no mention of Kearny having shared the command. Stockton estimated his losses in killed and wounded as "not exceeding twenty; the enemy's loss between seventy and eighty." He did not indicate how he had arrived at the latter figures.

Stockton's report pretty much conforms to Downey's recollections, in less colorful language, of the engagements at the San Gabriel River and The Mesa. Significantly, Stockton signed the report as Governor and Commander-in-Chief of the Territory of California. On the same date, he issued a "general order of commendation":

> The Commander-in-Chief congratulates the officers and men of the southern division of the United States forces in California on the brilliant victories obtained by them over the enemy on the 8th and 9th instants, and on once more taking possession of the *Ciudad de Los Angeles* . .
>
> The steady courage of the troops in forcing their passage across the *Rio San Gabriel,* where officers and men were alike employed in dragging the guns through the water against the galling fire of the

enemy, without exchanging a shot, and their gallant charge up the banks against the enemy's cavalry, has perhaps never been surpassed, and the cool determination with which, in the battle of the 9th, they repulsed the charge of cavalry made by the enemy at the same time on their front and rear, has extorted the admiration of the enemy, and deserves the best thanks of their countrymen.

Kearny's report of "but one private killed, two officers and eleven privates wounded," does not square with Dr. Griffin's "statement of killed and wounded," which lists three men dead and two officers and ten men wounded. Griffin identified the three dead as Frederick Strauss, a seaman of the *Portsmouth;* Thomas Smith, a seaman of the *Cyane;* and Jacob Hait, one of the San Diego volunteers. The two wounded officers were Captain Gillespie and Lieutenant Rowan, "contused slightly by spent balls." Of the ten men wounded, eight were sailors, one a marine and one a private of the dragoons.

But all this California marching and commanding and battling and celebrating and reporting constituted melodrama more than real war. In fact, even the melodrama lacked final substance, for its most picaresque figure had yet to arrive on the stage.

After considerable hardship, Fremont's battalion reached Mission San Fernando, north of Los Angeles where, on January 11, a courier announced defeat of the Californios and the occupation of Los Angeles by Stockton's force.

General Pico, caught in a *de facto* pincer between Stockton and Fremont, surrendered to the latter at Rancho Cahuenga, only some ten miles from Los Angeles. Fremont's late arrival on the scene, and his smug satisfaction in receiving Pico's sword, did nothing to endear him to Stockton and Kearny.

Political and personal differences among the three of them over who conquered California and who had official authority would continue for months, resulting ultimately in the court-martial of Fremont and a state of confusion and controversy that lasted for years.

Commodore Stockton ordered his men back to their ships. "As we celebrate our entry," gloated seaman Downey, "of course we were duty-bound to celebrate our departure." The exodus of sailors and marines from Los Angeles began on January 20. The night of the Nineteenth was apparently spent in revelry. "In fact," said Downey, "all hands were pretty royally corned."

Having seen his crews safely aboard the *Stonington* at San Pedro, Stockton left overland with an escort for San Diego. It is likely that Edward Beale and his troop of carbineers accompanied Stockton southward down El Camino Real.

Once aboard the *Congress* at San Diego, Stockton declared all Mexican ports to be under Naval blockade and ordered the *Portsmouth, Savannah, Cyane* and *Warren* to be in readiness at a moment's notice. After that, Stockton ordered Beale and Kit Carson to Washington with official dispatches, handing Beale his instructions aboard the *Congress:*

> I have selected you to be the bearer of the accompanying dispatches to the Navy Department in consequence of your heroic conduct in volunteering to leave General Kearny's camp, then surrounded by the enemy, to go to the garrison of San Diego for assistance and because of the perils and hardships you underwent during that dangerous journey, to procure aid for your suffering fellow soldiers. You will proceed without delay with Mr. Carson's party by the most expeditious route overland. On your arrival at Washington you will immediately deliver the dispatches to the Honorable Secretary of the Navy and receive instructions for your future government.

Beale and Carson set out with a ten-man escort that included at least two of Carson's mountain men, White Elliott and Baptiste Perrot. Besides Stockton's dispatches, Beale carried letters from Fremont to Jessie and Senator Benton, and a letter from Captain Turner to his wife, Julia, describing Beale as "a kind-hearted fellow, a good friend of mine." And so the sailor once again mounted a horse in the service of his country.

Stockton sailed on the *Congress* for Monterey to turn over his California command to Commodore William Branford Shubrick, who had arrived at that port on January 22 with the frigate USS *Independence.*

The continuing rivalry among Kearny, Fremont and Stockton

became sharply evident everywhere. Mariano Guadalupe Vallejo received three letters at Sonoma, all in one week. One came from Kearny at San Diego, the second from Fremont at Los Angeles and the third from Stockton at Monterey. Each man signed himself, "Governor and Commander-in-Chief of California."

And we can sympathize with Lieutenant William Tecumseh Sherman's honest confusion. Sherman arrived in San Francisco Bay on the storeship *Lexington* to learn of Kearny's insistence that he was "Governor and Military Commander" while Fremont and Stockton claimed the same office. Sherman asked, "Just who in hell is in command here?"

Beale was too junior in rank to have become personally involved in the Stockton-Kearny-Fremont controversy, but with every officer and jack in the Pacific Squadron he supported Stockton all the way. Except for Kearny's fifty-seven dragoons and Fremont's confusing Army-Navy status — not to mention his far remove from the scenes of battle — the conquest of California had been entirely an operation of the United States Navy.

As the bickering continued in California, Edward Beale and Kit Carson rode on toward St. Louis and Washington, D.C., and to a reception for which neither of them were prepared.

6

Coast to Coast

Edward Beale with Kit Carson and his party journeyed eastward from San Diego over the trail taken by General Kearny and the dragoons just a few short months before. Carson vowed this time to visit with his family at Taos, come what may. Beale felt quite equally determined to spend some time at home after an absence of eighteen months — and time with his childhood sweetheart, Mary Engle Edwards, daughter of Representative Samuel Edwards of Pennsylvania.

After Beale left San Diego, Captain Henry Smith Turner suffered a change of heart. He wrote again to his wife:

> I sent my letter by Lieutenant Beale of the navy, a person of whom I had at the time a good opinion. You will find Beale an apparently honest fellow, but he is untruthful and extremely deceitful. The truth is I find these navy officers greatly inferior to the army officers in everything pertaining to moral worth. There are but a few I would trust out of my sight.

We can only surmise that Turner learned Beale chose to stick to his own opinion of the San Pasqual fiasco and fully intended to report it that way. As to Turner's high opinion of Army officers, his journal is replete with utter disdain for them indivually and collectively. He had quarreled with every one of his fellow officers and even had words with General Kearny.

Beale and Carson crossed the Colorado River at its confluence with the Gila, where the city of Yuma now stands. During the first few days of travel Beale experienced a temporary return of the exhaustive condition afflicting him after San Pasqual. There were times when Carson had to help him onto his horse. Beale insisted on continuing until the weakness had passed, and his strength soon returned.

They followed the Gila River eastward through hostile Indian country in what is now southern Arizona, an arid land of barren mountain ranges and broad deserts cut by rivers which seldom flow with anything but wind-blown sand.

Carson's instinctive recognition of Indian signs kept them clear of trouble during daylight. After dark they often left their campfire burning and moved off a safe distance to sleep. Such lessons learned at the side of the master would save Beale's skin during future perils.

They reached the headwaters of the Gila, crossed the Continental Divide and dropped down into the valley of the Rio Grande where Carson had met Kearny's Army of the West coming down from Santa Fe. In a few days they arrived in Taos, New Mexico, where Carson rejoined his family and Beale rested a few days to restore his health.

The well-traveled Santa Fe Trail took them across the prairie to Fort Leavenworth, from where they proceeded by boat to St. Louis. Beale delivered Turner's letter to Mrs. Turner, and then Beale and Carson took letters from Fremont to the Benton home where the men were warmly received by Jessie. Recalling the visit, Jessie later said in an interview in *The Land of Sunshine:*

> Kit Carson was a man among men . . . When he was to come to our house for the first time . . . he was accompanied by Edward Beale then a midshipman . . . Carson was shy and reserved, and his welcome as one who had been Fremont's companion and right-hand man overwhelmed him. Yet he was not awkward. A perfect gentleman, his dignity and delicacy completely disarmed my mother. He had been "afraid the ladies might not care to have him there if they knew he had married a Sioux wife . . ."

Continuing by riverboat and train, Beale and Carson reached Washington in May of 1847, completing an overland journey of more than 3,000 miles in less than three months. They delivered their dispatches to the Secretary of the Navy and were amazed to find themselves in the national spotlight. Everyone wanted to meet the heroes of San Pasqual, especially Kit Carson the celebrated mountain man whose exploits were legendary. They were asked to tell repeatedly how American forces conquered California. In his own recollections, years later, Beale typically makes only casual mention of this visit to Washington: "I was sent across the Rocky Mountains with dispatches announcing the conquest of California, which occasioned great satisfaction to the people of the United States."

The Bentons remained in St. Louis until the arrival of Fremont in August. Fremont's reunion with Jessie after a two-year separation was dampened by General Kearny's order that Fremont consider himself formally under arrest and to proceed to Washington as a prisoner-at-large.

Beale and Carson were again lavishly entertained at the Benton's Washington home, where the Senator arranged for them to meet the most distinguished men of the day. There they learned directly from Fremont of his predicament and assured him of their support. Jessie related another recollection about Carson: "It used to delight him to go to the market . . . as my mother said, he who had so often had to risk his life for a mouthful could appreciate the abundance." Although mother Benton's remarks were undoubtedly well meant, such fawning condescension probably hastened Carson's return to the West.

Carson was lionized everywhere. When Beale went off to visit Mary Edwards at Chester — a significant visit which resulted in Beale's betrothal to Mary — widow Emily Truxtun Beale insisted Carson wait at Bloomingdale, the Beale home in Washington, D.C.

One day Jessie Fremont prevailed upon Carson to escort her to the White House where she presented the bashful frontiersman to President Polk. She expressed Carson's desire to again tender his services as courier back to California. As an apparent afterthought she asked that her husband also be allowed to return west where he had unfinished personal business. She produced Fremont's letter to her father that gave the Colonel's version of his conflict with Kearny. By her wiles she attempted to elicit from the President approbation of her husband's conduct.

Lieutenant Emory had long since arrived in Washington and delivered to the War Department Kearny's report that took sole credit for the California conquest. Emory on his own had published in the New York *Courier and Enquirer* of April 23 a scathing attack on both Stockton and Fremont. Kearny himself reported directly to Polk, so the President was fully briefed on the General's side of the matter. Polk had no desire to become embroiled in a controversy his cabinet had already resolved in Kearny's favor. Polk confided to his diary that he thought Kearny was in the right. "It was unnecessary, however, that I should say so to Colonel Fremont's wife, and I evaded giving her an answer."

Senator Benton, unaware of his daughter's visit, also made a call on President Polk. He demanded that a court of inquiry be appointed, confident such action would completely exonerate his son-in-law from whatever charges were brought against him. He was stunned to learn that a court-martial on a charge of mutiny had already been adjudicated by the Judge Advocate General. Preliminary proceedings were set for September 10 at Fortress Monroe.

Benton, never the most patient of men, lost his temper at this news. He swore he would see Kearny and his three lackeys — Cooke, Turner and Emory — brought before a court-martial to answer much more serious charges than any they might bring against Fremont. His threats reached the ears of Kearny, resulting in two additional charges appended to the original court-martial specifications: Mutiny from January 17 to May 9, 1847; disobedience of the lawful commands of a superior officer, and conduct prejudicial to good order and discipline.

Beale and Carson appeared at the Fortress Monroe preliminary hearing as defense witnesses. The proceedings were transferred shortly after that to the United States Arsenal at Washington, a location more convenient for witnesses and the press.

Both Beale and Carson had decided to return west as soon as possible after completing their testimony, and Beale prevailed upon Senator Benton to help expedite his return to active duty. Beale, meanwhile, still suffered spells of lingering illness. Benton petitioned Secretary of the Navy J. Y. Mason in August, 1847, on Beale's behalf:

> Passed Midshipman Beale, now ill in Philadelphia, desires the department to charge him with dispatches for the North Pacific. Being well informed by all those who have returned from California of his meritorious conduct there, particularly in the signal act of volunteering to go to Commodore Stockton for the relief of General Kearny, and for his manly daring in crossing the continent last spring amid great suffering and with heroic courage and constancy . . . Having a high opinion of the young man for honor, courage, truth, modesty, enterprise and perseverance, I should be happy to see him noticed and countenanced by the department.

Senator Benton received this reply from Secretary Mason:

> The department appreciates Mr. Beale's meritorious services and will give him orders to return when his health is sufficiently reestablished to undertake the journey. A bearer of dispatches is not required now but officers of Mr. Beale's character are much wanted. An opportunity will occur for him about the first of October.

Kearny's report of San Pasqual, introduced in evidence at the hearing, made no mention of Beale or Carson. Under Fremont's direct questioning, Kearny insisted he did not recognize Kit Carson as the guide who had led him and his dragoons from the Rio Grande to California. Possibly the General saw nothing about the neat, slight figure in broadcloth and starched linen to associate him with the scout he had seen only in greasy buckskins.

Beale testified that Carson was very well known to Kearny. He cited as one example of their intimacy an occasion at San Diego when Beale, Kearny and Carson engaged in target practice using the General's own pistols. Carson added that on first coming under Kearny's command he told the General of Commodore Stockton's intention to appoint Fremont to the governorship. Kearny had agreed in Carson's presence that Fremont's appointment should be made. Because of Kearny's slanted version of the San Pasqual action, which Beale and Carson knew to be false, neither held the General in high esteem.

True to the Navy Secretary's promise, Beale received orders in early October to return to the Pacific with Naval dispatches. Carson received instructions to take a detail of troopers from Fort Leavenworth to California. Jessie recalled Carson's impatience to leave Washington while they waited for Beale's orders from the Navy. "But at last he got away," she said, "and I accompanied him and Mr. Beale to St. Louis . . ."

Beale and Carson were on their way long before the court-martial formally convened in the first week of November. However, Beale suffered another relapse shortly after leaving Fort Leavenworth and had to be carried back to St. Louis. Carson went on without him.

A two-week rest saw Beale fit to travel again. He sailed in late October for Chagres and the Pacific with orders to report to the USS *Ohio,* flagship of Commodore Thomas ap Catesby Jones. Jones had relieved Commodore Shubrick on blockade duty in the Mexican ports and was back on his second tour of duty as Commander of the Pacific Squadron. Beale crossed the Isthmus of Panama and caught up with the *Ohio* at Callao, Peru, in January of 1848.

Archibald Gillespie and Commodore Stockton gave lengthy supporting testimony for Fremont during the court-martial. Additional defense witnesses included Alex Godey, Richard Owens, Thomas Williams, Risdon Moore and William H. Russell: The latter, Ordnance Officer in Fremont's battalion, attested:

> In consequence of the wise and humane treatment of Colonel Fremont toward the conquered population, his popularity became great in the country and enabled him to do what no other man, I confidently believe, could have done. I remember distinctly that General Kearny spoke of his intentions of appointing Colonel Fremont governor.

The court displayed not the faintest interest, however, in how Fremont had conducted his office or what Kearny's intentions may or may not have been. It concerned itself with whether Fremont had occupied the office with Kearny's official sanction.

Charges and countercharges flew back and forth between Kearny and Fremont for weeks on end, arguments often sinking to the level of petty irritations. The belligerent and bellicose Senator Benton continued to compound Fremont's problems by hurling charges against Kearny, Cooke, Turner and Emory, accusing them of the meanest intent to ruin Fremont through their jealousy.

To the public Fremont remained a hero, his reputation enhanced by most of the testimony in his behalf. But to the Army he became more and more a despicable figure guilty of rank insubordination.

In his final summation on January 24, 1848, Benton concentrated on immoderate charges of perjury and false testimony against Kearny, imputing his character, integrity and courage. It was a completely unwarranted attack on the Old Soldier. Despite his quarrels with Stockton and Fremont, General Kearny had served his country bravely and effectively for many years. Kearny's record was well known to the thirteen officers of the court. They found Fremont guilty on January 31 of all three charges and sentenced him to dismissal from the service. Six members of the court recommended him to the clemency of the President.

But under the articles of war Fremont's actions had not been mutinous. His only proven offense had been disobedience of orders that were at best confusing, and possibly so ambiguous as to be invalid.

Perhaps because of an appeal made by Edward Beale on Fremont's behalf, Secretary Buchanan advised the President to disapprove the verdict. Other cabinet members recommended approval of the verdict but remitting the penalty. Polk took a middle course. He declared Fremont innocent of the charge of mutiny but guilty of the other two charges. He remitted the punishment of dismissal from the service and ordered him released from arrest "to resume his sword and report for duty."

Fremont had no intention of resuming his sword or returning to duty. He could not in good conscience admit the justice of the verdict by accepting the President's clemency. He submitted his resignation, which the President accepted. Had Kearny's original charge of mutiny alone been prosecuted, the case would probably have been summarily dismissed. So Fremont had his intemperate father-in-law to thank for the verdict of the court-martial.

On January 24, 1848, the very day that Fremont gave his last statement to the court, an event took place on the south fork of the American River in California which would strongly direct the course of Edward Beale's life and forever alter the patterns of western expansion and settlement. On that date James Wilson Marshall, formerly of Fremont's battalion, examined the raceway for a water-powered sawmill he was building at Coloma for John Sutter. He discovered gold in what eventually proved to be almost unbelievable quantities. It would be many months before official news of the astounding find reached Washington. The courier bearing proof of the discovery would be Edward Beale.

Almost concurrently with the end of Fremont's court-martial, the Treaty of Guadalupe Hidalgo took formal effect and California became a United States possession.

Shortly after Beale reported aboard the USS *Ohio* at Callao in January of 1848, the ship departed for occupation duty on the coast of Mexico. On July 13, at La Paz, Baja California, Commodore Jones issued these orders to Beale: "You are hereby appointed an acting lieutenant in the Pacific Squadron. You will report yourself to Captain E. A. F. Lavalette for duty on board the *Congress* . . ." But before the end of the month Commodore Jones had a more important assignment for Beale. Jones needed a courier to go to Washington. Beale, perhaps tired of occupation duty in the sweltering heat, volunteered to go at his own expense. Beale's orders were contained in a letter from Commodore Jones dated July 29, addressed to "Acting Lieutenant E. F. Beale, U. S. Navy":

> . . . You will proceed to Washington via the City of Mexico, by the most expeditious route, and deliver to the Honorable Secretary of the Navy the four several dispatches now put into your hands to his address.
>
> At the city of Mexico, you will wait on our Minister at the Court and hand him the accompanying note addressed to him, receive his instructions and proceed without unnecessary delay anywhere to your final destination. After leaving the West Coast of Mexico let me hear from you by all favorable opportunities and particularly from the City of Mexico after you see our Minister.

Once more, then, the intrepid sailor switched from quarterdeck to saddlehorn and this time it was Beale's turn to make an historic ride that would rank with that of Juan Flaco. But Beale's ride, unlike that of Flaco's, would be an incredibly hair-raising experience in a savagely hostile country at great risk to his life.

7

Gold Fever

Gold hysteria claimed most of California by the summer of 1848, although the size and significance of the discovery had not yet become apparent in the East. Newspapers treated it as mere rumor at first, then as an amusing curiosity. But in the West gold created instant wealth and monumental chaos. Whole towns virtually emptied overnight as their inhabitants rushed for the mines. The lure of quick riches in the foothills affected the military, too. Desertions in the Navy left ships unmanned at San Francisco and Monterey, while Army posts stood with silent and empty battlements. One dispatch from Commodore Thomas ap Catesby Jones to the Secretary of the Navy described his concern:

> Nothing, sir, can exceed the deplorable state of things in all upper California at this time, and the maddening effect of the gold mania. Even men having a balance due them of over $1000 have deserted. For years to come it will be impossible for the United States to maintain any naval or military establishments in California, as no hope of reward or punishment is sufficient. To send troops out here would be needless as they would immediately desert.

The dispatches entrusted to Edward Beale from Commodore Jones and Consul Thomas Oliver Larkin dealt in substance with these conditions. It was Beale's own decision to take gold samples with him. Biographer Stephen Bonsal speculates that Beale approached a miner at La Paz who was on his way back to the States via Panama and traded 100 grains of quinine for a supply of gold dust and nuggets. Beale, still on occupation duty in Mexico, had not himself visited the gold country so a purchase of some kind seems likely. However he got hold of it, the gold belonged to Beale and not the Navy. Beale seemingly realized the momentous importance of the discovery and the urgency of convincing Washington that a bona fide gold panic appeared in the making.

Beale departed La Paz, on the Baja California peninsula, on July 29 aboard the *Congress* to cross the Sea of Cortez to Mazatlan. Traveling across Mexico was probably his own idea, inasmuch as he volunteered for the mission. Commodore Jones's instructions merely confirmed Beale's choice of a route. Beale, an expert horseman, knew the overland road would be much faster than a circuitous sea voyage and Isthmus crossing. It was the same route, in reverse, as that traveled successfully by Archibald Gillespie in 1846. Another U. S. Government agent, Thomas Jefferson Farnham, journeyed over the same road in 1840.

A storm battered the *Congress* in its passage from La Paz to Mazatlan on the mainland of Mexico. A tropical weather system had moved into the region, producing further storms that would both help and hinder Beale's journey for days to come. Anyone but a sailor might have been deterred, but wind-driven rain and salt scud pelting his face and stinging his eyes was not a new experience for Beale. He knew instinctively when to duck his head.

The *Congress* put him ashore at Mazatlan where he hired a small Mexican boat to take him 100 miles south to San Blas. The storm continued to rage. The little vessel received rough treatment from heavy seas pounding the coast. Five days passed before Beale finally landed at San Blas.

Beale's own account of his ride across Mexico is characteristically brief: "About August, 1848, I was sent through Mexico disguised as a Spaniard via Vera Cruz to Washington with dispatches, and arrived at Washington during September, 1848." Fortunately, he related the entire episode in detail to Senator Benton and the Senator's son-in-law, William Carey Jones. A third-person account of the ride, released by Jones, appeared in the *National Intelligencer*.

Although Mexico and the United States were officially at peace, Mexicans of the interior still regarded foreigners, especially Americans, as enemies. Deserters from the army of General Mariano Paredes swarmed the countryside, waylaying unwary travelers. Diligence coaches under military escort used the road, as did British couriers with armed guards. But the United States provided no such protection for its couriers at that time, and Beale regarded the regular *diligencia* as too slow for his purposes.

Beale's hair and bronzed features were as dark as a native's. His companionship with the Mexican vaqueros at San Diego had given him a ready command of colloquial Spanish. He supplemented these advantages by assuming Mexican garb consisting of a broad sombrero, bolero jacket, leather breeches, and boots equipped with the large rowelled spurs of the country. A painted portrait hanging at Decatur House in Washington, D.C., depicts Beale in his "Spanish disguise," as he termed it, with two of the "four six-barreled revolvers" with which he armed himself tucked into a broad leather belt.

The old pueblo of San Blas, a haven of sorts for sailing ships since the earliest days of Spanish exploration, lay at the base of a small hill. Adobes of varying description clustered around a cobblestoned plaza. In the most pretentious of these casas Beale found the local Governor. Fully aware of the dangers to be encountered along the unpoliced roads of the interior, the Governor advised Beale against traveling without an escort. "An American like yourself could not travel a dozen miles in Mexico without being robbed and murdered," the Governor told him.

But it would take time to organize such a troop. Beale knew he could travel much faster alone. He hired two saddle horses and set out from San Blas on August 12, accompanied by a single native guide provided by the Governor.

The going was difficult in the extreme. Recurring storms flooded the swampy lowlands. Streams ran dangerously high and fast. Once on higher ground on the road to Tepic, tropical heat, fatigue and swarms of insects became the enemy.

Three gunmen accosted Beale on the very outskirts of Tepic and shouted for his surrender. Beale, anticipating such an attack, drew two of his pistols, put spurs to his horse and charged down upon the startled *ladrones* at full gallop. His guide followed, literally riding for his life. This unexpected counterattack so rattled the bandits that Beale and his guide rode on past and out of range.

They reached the safety of Tepic. Beale, realizing the risk was every bit as real as the Governor had warned, made copies of all his dispatches. He addressed them to the U. S. Minister at Mexico City and entrusted them to the government mail. Beale headed for Guadalajara. He and his guide rode night and day, exchanging their spent horses for fresh mounts at way stations. Here Beale would often stretch out on the ground for a few minutes rest. Mexican hostlers shook their heads in wonderment at this loco.

Again they were attacked by a band of *ladrones*. This time the gunmen gave chase. Beale and his guide managed to outride them, but not before rifle bullets zinged close to their heads. They found fresh horses at the next station, where Beale learned that a group of eleven Mexican travelers were not far ahead. There would be safety in numbers if Beale could catch up and ride with them to Guadalajara.

Fierce storms struck again, but Beale and his companion pressed onward. They had to swim water courses swollen to raging torrents and make hazardous detours around avalanches of mud and rocks that often blocked the road. Beale kept on, for no *ladrone* in his right mind would be abroad in such weather.

It was just as well that Beale never caught up with the group ahead of him. They were ambushed by bandits who brutally murdered all eleven travelers and left their bodies on the trail. Beale forced himself onward, changing horses and riding night and day. He entered Mexico City on August 20, having ridden

725 miles in eight days, and reported to U. S. Minister Nathan Clifford. Mud spattered and close to total exhaustion, Beale and his guide had three days for what must have seemed like luxurious rest while Clifford prepared more dispatches for Beale to carry to Washington.

Beale is frequently described as having met Ulysses S. Grant in Mexico City. Actually, Grant had departed from Vera Cruz with his regiment on July 16 while Beale was still at La Paz. On August 22, while Beale rested in Mexico City, Grant exchanged marriage vows with Julia Dent in St. Louis.

Clifford completed his dispatches and prepared a "safe conduct" paper for Beale:

> To all whom it may concern: I, the undersigned Minister of the United States residing in the City of Mexico, do hereby certify that Edward F. Beale is a bearer of dispatches from this legation entitled to all the privileges and immunities to which agents are entitled. Given under my hand and seal of the legation at the City of Mexico this 21st day of August, 1848.

It is extremely doubtful that Clifford's "pass" would assure Beale of any "privileges and immunities" with Mexican highwaymen, but Beale accepted the document anyway. On August 23, Beale galloped off toward the Atlantic port of Vera Cruz. His faithful but bewildered guide rode right behind him.

They traveled the main road used by General Winfield Scott with his conquering army of 12,000 Americans. Destruction resulting from the just-concluded war was clearly visible all along the way — ruined towns, wrecked bridges and burned out buildings.

Beale underwent attack for the third time by a *banda de gente de camino* near Jalapa. This time he escaped by boldly heading his horse off the trail and plunging headlong down a precipitous mountainside, his terrified guide tumbling close behind him. Their horses barely kept their footing. They managed to regain the road further down the mountain and galloped off to safety. Beale executed the dangerous maneuver so suddenly that the bandits were left surprised and empty-handed in the roadway. He always prevailed, it seems, when it came to the final press of circumstances.

Beale reached Vera Cruz on the Twenty-sixth after traveling 270 miles from Mexico City in some sixty hours. His Mexican guide, forever nameless and unheralded, seems not to have arrived in an entirely sound condition. The loyal companion suffered a physical and mental collapse and, according to Bonsal, Mexican authorities were obliged to return him under guard to San Blas in a *diligencia*.

Beale rested and waited for four days at Vera Cruz where he finally boarded the sloop USS *Germantown* for Mobile, Alabama. From there he proceeded up the Mississippi and Ohio rivers to Pittsburgh, thence by stage to Washington. He arrived at the capital in mid-September. The various dispatches from Commodore Jones, Consul Larkin and Minister Clifford, and the samples of gold that Beale brought with him were the first positive news, the first hard evidence, of the great California discovery to be delivered by an official courier.

The news spread quickly. Once again Beale found himself a national hero. Stories linked his name with the gold discovery on the front page of every newspaper in the East, and ultimately in Europe and around the world. Benton again presented Beale to the United States Senate. And the news which Beale had brought to Washington formed the substance of President Polk's momentous State of the Union address delivered to a joint session of Congress on December 5, 1848. The nation at last succumbed to the gold fever which had gripped California for nearly a year.

Beale wasn't the only government courier to bear gold to Washington in 1848. Colonel Richard Barnes Mason purchased $3000 worth of gold in California and assigned Second Lieutenant Lucien Loeser of Company F, Third Artillery, to carry it to the Secretary of War. Loeser sailed for Panama on September 1, at about the time Beale departed Vera Cruz on the *Germantown* for Mobile. Andrew Hamilton in a paper for the U. S. Naval Institute titled, *Beale; He Won The Gold Dust*

Derby, attempted to make a race out of it for posterity. There is no evidence, however, to show that either courier was aware of the other, or that either commander knew the other had dispatched a gold-carrying messenger.

Loeser not only got a late start, but ran into bad luck. His ship carried him all the way to Peru, either by adverse winds or the unwillingness of its skipper to stop at Panama. Loeser had lost a month by the time he backtracked to Panama. He crossed the Isthmus and finally made his way to Washington, arriving there over two months behind Beale.

Half of Beale's gold went on display at the U. S. Patent Office. Beale had the remainder, a nugget, fashioned into an engagement ring for Mary Engle Edwards. The couple had little time together, for Benton whisked Beale off to New York where again he was wined, dined and lionized.

While on the East Coast, Beale called upon Commodore Stockton who, since turning over his command in California and returning east, had been elected U. S. Senator from New Jersey. Stockton carried on a business partnership with New York financier William H. Aspinwall. Beale would himself soon enter into a business venture for the two capitalists.

Beale received new orders to return to the West with dispatches for Colonel John M. Washington at Santa Fe, Colonel Mason in California and General Joseph Lane in Oregon. He left the capital on October 14 for Fort Leavenworth. The Mobile *Register* published a notice that Beale left Fort Leavenworth on November 20 with a company of seventeen raw Army recruits and a few adventurers. The recruits were not officially assigned to Beale. They were supposed to leave Fort Leavenworth in the spring as replacements for the Oregon garrison. Beale saw an opportunity to pick up an escort at no expense to the Navy. He convinced their Commander he could take the soldiers over the southern route in winter and get them to Oregon months ahead of time, thus relieving the fort of the cost for their keep during those months.

This "favor" for the Army would cause Beale far more

trouble than it was worth. In fact, this was the first of several unhappy confrontations with the bureaucracy in which Beale usually came off second best.

He engaged a well-known trapper, Andrew Sublette, as guide. The party proceeded westward from the Missouri River across the flatlands of Kansas. They followed the Santa Fe Trail into the gradually sloping uplands of eastern Colorado. They passed Bent's Fort on the Arkansas River, then turned southwest toward Raton Pass. From there Beale wrote a letter on December 3 to his friend and future brother-in-law, Harry Edwards:

> I have had a most unpleasant journey so far, and the men I have with me are so utterly worthless not a day passes that I do not punish two or three. There are thousands of Indians here, mostly of friendly tribes, but I have had two affairs in which I came so very near losing my hair that I am not positive at this moment that my scalp sticks to the top of my head. The weather is most cruelly, bitterly cold and freezing. It is said the Raton Mountains, which I am about to cross, are impassable but I have crossed impassable places before. Love to those who love me.

At least one of his affairs with the Indians received publicity in the Philadelphia *North American* for June 12, 1849. The Boston *Daily Advertiser* republished it on June 16. According to both articles, Beale was surprised by a band of Apaches while dressing the carcass of a deer he had shot a few miles from camp. He leaped onto his horse and rode hard for the camp. He managed to stay well ahead of the pursuing Indians. Upon cresting a hill and racing down the other side, Beale found one of his men on foot, petrified with fear. The man pleaded with Beale to save him, claiming to be the sire of six children. Beale reined up and slid from his horse. "Ride to camp," he shouted, sending the man on his way. "Have a party sent out to give me a decent burial."

With that, Beale threw himself behind a sparse clump of vegetation, drew his pistol and prepared to go down fighting. The Indians swept past in full cry after the fleeing horseman, apparently not seeing Beale and unaware they were chasing a different man. Their yells alerted the camp. As the mounted man rode in, a dozen rifles were leveled at the pursuing Indians. Apaches seldom let valor stand in the way of discretion. The band veered off and soon disappeared in the distance. Beale reached camp on foot just as a party started out to comply with his final request.

Several of Beale's troop suffered frostbite crossing the Raton Mountains. Some of the mules perished in the snow. They arrived at Santa Fe on Christmas Day of that severe winter. Beale described his condition as "on foot and nearly naked." He discharged seven men who were physically unable to proceed, then signed on eight to fill their places. Beale delivered his dispatches to Colonel Washington and headed his party south from Santa Fe on January 11, 1849.

They crossed the Sierra de los Mimbres in a blinding snowstorm. Beale's growing doubts about the character of the recruits were confirmed when a sergeant and six privates deserted and headed back to Santa Fe. They were never heard from again, either perishing in the snow or falling victims to the Indians.

Meanwhile, a second government courier made his way to California via Panama with duplicate dispatches while Beale struggled in the snow. A San Francisco newspaper article, reprinted in a February issue of the New Orleans *Picayune,* quoted the unidentified messenger: "Midshipman Beale left Washington with duplicate dispatches brought out by me and has not arrived, nor has he been heard from. He may be blocked by snow in the Sierra Madre."

Beale pressed onward across the Continental Divide to the headwaters of the Gila River, following the same trail he had taken in 1847 with Kit Carson. He crossed the Colorado River at Yuma, proceeded northwesterly over the Mojave Desert into the San Joaquin Valley via Tejon Pass and on to San Francisco. There he delivered his dispatches to Colonel Mason on April 10. Mason detailed another courier to take the remaining dispatches and the recruits to General Lane in Oregon. After

a respite of only two days, Beale received orders to carry dispatches back to Washington via the Panama crossing.

Commodore Jones, aboard the USS *Ohio* anchored at Sausa-
lito in San Francisco Bay, prepared a letter to be delivered, if
need be, to John Parrott, U. S. Consul at Mazatlan:

> Lieutenant E. F. Beale who will hand you this, is a bearer of im-
> portant dispatches for the government at Washington and is instructed
> in the event of accident or detention of the steamer from any cause
> on the coast of Mexico, to take the overland route through Mexico in
> which case you will be pleased to supply the ways and means he may
> be in need of.

Beale succeeded in boarding the ship, however — the steamer
California — and reached Panama City without undue delay.
He found the place choked with hundreds of anxious travelers
waiting for transportation to California. The steamer *Panama*
arrived from the south at the same time, compounding the noise
and confusion in the scruffy little city.

Near the Plaza, in the center of the scrambling mob, Beale
came face to face with Jessie Fremont. "Heavens, what a crib
for a lady!" Beale exclaimed. She had seen him from a window
of a private residence. Jessie and her daughter, along with Lilly,
her nurse and companion, had been waiting there more than a
month for a ship to take her to join her husband in California.
Beale learned from Jessie of the disastrous end of Fremont's
fourth expedition in the Rockies. She had heard that Fremont
survived but at that moment didn't know his whereabouts.

Jessie had been sick with fever. Beale told her of the wild
and convulsive gold-rush atmosphere at San Francisco, expressing concern for her safety. He urged her to return across the
Isthmus with himself as escort, thence on to St. Louis where
she could wait for Fremont in the safety and comfort of her
own home.

Before they could decide on a plan, however, a party arrived
from Chagres with sacks of mail. Jessie found a letter from
Fremont, sent from Taos, New Mexico: "I write from the

house of our good friend Kit Carson. How gratified you would be picturing me here in Kit's care, [he] constantly endeavoring to make me comfortable." Fremont wrote that he would take the southern overland route to California and meet her in San Francisco. Beale said goodbye to Jessie and continued eastward to Chagres, where he boarded a ship for the States.

On his arrival in Washington, Beale found a bill from the War Department charging him for the services of an "Army escort" from Fort Leavenworth to San Francisco. Beale's refusal to pay resulted in a flurry of correspondence in which he not only denied responsibility for the recruits he wet-nursed across the country, but requested mileage allowance for the journey. This is the way he put it to Secretary of War G. W. Crawford:

> I was ordered by way of Santa Fe to carry dispatches to the military commander at that place, and from thence to California. This was in the depth of winter and I was the only leader of a party, although five different ones started, who succeeded in getting through. This was before communication between our distant territories had become so frequent and easy and an escort was indispensably necessary. As the riflemen that composed it were to be stationed in Oregon and were to proceed there in the spring, it was no additional expense to the government and only caused them to be started on their way some months earlier than otherwise. I wish particularly to call your attention to the injustice that would be done me by checking this large amount, more than a year's pay, against me.
>
> It seems to me, sir, that my claim for mileage allowance is reasonable as I have not received a cent of compensation from your department, and I hope that on further deliberation you will conclude to allow it.

Beale was a reasonable man, and perhaps Crawford was too, but governments are not reasonable. Beale continued to stub his toe on this truth for years to come. The claim against Beale for escort services was finally dropped in mid-1850, but the War Department dismissed his claim for mileage expenses with a wave of its bureaucratic hand: "In the case of Lieutenant Beall [sic], whatever may be the equity of his claim, it is not within the power of the regulations and is therefore not approved."

Back home Beale found a letter dated May 29, 1849, from Barnum's Museum in Philadelphia signed by Phineas T. Barnum, the theatrical entrepreneur and showman:

> Mr. Harding of the *Enquirer* has just informed me that you have in your possession an eight-pound lump of California gold. As I am always anxious to procure novelties for public gratification, I write this to say that I should be glad to purchase the lump at its valuation if you will dispose of it, and if not, that I should like to procure it for exhibition for a few weeks.

Beale had carried back a chunk of gold on consignment from Alex Cross with the understanding that Beale would exhibit it and share the proceeds with Cross. Barnum's agent, Albert Case, wrote Beale that he would pay $100 per month for exhibition rights. Beale agreed to this, directing Barnum's Museum to make the payments to his brother, Truxtun Beale, as his agent.

Beale had other things than Alex Cross's gold to think about. He had received orders back to the Pacific, and his marriage to Mary Edwards at Chester was imminent. He wrote in haste to brother Truxtun:

> I am to be married in about an hour and shall leave at once for New York. Mary is very anxious that I should take her out with me but of course that is out of the question. Call on the Bentons and offer my services to carry letters to Fremont. I shall leave New York for the Pacific day after tomorrow. I have a great deal more to say but the minister has come and I must stop.

Edward Beale married Mary Engle Edwards in her father's mansion on the corner of Edgemont Avenue and Market Street in Chester, Pennsylvania, on June 27, 1849. Samuel Edwards, Mary's father, was a distinguished lawyer and for eight years a member of the House of Representatives. Some five years earlier, older brother Truxtun Beale had married Mary Ann Tillinghast, daughter of Representative Joseph Leonard Tilling-

hast of Rhode Island. So the Beale brothers were both married
to daughters of U. S. Congressmen.

Beale departed for the West again, leaving, if his memory
served, on his wedding day:

> Left Washington with dispatches for California overland for Com-
> modore Jones and Fremont on June 27, 1849, and arrived at San
> Francisco about August 17. Returned almost immediately with dis-
> patches and arrived at Washington during December, 1849.

Beale correctly recalled leaving on the 27th, right after his
wedding, but he didn't travel overland. He sailed from New
York on the Twenty-eighth aboard the *Falcon,* bound for
Chagres and the Panama crossing.

Beale left Truxtun to settle his accounts with the Navy,
having received no pay for several months. He had been carried
on the rolls of the *Congress* from 1845 to 1846 as Acting
Sailing Master, and from 1846 to 1847 as Acting Lieutenant
while still listed on his pay account as Passed Midshipman.
Through his civilian capacity as an executive in the Washington
Navy Yard, Truxtun learned that a certificate from Commodore Stockton regarding his brother's actual status would be
required. The Commodore complied and in due time the accounts
were properly adjusted to Beale's status as Acting Lieutenant.

A fellow passenger heading south from New York on the
Falcon was a boyhood friend of Beale's, Bayard Taylor. Out
of this journey with Edward Beale would come the first accurate,
full-scale historical and literary description of life in the California gold mines, Bayard Taylor's noted book *Eldorado*.

THE PORTRAITS OF
EDWARD F. BEALE

An early portrait of Beale
as a U.S. Navy Lieutenant
Courtesy, Huntington Library

Edward Beale in his "Spanish Disguise" worn during his
ride across Mexico in 1848. An oil painting which hangs
in the Decatur House, Washington, D.C.

Courtesy, National Trust for Historic Preservation

A portrait from the 1870's.
Courtesy, California Historical Society

An unpublished portrait, circa 1890.
Courtesy, Delaware County Historical
Society, Chester, Pennsylvania.

A portrait from a woodcut.
Courtesy, Huntington Library.

Edward Beale in Bronze.
Sculptured by Robert Hinckley.
Courtesy, Beale Air Force Base, Calif.

8

A Tour of the Golden State

At least two of the thousands of argonauts who descended upon California in 1849 were not in search of gold: Edward Beale, once again on assignment as a government courier, and his friend and traveling companion Bayard Taylor, a journalist for Horace Greeley's New York *Tribune*.

Taylor was born on January 11, 1825, at Kennett Square, Chester County, Pennsylvania. By 1849 he had been writing professionally for five years, two years of which he spent traveling in Europe writing for the *Saturday Evening Post, Graham's Magazine, United States Gazette* and the New York *Tribune*. As the author of a popular book recounting his European experiences, Taylor was well known to Greeley's readers. In addition, George P. Putnam had agreed to publish Taylor's California stories in book form.

With ample time on shipboard Beale and Taylor renewed their old friendship, recalling their boyhood years together in Pennsylvania. Taylor had read Fremont's published reports and Lieutenant Emory's story and wanted to hear Beale's version of the California campaign. He also was eager to learn of the sailor's various adventures in Mexico and the West.

They crossed the Isthmus to Panama City without incident but found over 700 emigrants waiting for passage to San Francisco. Beale recalled that he had made his first crossing in 1846 entirely alone. Many of those waiting for a ship had succumbed to one of Panama's periodic epidemics of cholera. Luckily, the steamer *Panama* stood ready to sail at once. Beale and Taylor were taken aboard, their passage having been arranged in advance. However, Taylor was not especially eager to leave:

I saw less of Panama than I could have wished. A few hasty rambles through its ruined convents and colleges and grass-grown plazas

— a stroll on its massive battlements, lumbered with idle cannon, of the splendid bronze of Barcelona — were all that I could accomplish in the short stay . . .

The *Panama* made scheduled stops for water and supplies at San Blas, Mazatlan and San Diego. Passengers were not permitted off the ship for fear of spreading cholera. The shipboard quarantine prevailed at Monterey, too, but Beale received special permission to go ashore in his capacity as government courier. He delivered dispatches to the Military Governor, General Bennet Riley, whom he found ill with a fever. Before returning to the ship, Beale walked to the upper end of town and called upon Jessie Fremont at the Castro adobe and delivered letters from her father.

Taylor described the end of their sea voyage on August 17, fifty-one days out of New York:

> At last we are through the Golden Gate, fit name for such a magnificent portal . . . southward and westward opens the renowned harbor, crowded with the shipping of the world, mast behind mast and vessel behind vessel, the flags of all nations fluttering in the breeze! . . . We glide on with the tide, past the U. S. ship *Ohio* . . . the signal is given, the anchor drops, our voyage is over.

The *Ohio* sent a boat for Lieutenant Beale. He took Taylor with him and reported to the ship with dispatches from the Navy Department. Later, the *Ohio's* boat put them ashore with their luggage at Clark's Wharf. They hired two Mexicans to carry their trunks to a hotel, "paying them each two dollars," noted Taylor, "a sum so immense in comparison to the service rendered that there was no longer any doubt of our having actually landed in California."

They obtained a garret room with two beds at the City Hotel on Portsmouth Square and set out to see the town. Bayard Taylor's description of San Francisco in 1849 is both vivid and accurate:

> . . . Hundreds of tents and houses appeared, scattered all over the heights, and along the shore for more than a mile . . . the greater part

of them mere canvas sheds, open in front, and covered with all kinds
of signs, in all languages. Great quantities of goods were piled up in
the open air, for want of a place to store them. The streets were full
of people, hurrying to and fro, and of as diverse and bizarre a character as the houses: Yankees of every possible variety, native Californians in sarapes and sombreros, Chileans, Sonorians, Kanakas from
Hawaii, Chinese with long tails, Malays armed with their everlasting
creeses, and others in whose embrowned and bearded visages it was
impossible to recognize any especial nationality.

Beale had dispatches for Fremont. He made arrangements
to leave for San Jose on the second morning, offering Taylor
"a seat on one of his mules." Beale secured animals for their
journey, an *alazan,* or sorrel horse, for himself and a brown
mule for Taylor. He bought two cream-colored mules for re-
mounts and a third pack-mule which Taylor named "Picayune,
a dwarfish little fellow with elfish character of cunning and
mischief."

Laying aside civilian attire for coarse flannel shirts and
Mexican serapes, they armed themselves with long sheath
knives and pistols, and buckled on immense Chilean spurs
with two-inch rowels that jingled at every step. Thus capari-
soned, they sallied forth from San Francisco to the sound of
the Ohio's guns booming a somber funeral salute to President
Polk, who had died on June 15.

Beale left Taylor at a hotel and located Fremont at the San
Jose home of Grove Cook, where he also found Andrew Sublette.
Before Fremont left California in 1847, he had given Consul
Thomas Oliver Larkin $3,000 to purchase a plot of land for
him near Santa Cruz, at the north end of Monterey Bay. Instead,
Larkin bought a remote mountain tract of several thousand
acres for Fremont. The land proved to be a grant made in 1844
to Governor Juan Bautista Alvarado named Las Mariposas
for the myriad butterflies found there. Alvarado sold the grant
to Larkin. Fremont thought the land to be worthless. He
castigated Larkin for wasting his money, but Mariposa timber
and gold eventually made him a wealthy man.

The energetic Fremont lost no time in developing his resources. He grubstaked a party of Sonorans in exchange for an equal share of whatever gold they might find along the Mariposa and Merced rivers. Pio Pico, returned from exile in Mexico, hired a group of Californios to mine the placer deposits near Fremont's party. Fremont also operated a steam sawmill at San Jose to raise money for supplies and equipment for Las Mariposas. Lumber brought $500 per thousand board feet and Fremont had enough contracts to keep the mill busy for a year.

Beale gave Fremont letters from Senator Benton, and a letter from President Zachary Taylor asking Fremont to serve on the Joint Survey Commission to "run and mark" the international boundary between Mexico and the United States. The two Democrats appointed to the Commission by President Polk had locked horns with their Mexican counterparts over interpretation of the treaty map. They were dismissed by President Taylor, who wanted two good Whigs to replace them. Fremont appreciated this show of confidence despite his court-martial, but declined. His mining and milling operations fully occupied his time. He would not even be able to attend the upcoming state constitutional convention.

After assuring Fremont of Jessie's well-being at Monterey, Beale rejoined Taylor at the Miner's Home, which the journalist described as a "decent-looking hotel where we lay down on the floor among a dozen other travelers and fleas which could not be counted."

Next day, Beale and Taylor headed for the town of Stockton, pausing long enough at Mission San Jose de Guadalupe to raid the old apple and pear orchards. They spent a night on the trail and then called upon Major Lawrence P. Graham, who had a camp about five miles outside Stockton. Graham brought the First Dragoons overland to California from Monterrey, Mexico, in 1848. One of his junior officers, Lieutenant Cave Johnson Couts, wrote in his journal that the Major stayed drunk during virtually the entire trip. Of this accomplishment Taylor made no mention, but did expound on Graham's hospitality. Graham welcomed Beale as he would an old friend and the two travelers remained his guests for four days.

Captain Charles M. Weber, a pioneer landholder on the San Joaquin River in 1844, established "Tuleburgh," a settlement of rude thatched huts that became the landing for gold-seekers traveling by water to the Mother Lode. Weber hired Major Richard P. Hammond in 1848 to survey a new townsite he called Stockton in honor of Commodore Robert Field Stockton. Beale and Taylor occasionally bestirred themselves from Graham's hospitality to gallop the five miles from camp to town astride two of the Major's fine horses. Taylor considered a view of Stockton something to remember:

> There is in the heart of California, where the last winter stood a solitary ranch in the midst of the tule marshes, I found a canvas town of a thousand inhabitants, and a port with twenty-five vessels at anchor! The mingling noises of labor abound – the click of hammers and the grating of saws – the shouts of mule-drivers – the jingling of spurs ... almost cheated me into the belief that it was some old commercial mart, familiar with such sounds for years past. Four months only had sufficed to make the place what it was, and in that time a wholesale firm ... had done business to the amount of $100,000. The same party had just purchased a lot eighty by one hundred feet, on the principal street, for $6000, and the cost of erecting a common one-story clap-board house on it was $15,000.

Beale chanced to meet White Elliott at Stockton, one of Kit Carson's mountain men who had been with them on their 1847 overland ride. Taylor noted:

> [Elliott] had been one of Lieutenant Beale's men on the Gila, and the many perils they then shared gave their present meeting a peculiar interest. Elliott, who, young as he was, had undergone everything that could harden and toughen a man out of all sensibility, colored like a young girl; his eyes were wet and he scarcely found voice to speak.

Beale and Taylor paid a visit to the Mokelumne River diggings. On their way the journalist recorded a characteristic peculiar to mules:

Sometimes a horse, sometimes an ass, captivates the fancy of a whole drove of mules; but often an animal nowise akin. Lieutenant Beale told me that his whole train of mules once took a stampede on the plains of the Cimarron, and ran half a mile, when they halted in apparent satisfaction. The cause of their freak was found to be a buffalo calf, which had strayed from the herd. They were frisking around it in the greatest delight, rubbing their noses against it, throwing up their heels, and making themselves ridiculous by abortive attempts to neigh and bray, while the poor calf, unconscious of its attractive qualities, stood trembling in their midst.

Hundreds of Americans, Sonorans and Hawaiians were hard at work along the Mokelumne. Taylor expressed his fascination with the actual process of taking gold from the riverbed:

When I first saw the men carrying heavy stones in the sun, standing nearly waist-deep in water, and grubbing with their hands in the gravel and clay, there seemed to me little virtue in resisting the temptation to gold-digging; but when the shining particles were poured out lavishly from a tin basin, I confess there was a sudden itching in my fingers to seize the heaviest crowbar and the biggest shovel.

Many Americans employed Indians and Mexicans to work for them, finding them in provisions as Fremont had done. Notwithstanding the enormous price of food, these workmen could be hired for about a dollar a day. The hundreds so employed soon exhausted the easily reached placer deposits.

Racial antagonisms mounted in a direct ratio to the amount of increased labor required to find the gold. No distinction was made between citizens of Mexico and those native Californios who had opted for United States citizenship. One victim was Andres Pico, who had a company of men digging along the Mokelumne. Learning of Edward Beale's presence, Pico hastened to visit his old adversary and Taylor again witnessed a scene of warm embraces and joyful reunion. Several of Pico's miners had been lancers at San Pasqual. They crowded around Beale, eager to shake the hand of the young Naval officer they remembered so stoutly defending his howitzer against their mounted attack.

Pico complained of the prejudice he had suffered. Several times his men were driven away from the diggings and allowed to return only after extensive explanations and arguments — sometimes only after a "trial" by a pickup jury elected for the purpose. There was little that Beale could do other than sympathize with Pico and the Californios.

Beale and Taylor rode south through the gold-rich foothills of the Sierra Nevada to Sonora, so named for the number of Mexicans from that province. The first man Beale saw was Baptiste Perrot, another mountain man who had been with Beale and Carson at San Pasqual and on their cross-country trek to Washington.

Again a scene of warm reunion ensued, Beale and Perrot pounding each other on the back. Perrot tethered their mules and made his makeshift accommodations their own. He operated a "hotel" consisting merely of an open space roofed with branches. A table of rough planks served for dining, another for the inevitable monte game. "Wherever there is gold, there is gambling," wrote Taylor. Seats were fashioned of logs on forked limbs. A bar of similar construction contained a stock of liquor and tinned goods. Taylor remembered these salient details:

> In the evening we sat down to a supper prepared by Baptiste . . . which completed my astonishment at the resources of that wonderful land. There, in the rough depth of the hills, where . . . we expected to live on jerked beef and bread, we saw on the table green corn, green peas and beans, fresh oysters, roast turkey, fine Goshen butter, and excellent coffee.

Actually, the meal cost them nothing, for Perrot wouldn't accept a penny.

Beale had spent all the time away from his official duties that he could afford. His departure was further prompted by an attack of poison oak which next to fleas might have been the worst plague of the mines. It might also be assumed that Beale's thoughts turned occasionally to the bride he had left practically at the altar. He and Taylor headed back to Stockton.

They found the trail filled with muletrains packing supplies to the mining camps. Each mule carried about 200 pounds. At the going rate of thirty cents per pound, the mules earned rich returns for their owners. One freighter disclosed profits averaging $3000 per month, a fact which Beale marked for future reference.

Beale embarked from Stockton by boat, arranging for Taylor to return overland to San Francisco with his horse and four mules. Beale took over navigation of the launch down the San Joaquin River and through the maze of delta sloughs. Through the vast inland sea of tules, across Suisun Bay and through the Straits of Carquinez he guided the boat, recalling his adventure in those same waters in 1846 when Commodore Stockton had sent him to find Fremont.

Taylor made his way to San Francisco, then south to Monterey where he attended sessions of the constitutional convention at Colton Hall, the imposing structure built by Beale's former chaplain on the USS *Congress*.

On September 30, Taylor wrote publisher George Putnam from Monterey that he would tour parts of California once more and then depart from San Francisco to arrive home in December. In typical literary optimism he promised the publisher to have his book finished early in the spring. Of Monterey he wrote:

> Quiet it certainly is, to one coming from San Francisco . . . The bustle of trade is wanting, but to one not bent on gold-hunting, a delicious climate, beautiful scenery, and pleasant society are a full compensation. Those who stay there for any length of time love the place before they leave it – which would scarcely be said of San Francisco.

Sometime during the happy interlude of these summer journeys Beale joined Fremont and his wife on a leisurely trip from Monterey to San Francisco. Jessie tells of it in the unpublished second volume manuscript of her husband's memoirs:

> The *Fredonia* touched in to Monterey and landed a traveling carriage for me and lots of household things sent around the Horn, and

Mr. Fremont coming down again for a little visit found me well enough for a turn of camping-travel, with the comfortable carriage for my house by night.

Problems arose in finding horses gentle enough for the carriage. They finally resorted to mules, with Edward Beale in charge. "Two Indians, fastening their riatas to the team, led as postillions, making an unusual but most effective six-in-hand outfit."

Jessie describes lovely valleys of the Coast Range with fields of yellowing wild oats, groves of live oak trees with groups of cattle grazing beneath them, and soft sea breezes under serene blue skies.

The days began early, she said, and overnight stops made in mid-afternoon:

> Then Mr. Beale would forage among ranches nestled away in the hills. Sometimes galloping back with a whoop of triumph when he had found fresh mutton or a small sack of pears and a handful of soup herbs. Once he dashed up bare headed, carrying something precious in his hat and shouting his call of victory, when the horse got his foot down a gopher hole and man and horse made a flying summersault. The three precious eggs were smashed on the ground and he was not to be consoled that I should lose such a rare dainty.

Beale accompanied the Fremonts on into San Francisco. Jessie termed the hotel "impossible," so Fremont bought a house prefabricated in China. Jessie said it "fitted together like a puzzle, no nails being used except for the shingles of the roof." Fremont placed the house among sand dunes "on some property owned by him, and where now is the Palace Hotel."

Beale stayed with the Fremonts for awhile in San Francisco while awaiting passage on a steamer for Panama. Jessie described picnics in the sand dunes attended by Sam Ward and,

> . . . our friends the Commissioners too, and fighting Joe Hooker then a slim young army officer; and pleasant Dr. Bowie with all the courtesy and generosity of his Maryland family, and eccentric Ned Beale . . .

Perhaps Beale's rich naval vernacular when he took the flying somersault with the eggs in his hat earned him Jessie's label of "eccentric."

Beale made his first attempt to purchase land in the fall of 1849. He authorized Abel Stearns to make an offer of $25,000 to Jose del Carmen Lugo for some 35,000 acres in Southern California. The transaction failed to materialize.

Beale finally caught a southbound steamer for Panama and the East Coast, at last rejoining his bride in Chester. Dispatches he carried to Washington included a preliminary draft of California's constitution.

By the time Bayard Taylor returned from Monterey to San Francisco later in the fall, 4000 new emigrants had swelled the city's population to over 15,000. He found Fremont at the United States Hotel, up from Mariposa and bubbling excitedly with his discovery of a rich quartz vein on the ranch.

Fremont hurried back to Bear Valley, the northern reach of his 43,000-acre Mariposa ranch and built a house. Jessie remained for the winter in Monterey, later relating:

> One night in December, Mr. Fremont came in dripping wet from San Jose, seventy miles on horseback through heavy rains to tell me he had been elected Senator and it was necessary we should go to Washington on the first of January steamer. At daybreak he was off again.

Taylor departed San Francisco for Mazatlan. He had missed the December steamer and rather than wait for the January sailing took passage on a Peruvian brigantine, the *Iquiquena*. She did not leave her San Francisco mooring for days, and when finally clear of the Golden Gate sprang a leak. For three days she tacked against adverse winds until finally regaining the entrance to the bay. Taylor found himself once more in San Francisco, but in his absence the city had suffered its first great fire and nearly burned to the ground.

Taylor finally left on the January steamer, the *Oregon*. He not only had the Fremonts for company, but California's newly elected Congressmen Edward Gilbert and George W. Wright, and the other Senator-elect, William McKendree Gwin.

Beale, enjoying leave from the Navy with his wife at her home in Chester, received a letter from Taylor dated March 26, 1850, written at the *Tribune's* New York office: "What has become of you? I was in Washington two weeks ago but you were not there . . . I had an odd, exciting adventurous ride through Mexico and should like to compare notes with you." Taylor wanted to dedicate the book about his western travels to Beale. "As the best friend and comrade I had on the trip, it is properly owning to you, and I shall try and make the volume such as you will be satisfied with." Permission was so granted and Taylor acknowledged his gratitude when his *Eldorado, or Adventures in the Path of Empire* was published in 1850. The dedication reads: "To Edward F. Beale, Lieutenant, U. S. N., this work is dedicated with the author's esteem and affection."

Beale became a father for the first time in March 1850, when his wife presented him with a daughter. They named her Mary, after her mother.

Beale's promotion to Lieutenant became officially confirmed on August 3, and by way of celebration he had his portrait painted in his new uniform. The picture now hangs in Decatur House and depicts the young officer as an alert, handsome navy man with clean shaven upper lip and a fringe of black whiskers adorning his chops, after the fashion of the day.

Upon his retirement from the Navy, Commodore Stockton had associated himself with New York capitalist William H. Aspinwall, and among other investments, they put funds into heavy equipment for a gold mining and milling operation on Mariposa land leased from Fremont. Stockton already owned mining properties in Virginia. Some of his machinery was shipped from there to the California mines. Returns from California proved disappointing. Knowing Beale to be just back from the West, Stockton solicited his opinion. Beale did not represent himself as a mining authority but had learned something from

Fremont about the complexities of quartz mining, reduction
and extraction. Beale offered to return west, consult Fremont
who was back in California campaigning for re-election, and
do what he could to relieve the situation.

The Navy granted Beale a year's leave of absence effective
November 1, 1850. Stockton's confidence in Beale can be taken
for granted. Aspinwall appeared reluctant to trust a twenty-
eight-year-old sailor who, as far as he knew, had no previous
business experience. Stockton finally wrote from Philadelphia:

> We have determined to consent to your going to California for the
> purpose of retrieving our affairs at the gold mines. You will therefore
> proceed by the first steamer to California and take upon yourself
> entire charge and superintendence of our gold operations in that state
> and all the property belonging thereto. You are fully aware of the
> great expense which has been incurred and the necessity to have those
> expenses stopped. You will immediately proceed to break up all mining
> operations, send the men home by the cheapest route, and sell the
> machinery and all mining property belonging to us. You will receive
> herewith a letter of credit for sending our men home and to pay other
> unavoidable expenses, taking care not to sell anything for a less amount
> than will cover costs and charges.
>
> You will ascertain if any party be in possession of a good mine where
> the machines can be erected, each party to own an undivided half of
> the mine and machinery. Any arrangement you may make must relieve
> us of any additional outlay. We look with confidence to your putting
> an end to all our expenses there as far as gold mining is concerned.

Edward and Mary Beale were soon on their way to California
by the Panama crossing.

Fremont had drawn the short term of only two months as
United States Senator, while William Gwin got the long term.
In the balloting of February, 1851, Fremont suffered a decisive
defeat for re-election. He once again turned his full attention
to developing his Mariposa property.

Great changes had altered San Francisco's appearance. Hundreds of frame houses and commercial buildings replaced the
tents and shanties. Families of men working the mines arrived
daily, and with them came the influences that built schools and

churches and the rudiments of an orderly society. But the city's politics were still densely laced with corruption. Widespread collusion among the police, criminal elements and shady members of the bar had paralyzed law enforcement. And fire remained San Francisco's greatest enemy.

While the Beales traveled west via Panama, Fremont disposed of the Chinese house. He set Jessie and Lilly up in a cottage on the Stockton Street hill where they commanded a sweeping view of the bay. There on April 15, 1851, Jessie gave birth to a second son, John Charles Fremont, Jr. On the evening of May 3, Jessie commanded a sweeping view not only of the bay but of a roaring fire that had started in a paint shop on the west side of Portsmouth Square. It spread rapidly to the adjacent buildings. Fed by a strong northwesterly wind, the conflagration soon leaped beyond control of the city's primitive fire-fighting apparatus. Still confined to bed, Jessie watched through a front window as the blaze reached the bottom of the hill.

Fremont was away at the Mariposa ranch, but neighbors stood ready to carry her out if the flames came any closer. Miraculously, the wind died and by mid-morning of the Fourth the fire had burned itself out. The hill house survived, but most of the lower end of town lay in charred ruins. At this point the Beales arrived to find San Francisco's central commercial area nearly wiped out.

Twenty-four-year-old Mary Engle Edwards Beale had great natural charm and grace. Her upbringing and education had been no less than that of her good friend, Jessie Fremont. Both their fathers were politically prominent. Their husbands were known throughout the land for their various exploits. Mary Beale, no stranger to the salons of the nation's capital, came not as a stranger to San Francisco. Several of her friends from the East were in residence and they gladly made her welcome. Mary was a skilled performer on the pianoforte. One of her admirers was author J. Ross Browne, also musically inclined. He would often accompany Mary in entertaining their friends, she playing the piano and he the violin.

Beale went to the Mariposa ranch. There he found Fremont

working his mine, and Alex Godey, one of Fremont's old scouts and a companion of Beale's at San Pasqual, running cattle to sell at mining camps along the rivers.

Indian Commissioner George W. Barbour had gathered the Mariposa Indians to council and negotiated a treaty. He promised they would be provided several hundred head of cattle, seed, farming implements, and agents to instruct them in farming the land which was to be permanently set aside for them. Barbour contracted with Fremont to supply cattle from the herd Godey was managing. He paid for them with drafts on the U. S. Treasury at the going rate of twenty cents a pound. He assured Fremont the treaty would be ratified by Congress and the drafts honored. Always in need of cash, Fremont sold the drafts at a substantial discount.

Congress did not ratify the treaty and the Treasury Department wouldn't honor the drafts, something Fremont didn't learn until much later. Luckily, Beale had witnessed Fremont's contract negotiations with Barbour.

The Indians were abandoned with little of Fremont's beef ever delivered to them, through no fault of his. They saw neither seed nor farming implements, much less agents to instruct them. Beale and Fremont agreed that colonization on farming reservations would be the safest and best life for the Indians. Generations of mission-bred Indians along the coast had worked as sheep herders and vaqueros on the ranchos. Indian house servants were practically members of the families they served — whether for better or worse. But the San Joaquin Valley Indians were neither civilized nor domesticated, hunters nor horsemen. They were mostly primitive diggers, gatherers and fish-eaters leading a stone age existence in an increasingly hostile environment. Their few contacts with the whites had been unfortunate. They were as eager to get away from the settlements as the whites were to have them go. Beale would have the opportunity before long to institute humane reforms in an effort to protect them.

Meanwhile, Beale learned from Fremont that the Aspinwall

and Stockton mining venture might eventually yield returns but would require a continuing outlay of capital for labor and equipment. He decided to dispose of their machinery. He made a tour of several mines where he might unload the equipment, but he had little knowledge of mining and declined to deal under that handicap.

There was one phase of California commerce which Beale did understand, however — the overland transportation of supplies to the mines. He recalled that freighters from Stockton to the Mother Lode region earned thirty cents per pound in 1849. That fee had grown to a dollar per pound.

Supplies for the most populous mining areas funneled through the two inland port cities of Stockton and Sacramento. The material was transported from there to the camps by overland means. Beale saw his opportunity. As Bayard Taylor had noted, one operation for which Beale seemed notably qualified was "mulecraft." No merchant or miner he, but with many of the requisites of a freighter his decision was made.

Beale disposed of the Aspinwall and Stockton equipment at a loss on the original investment, but for enough money to cover expenses. He found his letter of credit readily accepted in Sacramento. Major Graham provided pack-mules at Stockton. Beale's command of Spanish enabled him to hire Mexican packers. By diverting funds earmarked for sending ex-employees home, he could hire them back again as clerks and checkers, leaving one in each mining community. Beale then negotiated contracts with Adams Express Company and Palmer, Cook & Company to deliver supplies from the embarcaderos of Sacramento and Stockton to the mines.

Beale did his share of mule-skinning while establishing the freighting business, then later supervised operations by horseback and stagecoach. Deposits to his accounts were soon exceeding $10,000 per month.

The Navy granted him a six-months extension of his leave until May of 1852. Roads were so improved to the mines by the end of 1851, however, that pack-mules rapidly gave way to wagon freighting. Beale had skimmed the cream off the top of the business by then. His activities for less than a year had realized profits for Aspinwall and Stockton in excess of $100,000. The agreed-upon commission for himself, after expenses, amounted to $13,000. He wound up his affairs and returned to San Francisco near the end of the year.

Beale and his wife prepared to go East. The year in California, when he was virtually his own boss, had been an exhilarating experience. He earned more than ten times a Navy Lieutenant's pay and did it purely on his own initiative. He had accepted a personal challenge calling for new directions and purposes. The result was a smashing success.

Beale submitted his resignation to the Navy Department on November 1, 1851, without waiting for his leave to expire. It was not formally accepted by Secretary of the Navy John Kennedy until March 5, 1852, but for the first time since 1837 when he turned fifteen years of age, Edward Beale was a private citizen.

He and Mary took leave of the Fremonts and returned east by way of the Isthmus. Beale left Mary with her folks at Chester and reported to Aspinwall and Stockton in New York. Beale's pack-mules had pulled their financial chestnuts out of the fire as far as their mining interests were concerned. He had accomplished all that was expected of him, and more, confirming an emerging strength of character that would be his hallmark for the rest of his days.

But any commercial enterprises that might have been taking shape in Beale's mind would have to wait. He became aware of a more urgent call, a subtle but persistent plea for help. The message came on the west wind in the obscure tongue of aboriginal Indians, now experiencing death and dispersion in California's burgeoning growth. Beale heard their distant cry and he would become their champion.

9

Indian Superintendent

California's Indians fared no better under the advance of the white man's civilization than natives elsewhere in the Western Hemisphere. Their decimation simply came about in a little different way. Spanish colonizers operating under the sanctity of the Mother Church were interested mostly in saving souls through subjection. Generations of California mission Indians knew no other existence than miserable toil in the blessed fields. Material returns were measured by what they could steal. Escape meant pursuit, capture and flogging.

Secularization laws in the 1820's brought change to the Indians' condition. As restrictions were lifted most mission Indians fled to the hills. For the ones who didn't flee, something closely akin to slavery continued to prevail during the twenty-two years of Mexican rule in California. Many ranchos maintained small armies of Indian field hands, vaqueros and domestic workers. The wife of Mariano Guadalupe Vallejo of Sonoma, when asked how she employed her thirty household servants, replied:

> Each child has a personal attendant, while I have two for my own need. Four or five are occupied in grinding corn, six or seven serve in the kitchen, five or six are always washing clothes, and nearly a dozen are employed in sewing and spinning. They have no wages. We treat our servants rather as friends than servants.

Substitute the word slave for servant and the picture becomes clearer.

Yet, Mexican law considered Indians to be citizens, even if they didn't comprehend the fact. After the American conquest Indian rights were supposed to be protected under California law. Section XI of the Treaty of Guadalupe Hidalgo spelled it out:

> The sacredness of this obligation shall never be lost sight of when providing for the removal of Indians from any portion of the territories, but on the contrary special care shall be taken not to place them under the necessity of seeking new homes, by committing those invasions which the United States has solemnly obliged themselves to restrain.

In framing the California State Constitution in 1850, there were apparently not enough copies of the treaty to go around. Or nobody bothered to read it. The rights of California Indians guaranteed by the treaty were ignored.

Settlers and gold-seekers poured into the state and went about acquiring land largely by driving a stake into the soil and squatting. Encroachment on traditional tribal territories drove the Indians further into the hinterlands. Hostilities ensued, and then open combat on an increasing scale.

Edward Beale had seen enough brutal treatment to express himself strongly following the mass murder of Indians on the Trinity River in 1851:

> The river salmon constitutes the whole subsistence of the Indians. The whites took the river and when the Indians come to fish, they are usually shot. Last year some Indians were charged with taking cattle. A party went against their village, attacked at daybreak, and killed all the women and children, the men being absent. They carried home a bag full of scalps, and without loss to themselves, which proves the character of the operation.

It is sufficient to say that Beale absolutely abhorred such conduct. Others did too. What to do about it became one of the great emotional debates of the day.

Until 1824, the responsibility for Indian relations fell to the office of the Secretary of War. The Bureau of Indian Affairs was established in that year, with a Commissioner appointed by the President. The Bureau became part of the Department of the Interior in 1849 and Adam Johnston was appointed

Indian Agent for California. Lacking the resources of the War Department, Johnston adopted the philosophy that "to feed the Indians for a year would be cheaper than to fight them for a week." He recommended they be placed on reservations to be cared for as wards of the federal government.

That was one solution. John McDougal, California's second Governor, had another. Fearing the state lacked financial resources to control growing hostilities, McDougal told Congress the federal government should provide protection for whites by establishing forts to be garrisoned by United States troops. He made no mention of protection for the Indians.

Responding to Indian Agent Johnston's recommendations in 1850, Secretary of the Interior Thomas Ewing delegated three commissioners with a Congressional appropriation of $150,000 to go out to California, distribute presents among the tribes, make treaties, provide sustenance and determine what reservations should be established and where. But Governor McDougal didn't want commissioners, much less reservations. He wanted soldiers, and lots of them, to "chastise" the Indians or, better still, exterminate them. The idea of giving them presents he found preposterous. Alexander H. Stuart, the new Secretary of the Interior, agreed with McDougal and wrote to President Fillmore on November 29, 1851: "A temporizing system can no longer be pursued toward the American Indian. The policy of removal to reservations must be abandoned and the only alternative is to civilize or exterminate them."

But by then the three commissioners had already arrived in San Francisco. They were Dr. Oliver Meredith Wozencraft, Redick McKee and George W. Barbour. They met with Governor McDougal at San Francisco and were dismayed to learn their $150,000 appropriation had been whittled down by Congress to $25,000. They had already spent more than that amount in supplies and gifts for the Indians.

The commissioners visited tribes along the Eel, Klamath, Stanislaus, Merced and Tuolumne rivers, and in the Clear Lake country distributing presents and promises. By December, eighteen treaties had been signed and agreed to by the Indians. Redick McKee, acting as disbursing agent, approved unauthorized contracts amounting to $700,000 to provide sustenance for the Indians. One treaty read:

> It is agreed the ratification of this treaty by the President and the Senate of the United States, the tribe shall be furnished fifty brood mares, two stallions, sixty cows, five bulls, twenty-four plows, twelve sets of harness, twenty-four yoke of oxen, two hundred hoes . . . seeds for sowing, 3000 pounds of iron, 600 pounds of steel, 2000 blankets, 3000 yards of linsey cloth and the same quantity of cotton cloth and calico . . . fifty pounds of thread, 5000 needles, 500 thimbles . . .

In addition, the treaty promised a schoolhouse and teachers, and farmers, blacksmiths and carpenters to instruct the Indians in their skills. The Indians, in return, were to settle peaceably on reservations and all their worries would be over. McKee engaged, as interpreter, Robert Walker who ran a ferry on the Klamath River. Walker added to McKee's remarks that the Indians were also to take care of and operate his ferry. When all this promised under one treaty is multiplied by eighteen times, McKee's optimism takes on monumental proportions.

McKee sought out Beale, who had not yet left San Francisco, and asked for his endorsement of the plan. Beale did endorse it, enthusiastically. He added a written amendment to McKee's report to the Secretary of the Interior:

> There are men from Missouri, Oregon and Texas who value life of an Indian just as they do a wolf or coyote, and embrace every opportunity to shoot them down. I despair of seeing peace fully established until the government establishes military posts to protect the Indians from these attacks.

Here we have McKee, with Beale's endorsement, appealing for troops to protect the Indians, while McDougal is demanding the same protection for the whites. As to the efforts of the commissioners, McKee gloated: "Consider the results which must happily follow, the expenses are trifling. I doubt whether ever in the history of Indian negotiations . . . has been so much positive good effected." Little did he know.

Cattle were delivered by Fremont to Commissioner Barbour in the transaction witnessed by Beale. The cattle were then turned over to Major James D. Savage of the state militia for distribution to the Indians. Savage had several trading posts in the Mariposa region where he was known as "King of the Tulares." Savage, like so many of his contemporaries, took advantage of the Indians and when the Indians received less than promised — or received nothing at all — they retaliated with raids. Savage's trading post on the Fresno River became their first target. They murdered three men, ran off Savage's stock and burned his store to the ground. Sheriff James Burney of Mariposa County mounted a punitive expedition against the Indians with a party of seventy-four volunteers. It accomplished little. Governor McDougal authorized a second company known as the Mariposa Battalion, commanded by Major Savage. Their objective was to "drive the Indians back into the mountains, if it was not possible to exterminate them."

Back at Washington, the eighteen treaties were finally signed by President Fillmore on June 7, 1852, and submitted to the Senate for ratification. Commissioner McKee received the shock of his life when the Senate rejected all eighteen. The enormous unauthorized expenditures were cited as one reason. California's newly elected Governor John Bigler, as unalterably opposed as McDougal to reservations, claimed the commissioners were giving to barbaric savages the most fertile and valuable farm and mineral lands in the state. He warned the Senate that when the white settlers wanted the lands inside the proposed reservation, they would take them. The entire United States Army would be powerless to stop them.

Indian Agent Adam Johnston's position lost importance after arrival of the three commissioners. His reports became tardy and slipshod. He was dismissed from his office in 1852, leaving the Indians with gravely diminished sustenance, supervision and protection. The situation became critical. It was proposed that a position of Superintendent of Indian Affairs be created for California.

Edward Beale, back in Washington by January of 1852, had

his name placed in nomination for the appointment by Senator Benton. Beale received the immediate endorsement of former Secretary of State James Buchanan and other friends in Washington, including the California Congressional delegation.

The Fremonts were also there. Fremont had promised Jessie a trip abroad but charges suddenly arose that he had swindled the government in the beef contract with Commissioner Barbour. Beale rushed to Fremont's defense and on January 24 submitted an affidavit:

> This will certify that I, Lieutenant E. F. Beale of the United States Navy, was in California in 1851, engaged in business for Commodore Stockton and Mr. Aspinwall. I know that Mr. Barbour, the commissioner, was importunate with Colonel Fremont for a prompt delivery of cattle in June to keep the Indians friendly and peaceable. I know the commissioner constantly promised to have the treaty approved early at Washington and Fremont urged him to do so as the only means of keeping the southern Indians peaceable and quiet. I also know that Colonel Fremont negotiated the drafts Barbour gave him to pay for the cattle he bought, on the exhorbitant terms usual in California.

Beale further stated that the cattle had been delivered by Barbour to Savage for distribution to the Indians. What happened after that was beyond his knowledge.

Enemies of Fremont recalled that Beale was a witness for the defense in Fremont's 1848 court-martial. By inference they insinuated he was also involved in the beef deal for the financial benefit of both. Fremont leaped to Beale's defense. He denied the charges and emphatically stated, "Lieutenant Beale has never been associated with me in any business transaction whatsoever."

Fremont, cleared of the charges against him, left Washington for New York. He sailed with Jessie and the children on the *Africa* on March 10, 1852, for a year in England and France.

Governor Bigler declared in an 1852 message to the state legislature that the Indians ought to be removed beyond the confines of the state:

I condemn the reservations established by the commissioners as wrong, fraught with evil to the Indians and the whites, and calculated to produce instant collision and impose heavy burdens upon the government.

Bigler gave his opinion to General Ethan Allen Hitchcock, commander of the Department of the Pacific, that the Indians, with the ferocity of South Sea cannibals, hated the white race. He said the two races could never live together in peace. The only solution was the evacuation or destruction of the Indians by federal forces.

Hitchcock agreed with Beale's plan for reservations but his troops were too few and he feared their desertion to the gold fields if stationed at isolated posts. As to moving the Indians out of the state entirely, that was beyond his authority.

President Fillmore appointed Edward Beale Superintendent of Indian Affairs for California on March 4, 1852. Confirmation by the Senate was held up by Army brass who looked with cordial disfavor on a civilian — and a former Navy man at that — carrying out a commission certain to involve the military. Beale's appointment eventually received confirmation, but certain senators continued to mumble that it gave him *carte blanche* authority and vested in him powers "vice-regal in breadth and scope."

Beale waited several months for a Congressional appropriation to pay for his salary and implement the reservations. In the meantime, he appraised the eighteen treaties at the request of Commissioner Luke Lea of the Bureau of Indian Affairs. All were approved with the minor provision that Indian schools not be established because their state of development "was such as to preclude the possibility of their appreciating the benefits to be derived from such instruction."

Beale disagreed with Secretary of the Interior Stuart and Governor Bigler in their opposition to reservations. He petitioned the Senate to rescind rejection of the treaties. He pleaded,

To reject them without an effort to retain the Indians' confidence and friendship will undoubtedly involve the state in a long and bloody

war, disastrous and ruinous to her mining and commercial interests
and affecting the prosperity of our whole country.

Navy man Beale knew that a rising tide lifts all boats. Anything done to reduce tension would benefit Indians as well as
whites. And by pointing to the possible jeopardy to California's
mining and commercial interests, Beale demonstrated an instinct
for political motivation.

Meanwhile, the Indians stole horses, cattle, and anything
else they could get their hands on as a matter of survival.
Isolated camps were attacked and whites murdered and scalped.
Armed whites retaliated by wiping out entire Indian villages,
including those of groups innocent of the depredations.

Congress finally passed an Indian appropriation act, part of
which provided for Beale's return to California to investigate
conditions and submit recommendations on measures to assure
the future control and protection of the Indians. A sum of $14,-
000 was appropriated for his salary and that of a clerk, and
for limited expenses. For his clerk Beale hired his friend and
brother-in-law, Harry Edwards. He also employed Fred Kerlin,
his wife's cousin. They left New York on August 5 via Panama
and arrived at San Francisco on September 5, 1852, where Beale
took up his duties in the Indian Office at 123 Montgomery
Street.

The Fourth Infantry Regiment journeyed to the Pacific at
the same time, arriving in San Francisco soon after Beale.
Lieutenant Ulysses S. Grant served as the unit's Quartermaster.
Beale first met Grant shortly after arrival of the regiment.
They were of the same age and, as happened when Beale met
Fremont and Carson, their first acquaintance ripened into lifelong friendship. Of those days Bonsal, Beale's first biographer,
wrote, "They walked the Long Wharf together and ate their
meals at the What Cheer House." Knowing the propensities
of both men, however, it is highly unlikely that Beale and Grant
regularly patronized the What Cheer House. It was the city's
leading temperance hostelry and advertised, "No liquor on
the premises."

Beale wrote Commissioner Luke Lea after a month in the field:

> . . . Our laws and policy with respect to the Indians have been neglected or violated in the state. They are driven from their homes and deprived of their hunting grounds and fishing waters, and when they come back to get the means of their sustenance they are killed, thus giving retaliation to wars. The condition of the Indians is truly deplorable. They are caught like cattle and made to work, and then turned out to starve and die when the work season is over.
>
> To remedy this state of things and make some compensation for the country taken from them, several treaties were made, all of which were rejected. So now the Indians remain without protection from law or treaties. Supplies of cattle were contracted for but in their deliveries great irregularities occurred, to the great injuries of both Indians and government.

In response to Secretary Stuart's request that he investigate charges that Indians north of San Francisco were being mistreated, Beale reported:

> I went over to San Pablo rancho in Contra Costa County and found seventy-eight on the rancho and twelve back of Martinez, most of them sick and without clothes or food. Eighteen had died of starvation. They were the survivors of a band worked all last summer and fall, and as winter set in, when broken down by hunger and labor and without food or clothes, they were turned adrift to shift for themselves as best they could. Californians named Ramon Briones and Ramon Mesa have made a business of catching Indians and disposing of them in this way, and I have been informed that many Indians have been murdered in these expeditions.
>
> I have distributed the [healthy Indians] among families to clothe and protect them, and made provision for the sick to be fed and cared for. These people could easily be made to support themselves and their condition changed for the better. The grand jury of the county found bills against the Californians mentioned and I presume their trial will come up next term.

An example of the prevailing attitude toward Indians in California is described by a former shipmate of Beale's, Joseph

Warren Revere. In his book, *Keel and Saddle,* Revere relates how he, in company with Jose Armenteros, Juan Briones, Rafael Garcia and a party of their vaqueros stormed an Indian camp to recover stolen horses. They killed several of the Indians and captured several more to work as slaves on their ranchos. Revere kept two as laborers on his Rancho Geronimo in Marin County.

Beale estimated 15,000 Indians perished from starvation the previous winter. The remaining 70,000 diminished steadily. Whiskey and disease added to their senseless, brutal decimation. Beale believed, with Washington Irving, that the moral laws which govern the Indian are few, but he conforms to them all. The white man abounds in laws of religion, morals, ethics and manners, but observes them more in the breach than practice.

Beale called the attention of Governor Bigler to a massacre by whites of defenseless women and children in which the assailants were known to him. Beale applied to the United States District Attorney to issue warrants on charges of murder, but had to explain to Bigler that,

> As the gentleman who commanded the party in this unfortunate affair was the county judge, consequently I did not think it worth-while to prosecute him in his own county. The United States District Attorney informs me that he was not aware of any law that would apply in the case as the federal court had no jurisdiction in cases where life is taken.

Beale advised General Hitchcock that United States troops were in the vicinity of one such massacre and took no action. Their mission, as they understood it, was only to chastise the Indians should that be necessary.

No response came from Hitchcock, so Governor Bigler commissioned Beale a Brigadier General in the California State Militia to give him some "clout" in dealing with the Army. So, here's the sailor hardly out of his naval uniform suddenly made a Brigadier General. Beale didn't flaunt the title. That wasn't his style, but it seems likely he experienced a certain satisfaction in it. There seems little question the rank gave him clout when he needed it, and those times would come more frequently than he imagined.

Beale had returned to Washington by October of 1852 and reported directly to President Fillmore. He recommended that $500,000 be appropriated for the subsistence of the Indians; military posts be established on six reservations where the Indians could grow their own food; that the three agents employed in the Indian Service be dismissed; and that six new agents be appointed at annual salaries of $1,500 to live on the reservations and instruct the Indians in the cultivation of food crops. Beale had set up the first experimental farm for the San Joaquin Valley Indians and left it under the supervision of Harry Edwards. General Hitchcock thought Beale's plan would get both the Indians and whites off his back. He wrote the Secretary of War in November:

> I deem it necessary to express an opinion in favor of the plan proposed by General Beale, Superintendent of Indians in this division. The choice of the government lies between accepting General Beale's plan or giving the Indians over to rapid extermination. These Indians have never been recognized by the Spanish or Mexican governments as having any independent rights.

Hitchcock erred in his last statement. Indians did have the rights of citizens under Mexican law, and many Mexicans had more Indian blood than Spanish blood.

Hitchcock requested that if he was to be retained on duty in California, Beale also be continued in his office because,

> He has a more extensive acquaintance with the Indians than any other man in the country and brings to the performance of his duties an earnest zeal, a humane spirit, and untiring perseverance and honest independence.

As one of the last acts of his administration, President Fillmore on November 11 appointed Beale to the Superintendency of Indian Affairs in Nevada as well as California. One of the first acts of incoming President Franklin Pierce in 1853 was to confirm that appointment. At the same time, Pierce appointed Beale's friend Kit Carson Indian Agent for New Mexico and Tom Fitzpatrick agent for the tribes of the upper Platte and Arkansas rivers.

Governor Bigler addressed President Pierce in February of 1853 from Vallejo, then the state capital, subscribing somewhat less than wholeheartedly to Beale's plan. Bigler was to get his soldiers, Beale his reservations. In the same month, Senator William King Sebastian, chairman of the Senate Committee on Indian Affairs, told the Senate:

> The moment General Beale became satisfied that if the present order of things was permitted to continue the results would be disastrous, he congregated upon a small reservation a number of Indians, without interfering in the rights of property or occupancy of any citizen of California. Such has been the success of his experiment that hundreds of other Indians are absolutely importuning him to place them under his protection and allow them to work; $250,000 will suffice to carry out the plan. I have implicit confidence in the Superintendent and propose to let him carry out the details of his plan in his own way. Do not be startled by the amount asked, or the almost unlimited power to be conferred on General Beale, the sailor who has left the sea to become pilot of the plains and superintendent for the Indians.

Swayed by Sebastian's assurance, Congress passed a second Indian appropriation act providing funds for the Indian Bureau nationwide, $250,000 of it allocated to establish five California reservations — half the amount Beale had asked for and one reservation less. The reservations were to be set aside from the public domain in the State of California or in the Territories of Utah and New Mexico. Nevada at that time was part of Utah Territory and Arizona part of New Mexico, both bordering on California. Each reservation was to contain no more than 25,000 acres and was not to be established on any land inhabited by citizens of the United States.

Redick McKee resented Beale's appointment and his authority, and objected to his plan, but Beale persisted. President Pierce's Interior Secretary, Robert McClelland, advised Beale:

The President has approved the plan. For this purpose you will repair to California without delay and by the most expeditious route. The selection of the military reservations are to be made by you in conjunction with the military commandant of California. The $250,000 is to be devoted exclusively to the removal and sustenance of the Indians, and not to be applied to any other purpose whatsoever.

The department clearly intended to avoid a repetition of the unauthorized accounts of the prior three-man commission.

Beale's traveling expenses were limited to $2000. A drawing account of $30,000 was to be posted with the Collector of the Port of San Francisco. With all the restrictions cranked into his instructions, it is difficult to understand why some members of Congress still considered that Beale's appointment vested him with "vice-regal powers."

While Beale occupied himself with efforts to save the Indians from what amounted to a *de facto* plan of extermination, Congress in 1852 renewed its interest in transportation routes to the West. Five official surveys to be conducted by the U. S. Corps of Topographical Engineers were authorized for the following year to supplement prior explorations by John C. Fremont and others. Practical wagon roads were badly needed at once, and there had been tacit understanding for a long time that someday a railroad would span the continent.

In addition to the planned government surveys, two other parties headed by engineers were to be sent out in 1853. Edward Beale, on his way back to California as Superintendent of Indian Affairs, would lead one of these surveys under the urging and sponsorship of Senator Benton. He began immediate preparations for what has become known as the Beale-Heap Expedition. During its progress through some of the most remote and savage country in the United States, Beale would come to learn almost more than he wanted to know about Indians.

10

The Beale-Heap Expedition

Secretary of the Interior Robert McClelland ordered Edward Beale to California in 1853 "by the most expeditious route." He also instructed Beale to locate possible sites for Indian reservations along the way. Beale felt this gave him enough latitude to deviate constructively from the well-known trails to California and acquaint himself with unfamiliar parts of the West — all in the name of duty. At the same time he could scout a feasible central railroad route for Senator Benton, who dearly wanted St. Louis to be the "gateway" to everything west of there.

Preparations for this journey took on appearances of a major expedition into unexplored country. For at least part of the way it came close to being that. Most of the West had been penetrated by 1853, if not precisely mapped. Exceptions included irregular portions of what are now the states of Colorado, Nevada, Utah and Arizona. Beale determined, with Benton's urging, to lead his expedition right through the center of this still-wild frontier.

After a pleasant interlude with Mary at Chester during part of April, 1853, Beale recruited his troop. He hired an assistant in the person of Gwynne (frequently spelled Gwinn) Harris Heap, a neighbor and kinsman anxious to see California.

Beale, Heap and seven recruits left Washington on April 20. They arrived at Westport Landing on the Missouri River on May 6. Masses of westbound emigrants used this major supply base as a starting point on the overland trails — principally the Oregon Trail and the Santa Fe Trail and their various branches and extensions into California. Beale's intended route headed almost directly west in what he hoped would be a straighter and therefore shorter course than any of the existing routes.

He purchased horses and mules. He hired a pair of Mexican mule-skinners, Gregorio Madrid and Juan Garcia, and a Delaware Indian named Richard Brown. The expedition, now numbering twelve, departed Westport on May 15 after a send-off speech by Senator Benton. Heap recorded that "a party of ladies and gentlemen accompanied us into the prairie and drank a stirrup cup of champagne to the success of our journey." Beale's own report fails to mention this *bon voyage* delegation.

Beale and Heap kept daily journals. Beale logged each day's weather, temperature, availability of water, wood and grass, and miles covered in the day's march. Heap's is more of a personal diary. He gives us this word picture of wagon train emigrants they met along the trail:

> [There] were many women and children, and it was pleasant to . . . witness the air of comfort and [well being] they presented. Their wagons drawn up in a circle gave an appearance of security . . . Within the enclosure the men . . . were busy in repairing their harness or cleaning (weapons). The females milked the cows and prepared supper, and we often enjoyed the hot cakes and fresh milk they invited us to partake of. Tender infants in their cradles were seen under the shelter of the wagons, thus early inured to hard travel. Carpets and rockingchairs were drawn out, and what would perhaps shock some of our fine ladies, fresh-looking girls, whose rosy lips were certainly never intended to be defiled by the vile weed, sat around the fire smoking the old-fashioned corn-cob pipe.

The first part of their journey took them westerly toward the Rocky Mountains over the Santa Fe Trail, a well-traveled thoroughfare since 1822. Beale first rode over this road with Kit Carson in 1847 and later with the Fort Leavenworth Army recruits. This was Beale's seventh journey to California.

They left the Santa Fe Trail about ten miles west of Bent's Fort. The old trail turns sharply southward from the Arkansas River toward Raton Pass and New Mexico. The river turns northwesterly. Beale stayed with the river for a short distance, then headed off at Timpas Creek almost due west through little-known country. The party followed the Huerfano River into the heart of the towering Sangre de Cristo Mountains, a front range of the Rockies. They crossed the summit at Sangre de Cristo Pass near what is now North La Veta Pass and descended under the brow of 14,363-foot Blanco Peak. They struck Ute Creek and followed it down to Fort Massachusetts, arriving there on July 13, 1853. The fort, under the command of Major George Alexander Hamilton Blake of the U. S. First Dragoons, was built in 1853 — the first army post in Colorado.

Beale hoped to purchase additional mules at the fort and take on a guide familiar with the largely unexplored country to the west. Major Blake told him that neither mules nor guides were available closer than Taos, some eighty miles south. Beale left his party at the fort and headed for Taos, accompanied by Major Blake. As long as he was going to Kit Carson's home town, he would call on his old friend and ask him to guide the party. But Carson had left for California the month before driving a flock of 6500 sheep.

There were no mules to be purchased, but Beale succeeded in signing on two trappers acquainted with the country. They were cousins and both named Felipe Archulete. The elder Felipe bore the nickname Peg-leg for losing a limb in a skirmish with Ute Indians. He carried a makeshift wooden leg suspended from his belt. "Nothwithstanding his lameness," Heap marveled, "he was one of the most active men of the party, and was always foremost in times of difficulty and danger."

The expedition got underway again, moving westward from Fort Massachusetts into the broad San Luis Valley. The mountains were laced with Indian trails that led nowhere. Trappers like the Archuletes had traversed these ranges but their routes, too, led generally from one beaver stream to the next. Straight passages to far distant points were practically non-existent. Earlier explorers had seen some of this huge wilderness, but not much of it and their maps were sketchy and often unreliable. Heap's map of their journey became the first published map to show the middle Rocky Mountain region.

Beale's party struck the Rio Grande River and turned north for some fifty miles, then west into a side valley called Saguache. The climb was a gentle one through smaller valleys and wooded glades, up Saguache Creek and over the crest at Cochetopa Pass, "the pass of the buffalos." At 10,032 feet elevation, Cochetopa is the lowest Continental Divide pass in Colorado. The mountains here are known as the Cochetopa Hills, and they do in fact resemble rounded, forested foothills rather than the summit of the continent.

Had it been Beale's primary mission to find an easy pass over the Rockies, the expedition would have been an outstanding success. The fact that this route today is only a side road and not a main artery through Colorado is quite beside the point. It's a relatively gradual route all the way, considering the high elevations traversed. There is plenty of water and forage. During summer months the country abounds in game. All streams flowed westward now, toward the Colorado River and the Pacific Ocean.

They crossed Beaver and Willow creeks in rugged mesa country and found themselves on the south bank of a considerable river called the Grand but which would later be named the Gunnison. It was on the Gunnison that the party came abruptly upon a row of elk antlers thrust into the ground across the trail. Peg-leg interpreted this as a warning to stay out of Ute Indian territory. A group of whites some months before had ignored the warning and were massacred. Beale cautioned his group to remain alert as they continued down the Gunnison to Lake Fork, an icy stream tumbling out of the San Juan Mountains. They found the tributary too deep and swift to ford. Beale tied a rope to a tall tree. One of his men, William Rogers, took the other end and swam the swollen river. He secured it to a low rock on the opposite bank. The packs and saddles were slung one at a time high on the rope by a hook and sent sliding down to the other side. When all the packs and saddles had been transported across, the mules and the rest of the men swam the rushing stream.

Further west they left the Gunnison River, which roars down into an awesome gorge called the Black Canyon. The party crossed 8,000-foot Cerro Summit after a steep climb and dropped down into the broad valley of the Uncompaghre River. They turned north and reached the Gunnison again, after it issues from the Black Canyon. Heap described the river as "a mighty stream that flowed with a loud and angry current. As it was evident that this river was nowhere fordable, it was determined to commence at once the construction of a raft."

They found themselves opposite an old trading post built by Beale's friend Antoine Robidoux called Fort Uncompaghre, its ruins still visible on the north bank of the Gunnison. Peg-leg had been there before and remembered an easy ford downstream, near the present city of Delta where the Gunnison joins the Uncompaghre River. But there, too, the river was much too deep and swift to attempt a crossing. The men felled a large cottonwood tree and hollowed out the trunk with axes to make a canoe.

With Peg-leg at the steering paddle, four loads of supplies and four men were deposited on the north bank while the Delaware Indian, Richard Brown, swam one horse and three mules across. Darkness prevented further attempts and the split party camped on opposite sides of the river.

Next morning Peg-leg took another load across with George Sims, but in leaping ashore Sims upset the boat and it went hurtling down the river. With it went seven rifles, several pistols, ammunition, saddles, gifts for the Indians and the very axes with which the canoe had been hewn. Brown and Peg-leg swam back to Beale's side. They were successful in getting one of the horses back across, but the rest refused to enter the rushing waters.

The nearest settlement west of that point where supplies and weapons might be secured was the Mormon town of Paragonah, some 400 miles away through unknown country in what is now southwest Utah. To get there the expedition would have to cross the Gunnison, Colorado and Green rivers, all of them

expected to be swollen and turbulent. Hides must be obtained
to fashion a boat, but only five days' rations remained. Taos
was still the closest relief center. Beale instructed Heap to bring
the rest of the advance party back across the river. The horses
and mules on Heap's side were forced into the stream. They
swam across, battling the swift current all the way, and scram-
bled up the other bank. Heap's men spent a day lashing together
a raft. They climbed aboard with their gear and pushed off,
cheered on every watery foot of the way to safety by Beale
and his men.

Beale ordered Heap to Taos for equipment and supplies to
sustain the expedition until it could reach the Mormon settlements. Heap took Peg-leg and six men.

Three days out, Heap's party encountered a band of fifty
Utes. They proved friendly and gave the whites a quantity
of dried buffalo meat. With Peg-leg interpreting, Heap promised the Indians tobacco and other gifts on their way back from
Taos. Heap reached Taos on July 6. Supplies were purchased
and assembled, and Heap hired Thomas Otterby, a mountain
man and skilled guide. Otterby and Peg-leg had Heap's party
back at Beale's camp by July 16.

During the interval, Beale and his companions backtracked
some fifty miles and set up shelters at one of the tributary
creeks on the south bank of the Gunnison. Brown scoured the
country for game, bringing in an elk, a doe and a rabbit during
the first week. One day a dozen Indians rode into camp. Beale
recounted the episode in his journal:

> I gave them what little tobacco we could spare and some dried elk
> meat. They insisted on my accompanying them to their camp some ten
> miles off. Knowing that it is best to act boldly with Indians as if you
> felt no fear whatever, I armed myself and started off with them. A
> few hours ride brought us to their camp.
>
> Hundreds of horses and goats were feeding on the meadows and
> hillsides, and the Indian lodges, with women and children standing in
> front of them to look at the approaching stranger, strongly reminded

me of the old patriarchal times, when flocks and herds made the wealth and happiness of the people, and a tent was as good as a palace. I was conducted to the lodge of the chief, who welcomed me kindly and told me his young men had told him I had given of my small store to them, and to sit in peace.

Beale took out his pipe and they smoked together. In about fifteen minutes a squaw brought in two large wooden platters of fat deer meat and boiled corn, to which Beale did ample justice:

> One must have been two weeks without bread to have appreciated it as I did. Never at the tables of the wealthiest in Washington did I find a dish which appeared to me so perfectly without parallel. I scraped the dish dry with my fingers, and licked them as long as the smallest particle remained, which is "manners" among Indians. To leave any is a slight . . . After this we smoked again and, when about to start, I found a large bag of dried meat and a peck of corn put up for me to take to my people. Bidding a friendly goodbye to my hosts I mounted my mule, returned to camp late at night and found my men very anxiously awaiting my return, having almost concluded to give me up and to think I had lost my hair.

Beale moved his camp closer to the Indian village. Their lodges were pitched in a setting which he described in his journal as the most beautiful scenery in the world:

> It formed a hunter's paradise, for deer and elk bounded off from us as we approached and then stood within rifle shot, looking back in astonishment. In fact, it was an immense natural park, already stocked with deer and elk and only requiring a fence to make it an estate for a king.

In this idyllic setting Beale and his men settled down to await Heap's return. Beale described a morning hunt with the Indians, noting they were all well armed and mounted:

> . . . but God forbid that I should ever hunt with such Indians again! I thought I had seen something of rough riding before, but all my experience faded before today's feats. Some places which we ascended

it seemed to me that even a wildcat could hardly have passed over. Yet, their well trained horses took them as part of the sport, and never made a misstep or blunder during the entire day . . .

Beale noted on July 15 that two bands of Indians had assembled and were holding horse races. "They have been at it since morning, and many a buckskin has changed hands," he wrote. Some indication of Beale's growing understanding of the Indians and their acceptance of him is poignantly demonstrated by this incident from his journal:

> An Indian broke the main spring of his rifle lock. His distress was beyond the power of description. To him it was everything. The "corn, wine and oil" of his family depended on it and he sat for an hour looking upon the wreck of his fortune in perfect despair. He appeared so cast down by it that at last I went into our lodge and brought out my rifle, which I gave him to replace his broken one. At first he could not realize it, but as the truth gradually broke upon him his joy became so great that could scarce control himself, and when he returned that night he was the happiest man I have seen for many a day.

When Heap had not returned by the Tenth, Beale wrote that all eyes were turned constantly to the opposite side of the valley where the trail came in from Taos. After six more days of anxious waiting, Beale decided to ride out and look for Heap. He saddled his mule but rode only a few miles up the trail when he encountered Peg-leg, with Heap and the others not far behind. "Here," he wrote, "terminated the most unpleasant sixteen days of my life. But for this beautiful country to look at and explore, I think I should have gone crazy."

The next day Beale dispatched two men to the crossing place on the Gunnison River, there to make a boat. The rest of the party followed down the trail over which they had already twice traveled. As they approached the river, they saw along its bank a vast number of lodges being erected and numerous bands of Indians pouring in from the north. The Indians' horses were hitched to lodgepole *travois* packed with various properties on top of which rode the smaller children. The drags were unhitched and the animals driven to water. The squaws climbed down the bank to fill willow osiers, which they balanced on their heads. Braves stretched lazily on the grass, waiting patiently while the women put up lodges and prepared the evening meal. All the males, from the very old men down to lads of five or six, carried bows and arrows. Many of the warriors had rifles.

Peg-leg established communication and announced that the Indians wanted Beale to enter their camp and meet the chiefs. He did so, and told the Indians many white men would soon be passing through their country and if they were well treated the Indians would always be generously rewarded. The chiefs were much gratified to learn this and intimated they would be even more pleased to receive right then some of the presents of which he spoke. As Beale's party had passed through their country and had been fed by others of their tribe, was it not proper that some return be made for past favors?

The situation called for considerable tact. Beale explained he had no gifts to bestow because they had all been lost in the river. Nor would he part with his few remaining rifles, which the Indians considered a fair exchange for their hospitality. Tension mounted. Beale's remarks were far from acceptable. A group of young fire-eaters among the braves began to do everything they could to provoke a violent response. They galloped around Beale's party as it proceeded to the river and almost ran them down. "As we took little notice of them and affected perfect unconcern," he wrote, "they finally desisted from their dangerous sport."

Bypassing the Indian village, Beale's group joined his two advance men at the ford where the water level had dropped by six feet since their first attempted crossing. They got across the river without difficulty, but some 200 mounted warriors followed them. Heap described how the braves again tried to provoke a fight, and how Beale reacted:

> Their appearance as they whirled around us made a striking contrast with the half-naked condition in which we had crossed the river. They enjoyed many a laugh at our expense, taunting us and compar-

ing us from our bearded appearance to goats, and calling us beggardly cowards and women. Most of these compliments were lost on us at the time, but Felipe afterwards explained them.

They abused us violently for traversing their country without making any acknowledgement. Lieutenant Beale calmly explained again that all we possessed was a piece of cloth, a calico shirt and some brass wire that they could acquire by giving us a horse in exchange. Mr. Beale then said, "If you want to trade, we will trade. If you want to fight, we will fight."

He then directed all to dismount upon the first act of hostility, to stand each man behind his mule, and to take deliberate aim before firing. Those among the Indians who favored fighting found themselves in the minority and finally consented to give us a mare for our goods. After the trade was made we parted, much relieved at getting rid of such ugly customers.

Beale and his party were fortunate to be allowed to continue without a fight, due in large part to Beale's coolness and firm handling of the situation. Whites had been roughly treated by the Utes before, and would continue to be for many years afterward. No Indians were more proudly independent than the Utes, and none more ready to shed blood — preferably the enemy's blood — in defending their territory against encroachment.

Beale's party followed down the north bank of the Gunnison past the majestic Grand Mesa, a huge flat-topped mountain. On July 19, they reached the Colorado River a little above the site of present day Grand Junction. (The Colorado, known then as the Avonkarea, or Blue River, had its name changed in 1921 by an act of Congress.)

Here they put together the hide boat and used it successfully to cross the Colorado, although the river ran dangerously high and swift. The party continued down the north bank of the Colorado through Grand Valley, entered Utah and headed west toward the Green River.

About ten miles before reaching the Green, their path joined the main northern, or "summer," route of the Old Spanish Trail from Santa Fe to California. They would continue to follow that trail for the rest of their journey, in the footsteps of the earliest white explorers of the American Southwest.

The expedition reached the Green River on July 24. They found it broader and deeper than the Colorado, for the Green is truly the main fork of the Colorado River. They stretched the hides over a framework of willow branches to fashion a saucer-shaped bullboat again. It "answered admirably," Heap was happy to report, "buoyant, easily managed and safe." Indians lurked in the vicinity. Heap went across with the first load to guard the packs, then watched the others:

> Lieutenant Beale made great exertions to hurry the train over the river. He went across every trip, jumping into the river where it was shallow and taking the boat in tow until he was beyond his depth. He was thus for many hours in the water, encouraging the men by his example.
>
> We had now an excellent party. The men were daring and adroit. They exhibited no fear when we were so hardpressed by the Utes, and when exposure or toil was required of them not one flinched from his duty. Some appeared almost to rejoice whenever there was a difficulty to overcome . . .

Finally across the Green, Beale's party shared their camp with twenty-five friendly Indians who were given the boat hides. The Indians cut the skins up for moccasins. They warned Beale that the Mormons threatened to shoot any Americans passing through their country. Undismayed — and with little choice anyway — Beale pushed onward and entered the most difficult topography his party would see on the entire journey.

Great rocky mesas rose up out of the dry, rolling desert country. Water courses slashed deep, twisting canyons around and between the plateaus, each mesa and each canyon requiring a major effort to cross. Everything here drained in a southerly direction toward the deepest defile of them all, the Grand Canyon of the Colorado. The Old Spanish Trail veered to the northwest to escape the worst of these vast badlands.

Beale and his men crossed San Rafael Reef, a high mesa, and reached the San Rafael River, which they followed westerly toward the Wasatch Plateau. A zigzag trail through central Utah brought them on August 2 into the valley of Little Salt Lake and the Mormon settlement of Paragonah.

Contrary to the warnings, Beale and his party were most kindly received, but found the Saints in a state of alarm. The Indians were on the warpath and Brigham Young had ordered the abandonment of Paragonah and removal of its inhabitants to the comparative safety of Parawan, another Mormon town four miles south. The party saw houses being stripped and salvaged, and furniture and other possessions loaded on wagons. Beale followed the exodus to Parawan, a settlement of more than a hundred houses nestled against a range of hills. There they were again cordially welcomed and remained for two days to have their animals reshod and to procure supplies of flour and dried beef.

Colonel G. A. Smith, commander of the Mormon Militia, maintained headquarters in Parawan. He expressed amazement that Beale and his men had come safely through the Ute country without losing their scalps. Indeed, two months later Captain John Gunnison would not be so fortunate. On October 26, 1853, the Utes waylaid Gunnison's survey party and killed him and seven of his men near Sevier Lake.

Beale's party left Parawan on August 3 and continued southwesterly toward California. The Old Spanish Trail veered west to what is now Enterprise, Utah, then south again through Mountain Meadows to join the Virgin River near the present Nevada boundary. Heap noted that the Paiute Indians in this area had "reduced their costume to first principles" — which probably meant no costume at all.

The party left the Virgin River — so named by Jedediah Smith in 1826 for a fellow trapper, Thomas Virgin — on the Sixth and followed the old trail across the desert, shadowed constantly by roving bands of Indians on foot. They crossed Muddy River and came to the Ojo del Gaetan, or Vega Quintana. Heap called these spring-fed meadows "the diamond of the desert, so beautiful and bright does it appear in the center of the dreary desert that surrounds it." Vega Quintana today is Las Vegas, Nevada, a bright diamond of a different kind in that bleak desert.

They continued southwesterly, traveling mostly at night to escape the desert's broiling heat. The group reached the spring where Fremont recorded in the journal of his second expedition the massacre of a group of Mexicans on April 24, 1844. Heap mentioned it in his journal:

> A cruel tragedy, heroically avenged by Kit Carson and Alexander Godey, occured here in 1844, and has rendered this spot memorable. We found near the spring the skull of an Indian, killed perhaps in that fray.

It had been Beale's intention to split his party upon reaching the meandering Mojave River. He wanted to send the main group southwest through Cajon Pass toward Los Angeles. With a smaller group Beale would examine the northern Mojave Desert for possible reservation sites, then proceed into the San Joaquin Valley via Walker's Pass. He abandoned the plan because of exhausted supplies. The entire party continued toward Cajon Pass. Forage became more abundant as the dry bed of the Mojave River gave way to a running stream.

Brown shot two antelopes on August 19, the first fresh meat the expedition had seen for several days. Travel brought them to a grassy oasis and a pool of clear, cool water alive with fish. With the matter of thirst and starvation no longer a problem, Beale decided to take Heap and Brown and proceed as rapidly as the most fit of the mules could travel. The main party would follow in easy stages. "We thus crossed the desert," wrote Heap, "without abandoning a single animal which is, I believe, almost unprecedented."

Beale and his two companions entered Cajon Pass on August 21. The valley of San Bernardino broke upon their view, and never did so beautiful a sight gladden the eyes of weary travelers. Late that night they heard a dog bark. Another mile found them in the center of a cluster of buildings, welcomed

in the most friendly manner by the Mexican proprietor of a
rancho near present day Cucamonga. Heap's joy at their return
to civilization is reflected in his journal:

> . . . It was a pleasant sight to us to witness the satisfaction of our
> travel-worn mules in passing from unremitting toil and scanty food to
> complete rest and abundant nourishment.
>
> We obtained fresh horses, and a gallop of thirty-five miles . . .
> brought us to the city of Los Angeles, where every kindness and atten-
> tion was shown us by Mr. Wilson, Indian Agent, and his accomplished
> lady.
>
> . . . The remainder of our party arrived two days later, and thus,
> without serious accident to any of the men, and with the loss of only
> three of the mules, we accomplished the distance from Westport to
> Los Angeles in exactly 100 days.

Those aware of Beale's expedition but ignorant of the sixteen
days lost by Heap's detour to Taos became apprehensive at the
delay of his arrival. Fires were kept burning at Walker's Pass
by night, and smoke signals by day, to guide him in case he
had lost the trail.

Beale wrote to the Commissioner of Indian Affairs from Los
Angeles on August 2: "Sir, I have the honor to report my
arrival in this state." In September, the San Francisco *Daily
Herald* published a long account of the expedition.

Beale had kept Senator Benton informed of his progress
by letters sent back from the forts, and from Taos, letters
the Senator duly published in the *National Intelligencer*.

Benton addressed Beale from Washington on October 3:

> Colonel Fremont writes from St. Louis and desires me to send this
> message to you: "Please request Mr. Beale to put his animals at
> my rancho where they may recruit, and exchange them for mine. I
> had on my place, when I left California, upwards of twenty horses and
> mules." Our last advises from you are the letters from Mr. Heap at
> Taos. Hearing nothing more of you, I concluded that you had gone
> through.

Beale advised Benton of his arrival in California, to which
Benton replied: "Your expedition has been filling the U. S.

during all the summer and has fixed the character of the central route. The government expeditions seem to be forgotten." Benton displayed not the slightest interest in the primary purpose of Beale's journey, the location of Indian reservations. He had a railroad on his mind, a Pacific railroad anchored to St. Louis.

Benton again made available to the *National Intelligencer* last letters from the expedition:

> Two letters have just been received from Superintendent Beale and Mr. Harris Heap, giving information of their having reached the great Colorado of the West and found the country good for a railway and for settlement all the way out to the river. So that problem is solved, at least so far as summer is concerned. These letters from Beale and Heap cover the only debatable ground on the central route. The whole route has now been seen.

Benton wrote Beale again on December 3, still assessing the expedition from his own point of view:

> You have gained a great deal of credit by your expedition, and established yourself with the country, the more so from the massacre of Gunnison's party by the same tribe that was so hospitable to you. The *National Intelligencer* spreads it and it will be printed in pamphlet with a map, which will bring you a *deal de l'argent, beaucoup de l'argent.* Will also try to get Congress to reimburse you your expenses.

But Beale had other things on his mind. He turned his attention to the monumental task of establishing a secure home for the California Indians within a political system which he soon learned was not geared for success of that goal.

II

Battling the Bureaucracy

The Indian Appropriation Act of March 3, 1853, authorized the President to enter into negotiations with tribes west of the states of Missouri and Iowa, to "secure the assent of said tribes to the settlement of citizens of the United States upon the lands claimed by said Indians, and to extinguish the title of said tribes, in whole or in part, to said lands."

Colonel George W. Manypenny, Commissioner of Indian Affairs, personally conducted these negotiations. He went to Indian territory and held council with eight of the plains tribes. Among them were remnants of tribes that had been moved from east of the Mississippi to Ohio and Illinois, thence to Missouri and Iowa, and again westward to new territory. With each relocation they were promised that the new place would be their permanent home "as long as the rivers ran and grass grew along the banks."

Manypenny's activity on the plains occurred at the same time as Edward Beale's initial efforts with his test farm in California. Manypenny submitted a report to the Secretary of the Interior on November 9, 1853, in which he said:

> The Indians generally adhere to the customs of their fathers and the heathen traditions descended to them. They prefer indolence to labor, vice to virtue, and such is their thirst for ardent spirits they will make any sacrifice to obtain it. They were shown that they must make up their minds to dispose of their lands to their Great Father, and receive from him new homes . . .

Manypenny said he found it difficult to calm the Indians because of their "apprehension that their country was about to be taken from them." That their apprehension was fully justified seems not to have occurred to the Commissioner. He went on to report that,

It is very desirable for the interest of both red and white men that no reservations be made, but that the different tribes be removed from the borders of the states and located in some less exposed places. I was of the opinion that treaties could be made after they had time for discussion and reflection, and I therefore deemed it best to leave the subject with them.

Having kicked the Indian problem under the rug, Manypenny departed the Great Plains and scuttled back to Washington.

Beale reported to Manypenny by letter on the arrival of his expedition at Los Angeles in August of 1853, and said he had been occupied since then,

. . . examining lands from the state line to this place [Los Angeles], which might be suitable for the Indians. The country south of Walker's Pass I find utterly unfit for the purpose and am about to examine the great Tulare [San Joaquin] Valley in the hope of meeting with better success . . .

I find numerous obstacles which had not previously occurred to me. The principal of these is the peculiar wording of the Act of Congress making the appropriation, which embarrasses me more than I can express. My plan proposed the abandonment of three agencies and the substitution of six sub-agencies. The agencies were abolished, but no provision was made for the sub-agencies and without the assistance of such subordinate officers it is impracticable for me to carry into execution an entire change in the hereditary mode of life of 100,000 persons scattered over a distance of 700 miles . . .

Beale complained that the same difficulty presented itself in the employment of blacksmiths, farmers and carpenters for necessary construction. He simply didn't have clear authority to hire workers and pay them.

It was a bit late for Beale to be discovering this crimp in his "vice-regal authority." Because of the great amount of time he spent in the field, he said it was impossible for him to keep accounts with precision and regularity or to submit quarterly reports. He asked the indulgence of the department in the delay of his reports, and continued:

As soon as I have selected the locations of reservations I shall request the sanction of the department to the appointment of such sub-agents as I shall be obliged to make in pursuance of the plan proposed. My instructions render it imperative that I should abolish the present agencies, yet it is impossible to dispense with the services of Mr. Benjamin D. Wilson at present as I shall employ him to superintend the removal of the Indians and to aid in locating reservations, his knowledge of the country being perfect, and to use his paramount influence to induce the Indians to remove in peace.

Wilson, known as Don Benito, arrived in California in 1841 with the Workman-Rowland Party from New Mexico. He had been a staunch supporter of the American cause during the Mexican war, although a naturalized Mexican citizen. He was a former Mayor of Los Angeles and the husband of Ramona Yorba. The Indians had no better friend than Wilson.

Harry Edwards remained employed, ostensibly as Beale's clerk but actually in charge of the Indians on the small reserve on the Fresno River which Beale intended to serve as a prototype for the larger system he hoped to install.

The San Francisco *Daily Herald* for September 5, 1853, devoted a full page to Beale's cross-country journey, then noted that,

> Beale left Los Angeles on an expedition through the San Joaquin Valley to have a talk with the various Indian tribes, and to look out lands for reservations, accompanied by Don Benito Wilson, Indian Agent for that section of the country, and several members of the expedition.

General Hitchcock read the article and wrote to Beale from San Francisco:

> The *Herald* has just announced the anxiously looked-for news of your safe arrival in California once more. As some measures of a military character were contemplated in your locating Indian farms or reservations, it was thought proper that the military commander of the district should have a voice on this point. Otherwise the superintendent would virtually have the troops under his control, by selecting sites and compelling troops to occupy them.

To which Beale might have replied, "heaven forbid!" Hitchcock suggested that Beale see Captain Thomas Jordan at Fort Miller, a post established in Fresno County at the site where one of the eighteen unratified treaties had been signed by Barbour.

The General warned Beale not to exceed his appropriation, and "on no account to begin with the Indians on a scale beyond your ability to carry it through." He was well aware that $250,000 would hardly get Beale off the ground establishing one reservation, let alone five. He had approved the plan and would bask in its success, but he did not intend to become involved should it fail.

Manypenny was something less than ecstatic to receive Beale's report of August 22 advising him of the many unfortunate hitches to the plan which he also had approved. It galled him to realize that failure would rest heavily on his shoulders and he feared another McKee fiasco. Beale's second report, dated September 30, outlines in detail his activities for the month — activities that threw Manypenny into a tailspin:

> I left Los Angeles on the 30th ultimo, arrived at Tejon Pass on the 2nd instant and found the Indians in that quarter quietly engaged in farming, but anxious to know the intentions of the government toward them. Mr. Edwards, with great tact and assistance from Mr. Alexander Godey, had traveled from tribe to tribe, talked constantly with them and succeeded in preventing any outbreak or disturbance in the San Joaquin Valley. I collected together the chiefs and headmen of the mountains and plains . . . and they agreed to accept the terms I offered them . . .

Beale's plan called for a system of farming and instruction which would in time "enable the Indians to support themselves by the produce of their own labor." He proposed to furnish the Indians with seed and provisions to sustain them in the interim. "To all this," Beale wrote, "I had no difficulty in bringing them to assent."

Beale selected the southeastern corner of San Joaquin Valley south of present day Bakersfield, locally called Tejon Valley, as the site for his first full-scale Indian Reservation. He told Manypenny he secured the prior blessings of three Army officers — Lieutenants George Stoneman, John G. Park and Robert S. Williamson — who had done some preliminary survey work and were familiar with the country. Beale asked them if they preferred a reservation north of the Sacramento River delta in country already heavily settled by whites, or in the remote south. They were unanimously against settling Indians in the north and thus Beale got Army approval for the Tejon by default. The officers also recommended against locating a reservation east of the Sierra Nevada.

Beale's report to Manypenny shows a sincere, humane consideration for the plight of the Indians, something most bureaucrats of the day — including Manypenny himself — sorely lacked:

> A large portion of the Tejon Valley is said to be covered by a Spanish grant, but I found no evidence that it had ever been settled and there was no other place where the Indians could be placed without the same objection as there is not sufficient public land for a single reservation of the quality required. The land must be of the best quality, since the failure of the first crop might so discourage the Indians as to render subsequent attempts abortive.

Beale said the reservation should be adjacent to mountainous country, "for it is not to be supposed the habits of a race . . . can be suddenly and entirely changed." His report went on to call for removal of northern California Indians to the southern part of the state "which is thinly settled and possesses little or no mineral wealth." To do this, he wrote,

> . . . it will be necessary to purchase land and I recommend that authority for the purchase of Spanish grants be given at government price, or for much less. Law in relation to Indian affairs in California gives me no authority to purchase lands for the Indians and I conclude to leave it to Congress to purchase the land should the title prove good.

Beale added that he had consulted the state's Congressional delegation before making his choice and had been governed by their advice. He expressed the satisfaction he felt in the success of his experimental farm "commenced with Indians of the wildest and most uncivilized character" and kept the kicker for his last paragraph. To carry out his plan would take an additional $500,000. This left Manypenny in a state of shock.

There were no Spanish land grants in the area he selected. There were five Mexican grants, however, but Beale had no time to worry about such things. Indians already lived on the land in scattered bands and had been there long before the grants were made. They, at least, would not have to be relocated. Beale had to act quickly to get the reservation established before the Congressional authorization with its financial appropriation expired on June 30, 1854.

Along with his second report he included a list of results achieved by Harry Edwards at the farm on the Fresno River: 350 acres plowed and sown in wheat; 7000 pounds of potatoes planted; 200 acres in corn, watermelons, pumpkins and muskmelons; 100 tons of hay made; and two miles of ditches dug surrounding the planted fields and cattle corral. Not bad for a trial effort.

Lieutenant Williamson's survey party stopped at Woodville, the county seat of Tulare County, in August of 1853 and Williamson filed this report:

> Here I was fortunate enough to meet with Mr. Alexander Godey, who knew more about the mountain passes which I was about to examine than anyone in the country. He had just returned from the Tejon where he had been with the hope of meeting Mr. Edward Beale, Superintendent of Indian Affairs, who had been expected for some weeks. I proposed to him to accompany me and he agreed, with the understanding he be allowed to leave as soon as Mr. Beale should arrive.

Upon learning Beale was on his way back to California, Godey gave up the ferry he was operating on the San Joaquin River and management of Fremont's cattle herd at Las Mariposas so he could work for Beale. Godey would remain in Beale's employ as sub-Indian Agent during the days of the Tejon reservation. "After leaving Fremont," he was quoted,

"I located at the Tejon and had all the Indians in that section under my control." Maybe that's the way he saw it. Godey was in many respects a "natural Indian" himself and was perhaps better liked by them than any white man who ever lived in the Tejon country.

Beale addressed letters to U. S. Senators William M. Gwin and John B. Weller and former Governor John McDougal advising them of his intention to proceed with his plan. Gwin answered guardedly that he should "make arrangements, subject to the approval of Congress, as in his opinion were indispensable" — whatever that meant.

Weller objected to reservations of more than 8000 acres. As to land claimed under Spanish [*sic*] grants, "I would not hesitate to take it. The government, having taken private land for public use, will have to make compensation therefore," adding on second thought, "subject, of course, to the confirmation of Congress."

McDougal mulled over Beale's letter for two weeks, then assured him on October 14, "Your familiarity with the business you have in hand commands from me complete confidence in such policy as you may suggest with regard to our Indian affairs." A masterpiece of ambiguity.

After no response from Commissioner Manypenny to his first two reports, Beale submitted a third in which for the first time he rendered an accounting. He had moved 500 Indians from the Feather River in northern California to the Tejon reserve, which he now called the Sebastian Indian Reservation after Senator William King Sebastian. He had spent $125,000 to provide them with cattle, horses, mules, farming implements, provisions and clothing. He had engaged laborers and mechanics. Beale intended to draw on the remaining $125,000 to establish a second reservation. That would use up his appropriation and leave three reservations to go. "When it is remembered these supplies are for two reservations of 25,000 acres each to ultimately support 10,000 Indians, the expenditures will not be found extravagant," he optimistically wrote. Beale had gone on his way blithely ignoring instructions. Like McKee before him, he steered a collision course with bureaucratic reality.

Manypenny's failure to respond was not due to neglect. His meeting with the plains Indians had kept him away from Washington. His own failure with the Indians, where Beale had succeeded, stemmed at least partly from his position as a stranger who filled them with fear and distrust. Their distrust, if we can judge from Manypenny's report to Congress, was not unfounded. When an Indian objected to working like a white man, Manypenny attributed his attitude to laziness, whereupon the Indian asked with considerable disdain, "Did you ever skin a buffalo?"

Beale held council with the tribes as a friend. He never required the Indians under his care to abandon their ancient customs and rituals. Not a missionary, he directed his interest to their physical well being, leaving them to find spiritual comfort after their own fashion. As a consequence, Beale had the confidence and respect of all the Indian tribes. One of Beale's "wild" Indians once told him, with a display of good humor:

> At the time the white man discovered us, we also discovered the white man. We did not know there were lands across the sea. If I should ever go there I would claim the land for my Indian people, for it would be the first time I had ever seen it, so therefore I would be discovering it.

Manypenny returned to Washington in early November of 1853, discouraged by his lack of success. He looked with jaundiced eye upon Beale's report of favorable negotiations with the California tribes. He was particularly disturbed by the request for an additional half-million dollars accompanied by an assurance almost echoing McKee's comment in a similar situation, "the estimate will not be found extravagant."

The Commissioner addressed Beale in a letter on November 18 that for the first time made the former sailor aware that he was entering waters filled with rocks and shoals:

. . . In the instructions given you by the department you were informed the $250,000 appropriated by the Act of 3 March, 1853, is to be devoted exclusively to the removal and subsistence of the Indians and not to be applied to any other purpose whatsoever, and it is therefore not within the province of this office to direct otherwise. If the wants and necessities of the Indians will not admit of their being colonized on the "public domain," it would seem to be prudent that you should postpone all action and await further legislation on the part of Congress. Under no circumstances can the department sanction the purchase of any lands or claims laid thereto for the purpose indicated.

At the same time, Manypenny advised in a report to Congress that suitable locations could not be found for the Indians in northern California:

Their removal and colonization will, therefore, be attended with greater difficulty and expense than was expected. Instead of there being ample territory belonging to the United States, as was supposed, we may be compelled to incur considerable expense in making extensive purchases of existing claims to lands founded upon pre-emption rights and Spanish and Mexican land grants. The superintendent reports that under the counsel of the Congressional representatives of the state, he shall proceed to purchase the individual rights to lands embraced in the reservations, and in addition to subsistence he is making arrangements to supply the Indians with stock, agricultural implements, seeds, and other means of self-support and improvement.

These proceedings are not warranted either by law or his instructions, but are in contravention of both . . .

Beale had not written that he intended to purchase the land rights, but would leave that to the government. Matters had progressed too far to "postpone all action pending further action of Congress." Beale had already entered into contracts exceeding the $250,000 appropriation.

The one instruction with which he faithfully complied was the dismissal of the three agents. Don Benito Wilson did not want to be retained. The complaints of the other two, who were political appointees, were soon heard in Washington.

They were supported by many of the settlers, who were violently opposed to Beale's plan for colonizing the Indians. Obviously becoming aware of his precarious position, Beale revealed to Manypenny in a letter on December 28 his weariness and anxiety: "Jealousy, envy, and detraction is the fate of anyone who attempts an innovation on any old fashioned custom, and I am not vain enough to suppose I may escape this inevitable fate."

Manypenny had not ordered Beale to cease operations but merely thought "it would seem to be prudent" that he did so. Hearing nothing further from him, Beale proceeded with his plan. In February of 1854, he submitted a fourth report citing 2,500 Indians employed on the Sebastian Reservation; twenty-four plows in operation; 2,000 acres planted to wheat, 500 to barley and 150 to corn; twelve whites employed, including Harry Edwards and Gwynne Harris Heap; and other projects of a constructive nature. Groups of Indians occupied seven separate rancherias scattered over the reservation, each under its own chief. At Senator Benton's suggestion, Beale prevailed upon Mary to join him. The Indians gave her a dance of welcome when she arrived at the Tejon on June 24.

Beale had been appointed by Whig President Millard Fillmore. Incumbent President Franklin Pierce entertained no obligation to become embroiled in a matter of patronage by reappointing him when the Act of 1853 expired on June 30, 1854. Several deserving Democrats jockeyed for this choice bit of pork. They were prompt to take up the cudgels against Beale's reappointment. They charged him with unauthorized expenditures in excess of appropriations and accused him of profiteering.

So rampant was graft under the prevailing spoils system that these charges found acceptance in Washington. Senator Benton made light of it, writing Beale, "They cannot remove you on account of the hold you have on the public mind. Your . . . success . . . does the business for you." Unfortunately, Benton's own political star had begun to wane. Influences stronger than his were at work plotting the downfall of Beale.

The Indian Bureau asked Special Treasury Agent J. Ross

Browne, a friend of Beale's, to examine Beale's accounts. Browne found nothing to suggest fraud or peculation, although he did not defend Beale's unwise expenditure of government funds.

The Beales had scarcely set up housekeeping at the Tejon when the charges were published in Eastern papers, copies of which soon arrived on the West Coast. Beale left his post immediately and returned to Washington to face his accusers. He took the quickest route across Panama, accompanied by Mary, Harry Edwards and Gwynne Heap. He took along all his vouchers and records. Just before leaving for Washington, he addressed a letter to Don Benito Wilson:

> This letter will introduce my friend, Mr. J. Ross Browne, for whom I speak your cordial reception in Los Angeles. I beg you will render him every assistance in your power and endeavor to make his visit to your city agreeable. Mr. Browne may require information on a variety of subjects and I have referred him to you as one whose position has placed it in his power to afford him all that he requires.

Browne entrusted Beale with letters to Mrs. Browne in Washington, one of which says:

> This will be handed to you by my old friend, Ned Beale, who will tell you all about my doings in this quarter. I have fallen quite in love with Mrs. Beale, who is the most amiable and accomplished lady I have met in California. If you can prevail upon her to spend an evening at our house, and her perform on the piano, you will I am sure excuse my weakness and believe me.

Beale had gained great popularity in his home town of Washington, D.C., and on his return with Heap the city tendered them a banquet at which Senator Benton was the principal speaker. Benton extolled the virtues of the two in his usual extravagant rhetoric:

> There before you, gentlemen, sit the heads of this remarkable party [the Beale-Heap Expedition], young in years but old in experience and well tried in all the hardships and dangers of distant travel. The superintendent, Mr. Beale, has made at least a dozen voyages by land and water to California, has been the companion of Fremont, Carson and other mountain men, and yet is only twenty-eight. They were not

yet a government party, equipped at public expense, and did not graduate at West Point.

That Beale and Heap were not West Pointers was one of the few factual statements in the garrulous old gentleman's long-winded discourse. Beale had made seven, not "at least a dozen," journeys to California; he was thirty-two, not twenty-eight and the Beale-Heap Expedition had indeed been a government party equipped at public expense.

While Beale's tardy accounts were audited, he stepped down from his duties. He was replaced on July 1, 1854, by Thomas Jefferson Henley as Superintendent of Indian Affairs for California and Nevada. Henley was a strong supporter of Senator Gwin, who in 1852 had wrangled Henley the appointment of Postmaster of San Francisco. On taking over Beale's office, Henley wrote Commissioner Manypenny:

> Not deeming it my duty to allude to what might be considered the delinquencies of my predecessor, which could be unpleasant to Mr. Beale's feelings, I send herewith a letter just received from one of my assistants on the Tejon. The statements may be relied upon to be strictly true.

The enclosed letter was written by Alonzo Ridley, a trader Beale had run off the reservation for selling whiskey to the Indians. Ridley claimed Beale brought but few groups of Indians to the Sebastian Reservation and they had all run off with stolen horses. According to all the information he could get on the subject, "800 Indians great and small, old and young, is the highest number estimated or can be proven to have been here at any one time."

This contrasts sharply with Beale's accounting of 2500 Indians on the reservation in February. To justify Ridley's letter, Henley began to return the northern bands to their places of origin until he had cut the number down to 700. He sold off the cattle they were raising for their sustenance. It was unthinkable to Henley that Indians raise their own cattle, depriving him of the opportunity to contract for such provisions.

J. Ross Browne returned to Washington in January of 1855 to testify in Beale's behalf before the Treasury Department. An article in the Washington *Evening Star* elaborating on the alleged delinquencies inspired the accounting officers to examine Beale's records with more than usual thoroughness. After an investigation lasting eight months, all of Beale's accounts were finally approved. The Secretary of the Treasury allowed every claim he had made in expending some $360,000, not a cent of which accrued to Beale's personal benefit. The Tejon reservation stood as an outstanding success, but Beale had exuberantly spent $110,000 more than his authorized appropriations. The bureaucracy could not forgive a sin of such cardinal proportions, but Beale had committed no fraud, no crime, hardly even an indiscretion. The Treasury Department printed Beale's complete vindication on April 20, 1855.

Beale also found his chance to square accounts with Commissioner Manypenny, as reported in the *Evening Star:*

> After the article charging Mr. Beale with being a defaulter appeared, and his accounts were admitted to be correct, a number of his personal friends called upon the editor of the *Star* and were frankly informed the information was furnished by the commissioner [Manypenny], who had himself written the article charging Lieutenant Beale with the defalcation . . . Mr. Beale embraced an opportunity to meet his accuser. He encountered Manypenny in front of the Willard Hotel, upon whom he inflicted a severe castigation with his fists.
>
> If an assault can be justified in any case, then was this public castigation right and proper. An attempt had been made to ruin the reputation of an honest man in his absence; and now the vindication of the charges, extorted from the accuser, and his public punishment go together.

Other newspaper accounts relate that Beale accosted Manypenny inside the Willard Hotel and slapped him twice across the face with his open hand. The men wrestled to the floor. Manypenny attempted to hit Beale with a chair. Beale challenged him to a duel, but Manypenny never responded.

Satisfaction having been obtained from both the Treasury

Department and Commissioner Manypenny, the Beales continued with their plan to return to California and settle in the
Tejon country.

As a token of their regard, Beale's friends presented him
with a ten-piece silver coffee set made by Bailey & Company
of Chester Street, Philadelphia. It is now on display at Decatur
House in Washington, D.C.

The Beales sailed from New York aboard the steamer *George
Law* on May 5, 1855. Fellow passengers were J. Ross Browne,
his wife and five children. Browne, returning to continue an
investigation of the Revenue Service on the West Coast, had
also decided California was the place to raise his family. Beale
and Browne resumed their friendship despite friction between
them which had developed during the Treasury Department
investigation.

Superintendent of Indian Affairs Henley received an advance
of $250,000, but the *Alta California* for July 6, 1855, com-
plained that he devoted all his time to politics in Sacramento,
"while his reservations were left to the care of irresponsible
agents. The appropriations . . . provide places for several
members of the superintendent's family, but the poor Indians
get nothing."

Beale attempted at first to help Henley in carrying out the
complex agricultural program. Henley refused to follow his
advice and pursued a course which almost seemed designed to
ruin the reservation. By late 1855, only 437 adult Indians
remained at the Tejon. A year later the number had fallen to
150. The Sacramento *Union* deplored the situation with this
article:

> The Tejon reservation, for which so much was hoped, is nothing
> but a byword. It is a year since Henley stepped into the shoes of Lieu-
> tenant Beale, who had carried out to the fullest extent the designs of
> the government. Henley's mismanagement of Indian affairs has resulted
> in the thorough and complete wreck of this once flourishing establish-
> ment.

Beale had no idea how complicated the land ownership was

in Tejon Valley. He had situated the Sebastian Reservation on some 75,000 acres which he considered geographically suitable for the purpose. No whites lived on the land and the only sign that any had ever been there was a single small adobe building which had been abandoned. Beale eventually learned he had preempted not just one piece of private property, but portions of four old Mexican land grants. What's more, Beale's site for a military post also occupied land grant property.

Mexican Governor Micheltorena had awarded the first grant in the far southern San Joaquin Valley to Jose Antonio Aguirre and Ignacio del Valle on November 11, 1843. It consisted of twenty-two *sitios de ganada mayor, mas o mano* — 97,617 acres. It was named Rancho el Tejon. The alcalde of Santa Barbara, Jose Maria Covarrubias, refused to verify the map, however, and the land remained inhabited only by indigenous red men. Dr. E. D. French attempted to run a small herd of cattle on the land for awhile, but Indians drove him out. It was Dr. French who had built and abandoned the single adobe on the land. A pair of squatters moved onto the ranch in 1850 — an old mountain man named David McKenzie and the aforementioned trader, Alonzo Ridley. Title to the rancho remained with Aguirre and del Valle.

Alcalde Covarrubias himself received the second Tejon grant from Governor Micheltorena, a 22,000-acre parcel called Rancho Castac (also spelled "Castaic"). Covarrubias made no effort to settle on the land. He sold it in 1853 to Alfred Packard, City Attorney of Santa Barbara.

Jose Maria Flores came up from Mexico in 1842 as secretary to Governor Micheltorena and remained after the Governor's departure. Governor Pio Pico awarded Flores the third Tejon area grant, 49,000-acre Rancho la Liebre, on April 21, 1846. It was Flores, acting as Pio Pico's representative, who surrendered Los Angeles to Commodore Stockton in August, 1846. And it was Flores who violated his parole to lead the short-lived Californio uprising that culminated in the final capitulation of Andres Pico to John Fremont at Cahuenga Pass. Flores fled to Sonora, Mexico, but Rancho la Liebre remained in his name.

The last of the four Tejon grants was made by Governor Pio Pico to Francisco Lopez, Luis Jordan and Vicente Batello on May 27, 1846. Called Rancho los Alamos y Agua Caliente, it embraced 34,560 acres. Three other men later joined in ownership of the ranch, J. Lancaster Brent, Cristobal Aguilar and Agustin Olvera.

These four ranches, situated partly in the fertile valley and partly in the steep Tehachapi Mountains, all joined one another. Beale's Sebastian Indian Reservation overlapped portions of all of them. Fort Tejon was located on a portion of Rancho Castac. Beale's involvement with these four Mexican land grant ranchos, as we shall see, did not end with the loss of his job as Superintendent of Indian Affairs.

The U. S. Attorney General, after extended litigation, finally cleared the government's title to Sebastian Indian Reservation and Fort Tejon by ruling: Because the original Mexican grants of 1843 stipulated that existing Indian rancherias were not to be disturbed, and the Mexican government might take as much land as may be required for military establishments, these same conditions devolved upon the United States, allowing both the reservation and Fort Tejon to be so established.

The ruling let Beale off the hook for moving his Indians onto private lands. At the same time, the owners of record gained clear title and could go about developing or disposing of lands not preempted by the government. By that time, the Sebastian Reservation had shrunk from 75,000 acres to 25,000 to comply with Congressional authorization, and seemed likely to shrink to 8000 because of pressure in Sacramento.

Major General John Ellis Wool, commander of the Department of the Pacific, issued the order to establish Fort Tejon on June 24, 1854:

> The quartermaster department will, without delay, erect quarters
> for one company of dragoons and one of infantry on the site, in the

military reserve for the Indians near the Tejon Pass designated by
E. F. Beale . . .

Colonel Joseph K. F. Mansfield, Inspector-General, approved
the selection of the site in a letter to General Wool in July.
Mansfield explained that the fort would have no strategic advantage for defense, nor was any advantage needed, for its
primary purpose would be "the protection of the Indians of
the southern San Joaquin Valley." As far as the Army was
concerned, all details were official and properly authorized.
No concern had been given to the possibility the site may have
been preempted from private lands.

Fort Tejon, situated in oak-studded Canada de las Uvas,
is some seventy miles north of Los Angeles (on what is now
Interstate 5, the main north-south freeway in California).
It remained a tent camp for more than a year while William
Hamilton of Los Angeles made adobe bricks under contract
for the permanent buildings.

The Beales returned from the East in midsummer of 1855.
Beale was temporarily out of a job, but now he and Mary
could settle down after a year's absence and plan their future.
It didn't take long for them to decide on a course of action.

On August 8, 1855, they purchased, in Mary's name, the
48,825-acre Rancho la Liebre. The Flores title had been
validated in court. Flores sold the property to William Walker
of San Francisco, and Walker, undoubtedly acting as agent for
the Beales, sold it six days later to Mary Edwards Beale for
the same price Walker paid for it — about three cents per acre.

By this transaction Beale became patron of the scattered
Indian rancherias on the property. He immediately encouraged
the inhabitants to remain, promising employment for all who
desired to work. He set about constructing in the hills a large
adobe that was to be ranch headquarters and their home for
the next seventeen years.

Beale's successor, Superintendent Henley, maintained his residence and headquarters at San Francisco. Without Beale's care,

discipline, and personal direction, the Indians performed little if any work on the promising reservation farms Beale had started. Cattle bought for the Indians wound up at the Fort Tejon commissary. Alex Godey acted as Henley's agent, and both profited at the red man's expense. So many Indians had left the reservation by November of 1855 that the original purpose of Fort Tejon, established for their protection, no longer seemed valid. Construction on the nearly completed fort was suspended and the unroofed adobe walls left standing.

Beale has occasionally been accused of "stealing the Indian's land," but by that time the federal bureaucracy and public indifference had already allowed Sebastian Reservation to fail. He paid the legal owner for the rancho and allowed the remaining Indians to stay — perhaps a kinder fate than they would have experienced otherwise.

When Beale first moved the Indians down the San Joaquin Valley to Sebastian Reservation in 1854, the assistant Beale engaged to be in charge of the trek was a forty-niner, Samuel A. Bishop. During Beale's absence in Washington, Bishop established himself as partner of Alfred Packard on Rancho Castac, put up an adobe house and corrals, and raised cattle and sheep. Beale renewed his acquaintance with Bishop and entered into a joint venture with him in stock raising. The ever-enterprising Alex Godey also associated himself with Bishop at this time, contracting to supply beef to Fort Tejon.

And so Edward Beale settled into the life of a private citizen and cattleman on his own ranch. This state of relative serenity didn't last long, however. Mary Beale neared the birth of their second child and they decided to take up temporary residence in San Francisco — a city perpetually rocked with such criminal violence and political corruption that a citizens Committee of Vigilance had taken the law into its own hands. Not only that, Superintendent Henley was losing his grip altogether on the San Joaquin Valley Indians.

12

Life in San Francisco

Edward Beale left Alex Godey in charge of Rancho la Liebre and took Mary to San Francisco. They had just settled in temporary quarters when on March 6, 1856, Mary gave birth to a son. They named him Truxtun, after the boy's illustrious great-grandfather Commodore Thomas Truxtun.

In the early 1850's, San Francisco experienced a period of widespread political corruption and criminal activity of such boldness and violence that outraged citizens were compelled to take the law into their own hands. A Committee of Vigilance captured and "tried" some ninety-one alleged miscreants in 1851. They hanged four of them and banished another twenty-eight from the state. Now, in 1856, the Vigilantes were about to experience a blood-drenched renaissance.

Handsome Charlie Cora, a New Orleans cardsharp, took his paramour Arabella Ryan to San Francisco and by 1855 had become solidly established as a gambler. It was their habit to attend performances at the popular American Theatre, but such unseemly boldness scandalized certain moral sensibilities. Among the sensibilities most scandalized were those of the wife of United States Marshal William H. Richardson. Mrs. Richardson prevailed upon her husband to suggest to Charlie Cora that he should seat the glamorous Arabella more discreetly — perhaps in one of the curtained stalls. Richardson dutifully approached Cora the next day. Cora took not at all kindly to Richardson's suggestion. A violent quarrel ensued. They went into the street. Cora ended the fight by drawing a pistol and shooting Richardson dead on the spot. Richardson's funeral notice lists Beale as a pallbearer.

Cora was arrested and tried, but the jury failed to agree on a verdict. Meanwhile, another murder took place which galvanized the populace into demanding action more resolute than the constituted authorities were able to deliver.

On May 14, 1856, San Francisco Supervisor James P. Casey, a man of shady reputation, shot and killed a popular crusading journalist named James King, who called himself James King of William. News of the shooting spread quickly through the city. The people had found a champion in King, a fearless voice calling for decency and social responsibility. A shocked citizenry poured into the streets. By nightfall a crowd had filled Portsmouth Square, shouting for both Cora and Casey to be taken out and hanged.

Members of the original Committee of Vigilance were called together and they quickly reorganized. They moved on the city jail and placed it under siege.

Governor John Neely Johnson appointed William Tecumseh Sherman a Major General in the state militia, hoping to control the Vigilantes. Neither Sherman nor the militia were effective in doing so. The militia lacked manpower, equipment and organization.

Vigilantes stormed the jail and took Cora and Casey to "Fort Gunnybags," their headquarters at First and Sacramento Streets. There the two men were "tried," found guilty and summarily hanged from the second floor windows.

Edward Beale served on the coronor's jury to determine the cause of death. The panel listened to Dr. Dupuytrym testify that he had examined the bodies and found that "life was extinct." The jury foreman reported:

> This testimony is quite sufficient for the purpose of our investigation. The deceased came to their deaths by hanging, committed by a body of men styling themselves a Vigilante Committee. As no witness could be produced to identify any member of the committee, the case is closed.

The jury could do little else. Its verdict was identical to that which followed the 1851 hangings. The San Francisco Committee of Vigilance disbanded for the second and last time.

While this agony of social conscience ran its course, violence of a different sort had reached crisis proportions in the San Joaquin Valley. The Indians failed to receive the benefits promised them. They stood helplessly by as settlers and miners encroached on their land, threatening to wipe them out. Finally driven to the wall by impending starvation, Indians in the Four Creeks and Tule River region went on the warpath. They attacked white camps, farms and settlements, ran off horses and cattle, burned homes and crops, and destroyed a sawmill.

Governor Johnson asked Edward Beale to help quell the uprising. Beale agreed, and Johnson commissioned him a Brigadier General in the California State Militia, just as Governor Bigler had done four years earlier. Johnson issued formal orders on May 26, 1856:

> Some fifteen days since, I became advised of seriously threatened disturbance between our people residing in the Tulare section of the state and the Indian tribes in that region and, at the request of a special agent sent for the purpose, complied with the wishes of those people by forwarding them arms and ammunition for their defense against Indian hostilities. A few days since I was informed that it would be impossible for General Wool to send any additional U. S. troops to that section and, learning the number and disposition of those already there, I was satisfied that they would be unable to render efficient aid, and of the necessity of calling out a volunteer force.

Governor Johnson explained, somewhat circuitously, that he didn't have the funds to field a volunteer army. He had already mobilized the militia under Sherman in the San Francisco civil debacle — for which he received pointed criticism — and didn't feel inclined to further lay his political neck on the line. His orders to Beale reveal fond hope that the Indians could be pacified with the help of federal troops but without the need for a state-funded volunteer force:

> . . . You are hereby ordered to proceed with all celerity to the seat of those Indian disturbances and so act as you would be authorized as the General commanding that brigade and the special authority hereby given you as will tend to suppress further hostilities . . .

> In the performance of those duties, you will cooperate with the authorities both civil and military in such wise as will most speedily and efficiently attain the paramount objective of your mission to secure peaceful relations between the whites and Indians . . .

Then came the kicker. Governor Johnson wanted a war stopped, but only if it wasn't going to cost him anything.

> As I have at my disposal but a limited sum of money from which can be drawn the necessary expenses of your trip, I can only presume you to have drawn in your favor warrants on the state treasury to an amount not exceeding $500, and if those expenses should exceed that sum, the residue will have to await the action of the next legislature, which will without doubt make a reasonable appropriation for the purpose.

Johnson searched out Beale in San Francisco for this mission. Beale's successor, Superintendent Henley, had gone east on Bureau business, but returned to California at about this time. An article in the Placerville *Mountain Democrat* on May 31, 1856, noted Henley's return on the "last steamer" from Washington where he had been vindicating his character against "Know-Nothing revilers."

Although Beale and Henley were acknowledged enemies, Beale carried out his orders to "cooperate with the authorities both civil and military" by advising Henley that the Governor had authorized him to deal with the Indians. Realizing the limitation of his funds, Beale asked Henley for $100 in expenses to give the Indians a "feast," as customary when assembled in council. Henley responded that Beale's authority did not emanate from the Bureau of Indian Affairs. Feasting for the Indians should be determined by his sub-agent in the field, M. B. Lewis, and not by Beale.

In a brief communique to the Governor from Camp Easton, Tulare County, Beale reported that he had met with twelve of the Indian groups living between the Tule and Kings rivers and had concluded a term of peace with them. He told the Indians they must retire to established reservations and stay there. The Indians were to be fed by the Indian Agents "until the arrival of the Superintendent of Indian Affairs."

Beale submitted a final detailed report on July 12. His activities, meanwhile, had aroused the wrath, petulance, and concern of the Indian Agents and their Superintendent. They busily engaged themselves in writing letters back and forth regarding Beale's usurping the authority of their respective offices.

In a brief commentary on Beale's part in this campaign, biographer Stephen Bonsal expressed the opinion that "the most remarkable feature was the fact that United States officials and troops acted throughout in perfect subordination to General Beale in a happy and most unusual cooperation." Such was not the case, however. Beale had secured an escort of federal troops from Fort Tejon, but the United States "officials," in this case the Indian Agents, were strenuously opposed to the action he took. Agents Lewis and Campbell both complained to Henley in letters written on June 14. A week later, Lewis even implied to Henley that the Indians had been peaceful under his administration but Beale had stirred them up.

The relationship between Beale and the agents stood far short of "happy and most unusual cooperation." It seems likely that, in fact, Beale experienced certain satisfaction in seeing Henley in an awkward situation.

Henley complained bitterly to Governor Johnson about Beale in a letter dated June 24, closing with these remarks:

> . . . Should it hereafter be deemed advisable by your excellency to make treaties with the Indians independent of this department or its agents, it will facilitate very much the object sought to be obtained if this office can be immediately furnished with authenticated copies of the treaties made, the number of Indians proposed to be provided for, and the extent to which the Superintendent of Indian Affairs is expected to furnish means to consumate such treaties.

Having gotten that off his chest, Henley let his hair down

with a private letter to the Governor on the same date. He
acknowledged receipt of a copy of Beale's report of June 10
in which Beale,

> . . . professes to have made treaties with the Indians in the Tulare
> Valley. I cannot give you in an official letter the true state of the case
> in regard to Beal's [sic] mission to the south. I therefore make this a
> private letter. But the truth is that if Beal has any ambition in the
> world it is that the Indian affairs in that portion of the state under
> my administration shall be a failure.
>
> From the time of Mr. Beal retiring from office to the present mo-
> ment, several of his late employees have lounged about in the vicinity
> of the Tejon reservation using most untiring efforts to disaffect the
> minds of the Indians, and induce them to leave the reserve and aban-
> don the protection of the government.
>
> General Beal professes to have made treaties with the Indians, and
> to have made certain stipulations for giving them food, etc. Now, no
> one knows better than Mr. Beal how embarrassing it is to the Super-
> intendent to have promises made to the Indians which cannot with
> certainty be complied with. I have great fear that his operations in
> that quarter will give me infinite trouble. The Indians were at peace
> before he arrived there . . .

If Henley thought by this objection to the Governor's sponsorship of Beale's actions he was putting Johnson in his place,
he couldn't have been more mistaken. The Indians were most
certainly not at peace, and that was the reason for Beale's
actions — and the Governor's. Henley's quavering paranoia
makes a revealing point about the Indians' chances for humane
treatment under the impersonal minions of civil service.

A few days later Henley penned a letter to "General E. F.
Beale at Visalia," requesting all pertinent information regarding
his treaties, but didn't send it direct. He preferred to have the
Governor forward it together with the latter's own instructions
to Beale to "furnish the information sought for." Henley's
letter said:

> Recently I have been informed by Governor Johnson . . . that you
> had made treaties with the various Indian tribes . . . but I am not

informed as to the terms of those treaties, or the probable cost of carrying them into effect.

Although your authority did not emanate from this department, yet as the Superintendent is expected to make provisions for carrying into effect the treaties in question, you will perceive it to be indispensable before definite action can be taken, that this office should be furnished with copies of the treaties, a statement of the pledges given, and promises made to the Indians, so as to determine the questions that may arise in connection with this subject.

Old sailor Beale must have thought there was more sail than ballast to this man. The only pledge he had extracted from the Indians was that they agreed to stay put. The only promise he made was that Superintendent Henley would come and take care of them. But Henley ignored the Indians. He professed complete ignorance of Beale's activities in the San Joaquin Valley, although his agents had already given him the full particulars.

The Governor duly forwarded Henley's letter to Beale but there is no record of his instructing Beale to comply with the request, or of Beale ever doing so. Johnson had no intention of becoming involved in their controversy. He felt quite content with the manner in which Beale had conducted his mission, dumping the entire Indian problem back on the federal government and relieving the state of the expense of augmenting the federal troops with a detachment of the state militia. Except for his modest personal expenses, Beale had charged the entire cost of the expedition — including gifts and provisions for the Indians — to the Bureau of Indian Affairs. He advised Governor Johnson that all such goods "were given by the sub-Agents of the federal government and are not chargeable to the state."

Beale thought Henley should get the treaty information from his own agents, who had been present at the councils. As to the number of Indians to be provided for, Henley could determine that for himself.

Hostilities had been suppressed in the San Joaquin Valley and peace restored. In his own way, Beale had "cooperated

with the authorities both civil and military," which was all
Governor Johnson had ordered him to do. From there on, the
problem was Henley's. As he might have expressed in Navy
jargon, Beale had Superintendent Henley in the bight of his
line.

The are two versions extant of Beale's final report of July
12. One is given in Bonsal's 1912 biography of Beale, the other
is a holographic copy in the California State Archives. Because
of certain discrepancies and omissions in Bonsal, the archives
copy was used in preparing these pages. In Bonsal, the date
of the report is July 12, 1855, instead of the correct year, 1856.
Bonsal gives the number of Indians assembled at the first
council meeting as sixty or seventy when the number was 160
or 170. Bonsal's most important omission is the last paragraph
of the report in which Beale resigns his "commission of Brigadier General, First Brigade, First Division" in the state militia.

Beale's long report details a series of successful meetings
with Indian leaders. In each case, the Indians complied with
Beale's verbal instructions and returned peacefully to their
homes and reservation farms. He makes no mention of written
treaties. Along with his report Beale submitted vouchers for
"traveling expenses to the seat of the late Indian war" and a
personal note to the Governor:

> You will find [the expenses] I am sure as moderate as possible,
> considering the time occupied in the service and the important char-
> acter of the result. You may have seen in the *Herald* a publication of
> my report before it was sent to you . . . made entirely without my
> knowledge. Please send check for the enclosed vouchers by mail.

His vouchers totaled $924, of which $704 was for hiring
a wagon and horses for forty-four days at $16 per day, and
$220 for subsistence for himself and his horses for forty-four
days at $5 per day. Beale claimed nothing at all for his personal
time and services. Governor Johnson held him to the original
stipulation of $500, however, for which he sent a warrant on
September 1, made out to "General Ed. H. [sic] Beale" with

the notation: "The next legislature will doubtless meet the deficiency in your expenditures." There is no indication in the state archives that Beale ever received the other $424.

That Beale's conduct had met with the complete approval of the Army is made manifest in a letter addressed to him by General Wool:

> Being apprehensive that the attack of the white inhabitants on the Tulare Indians in 1856 might lead to an Indian war in Southern California, and from my knowledge of your great efficiency of character and your influence over the Indians in that section of the country, I had no doubt . . . you would be able to prevent so great a calamity. It was therefore that I not only urged your employment, but, in order that you might more effectively control the whites, especially the militia, who seemed determined on war against the Indians, I urged upon the Governor your appointment as Brigadier General . . . The course you adopted and pursued on the occasion referred to, I cannot doubt, settled the difficulties with both whites and Indians.

Beale returned to San Francisco on July 10 to find the city still in the hands of the Vigilantes. Meanwhile, under the consolidation act of April 19, 1856, the State Legislature carved San Mateo County from the southern portion of San Francisco County. All San Francisco city and county officials were required to post bonds with the Board of Supervisors for the faithful performance of their duties within two days after July 1. The board was authorized to fill any vacancies in office by appointing "some suitable person, an elector of the county, to fill the vacancy until the next general election."

San Francisco Sheriff David Scannell submitted a bond underwritten by Charles W. Cook of Palmer, Cook & Company on July 10. The Board of Supervisors rejected the late posting and declared the office of sheriff vacant. Scannell appeared before County Judge Thomas W. Freelon and again offered the bond, but the judge refused to accept it. Scannell in turn refused to relinquish his office and appealed directly to the county court. But Charles Cook, apparently giving in to political pressure applied by Scannell's opponents, petitioned the court on August 6 to release him from bonded responsibility for Scannell, who was unable to secure another bond.

The board wanted a man of courage and integrity to assume the office — someone like, say, Edward Beale who had just returned from the Tulare campaign popularly acclaimed a triumphant peacemaker. The success of his mission was well known to the Supervisors. Thus, they elected Beale Sheriff of San Francisco on the board's first ballot.

Beale's official residence was his ranch in Los Angeles County. It seemed to make no difference to the Supervisors that he was not an elector of San Francisco County. They wanted Beale and were willing to overlook certain fine points of the law. William C. Kibbe, Adjutant General of the state militia, wired Governor Johnson of the board's action,

> . . . which election gives great satisfaction. I would suggest that you recognize General Beale as sheriff, authorizing him to call upon the military if required. Beale's appointment would do more for the success of law and order than any act which could be done. All have confidence in Beale as the proper man, he is very popular among all classes.

Governor Johnson, himself so recently aided by Beale's willingness to serve in a time of need, happily obliged.

But confusion reigned. The Court of Sessions, ignoring the action of the Board of Supervisors and recognition by the Governor of Beale's appointment, selected Charles L. Strong to fill the office of sheriff. And Scannell continued to clamor in defense of his incumbency. The *Herald* did not share Kibbe's glowing opinion of the board's choice or its authority and decried its action:

> The Board of Supervisors are of the opinion they have the power to elect a sheriff, the appointment of the Court of Sessions notwithstanding. It is probable that we shall have three gentlemen in the field, each claiming to be the legal sheriff . . . Mr. Beale may make a very good sheriff, but he was peculiarly unfortunate in his selection of Stephen G. Whipple for his bondsman.

We are undecided as to who had the most impudence, Mr. Whipple in coming from his gilded den of vice and infamy to insult our community by offering his ill-gotten gains as a bond for a public officer, or our beautiful board of city fathers accepting a notorious gambler as a surety . . .

The *Herald's* condemnation of Whipple may have been a narrow political exercise, as were many of its editorials. Despite his ownership of a sporting house on Commercial Street, Whipple's reputation seems not to have been entirely negative. He owned a Mt. Diablo coal mine for awhile, and a Sacramento River steamer named *S. M. Whipple,* after his sister. He also raised fine race horses, among them the noted "Whipple's Hambletonian." Business conducted in his Commercial Street establishment, according to his July 8, 1888, obituary, "never exceeded the bounds of propriety."

Beale never explained his selection of Whipple for a bondsman, but then why should he? Beale was perfectly inclined to accept a man's bond as easily as his word, or his friendship, and to consider if others didn't approve, that was their problem and not Beale's. Besides, a dozen other prominent businessmen had joined Whipple as bondsmen for Beale. The issue of Whipple's moral suitability constituted but a single grain of sand on a vast political beach.

A commission consisting of the County Judge, County Auditor and President of the Board of Supervisors met to pass upon the bonds of county officials. Beale appeared before the commission on August 9 with Whipple. Judge Freelon delayed Beale's appointment for two days, hoping that Strong could post bond. When Strong failed to do so, Beale duly received the appointment as Sheriff of the City and County of San Francisco. Or did he? Scannell never actually vacated the office.

Beale's tenure, if any, was short-lived anyway. He didn't run for a "second term" in the general election of November, 1856. Scannell did run, and was elected. Another activity had already claimed Beale's attention. He had been politically active in San Francisco, and now accepted chairmanship of the State Demo-

cratic Committee meeting in Sacramento to elect delegates to
the national convention for the Presidential election of 1856.

All three major candidates for President were close friends
of Beale. James Buchanan, recently returned from the post
of United States Minister to the Court of St. James, was a
lifelong politician. He had served in both houses of Congress
and as Secretary of State. Upon demise of the Federalist Party
he became a Democrat and perennial contender for the Presidential nomination. He tried in 1844, 1848 and 1852. He finally
made it in 1856 — on the seventeenth ballot at the Cincinnati
convention. Buchanan had been instrumental in furthering Beale's
career ever since recommending him for a Midshipman's warrant in 1836.

The tremendous national popularity of John C. Fremont was
evinced by all three major parties. Each sought him as its
candidate. A coalition of Whigs, Free Soilers and other anti-
slavery groups had united in a new Republican Party. Its two
main objectives were opposition to the extension of slavery
and promotion of a transcontinental railroad. Fremont wholeheartedly supported both these planks in the Republican platform and agreed to be the party's candidate. As one of Beale's
closest friends, Fremont could normally have counted on his
energetic support.

Former President Millard Fillmore had lost the nomination
of the Whig Party for reelection in 1852, and this time accepted
a bid by the American Party, a group of disgruntled Whigs and
Northern Democrats. Beale felt somewhat obligated to Fillmore
for his appointment as Superintendent of Indian Affairs in
1852, but could not otherwise rouse himself to support the
American Party.

Beale went to work for the nomination and election of James
Buchanan. His obligation was not to Buchanan alone, but also
to the Democratic Party. Under the Democratic administrations
of Presidents Jackson, Van Buren, Polk and Pierce, Beale had
progressed and prospered. Besides, it's altogether likely that
Beale found in James Buchanan a father figure. His loyalty to

Buchanan went back to his youth and to the very grass roots beginnings of his own career in public service. And Buchanan was a gentleman of the first order. There seems little doubt that the qualities of honesty, loyalty and perseverance which Beale found in Buchanan were the substance of his own fiber.

When the November returns were in, Buchanan carried nineteen of the thirty-one states, Fremont eleven and Fillmore one. Although the campaign was heated and at times exceedingly abusive, Fremont did not lose his dignity and restraint, but it did effectively cost him his political career. Accepting defeat calmly, Fremont returned to California in the spring of 1857 to look after his mining and ranching interests.

Edward and Mary Beale divided their time between Chester and the California ranch. For Mary, it might have looked like Edward could finally settle down. But that was not to be. She would soon see him off again, this time on one of the strangest expeditions in the history of the West.

13

Camels Across the Continent

The use of camels by the Army for transportation in the southwestern plains and deserts was first proposed in 1836 by Major George Hampton Crossman. Edward Beale is often credited with conceiving the plan, but in 1836 Beale was only fourteen years old and mostly interested in joining the Navy. Crossman viewed the matter seriously but around Washington it was treated more with jocularity than respect.

Later, in 1847, Major Henry Constantine Wayne liked Crossman's idea well enough to propose it to Mississippi Senator Jefferson Davis. The war with Mexico blazed on all fronts by then, however, and the Army preferred to stick with its proven methods of mobility — horses, mules and the shuffling feet of its soldiers.

Major Wayne revived the camel idea in 1853. The great deserts stretching west of Texas all the way to the Pacific had become part of the United States. All-weather roads were badly needed, and there was increased talk of a transcontinental railroad. A southern route seemed the most feasible for both purposes. Camels, proponents reasoned, would take to the American desert as readily as to their own desert at home.

President Franklin Pierce appointed Jefferson Davis Secretary of War in 1854. Davis still liked Wayne's plan to use camels and discussed the idea with several men considered knowledgeable on western travel. Among these were John Russell Bartlett, Captain George B. McClellan and Edward Beale. Beale expressed enthusiasm for the idea. Davis told President Pierce on December 1, 1853, what he thought about it: "Importation of camels for military purposes and for transportation with troops would remove an obstacle which now serves to greatly diminish the value and efficiency of our troops on the western frontier."

The President made no response. Davis repeated the appeal in his annual report of 1854. Senator Shields of Illinois added an amendment to a military appropriation bill which would provide $30,000 "to be expended in the purchase and importation of camels." The bill passed, and the United States went into the camel business.

News of the Army's novel enterprise soon reached the West Coast and on April 11, 1854, the San Francisco *Herald* optimistically informed its readers:

> The camel will not long be an object of curiosity. An enterprising company is about to introduce the camel into this country as a beast of burden . . . Kentucky and Ohio will quite likely enter largely into the raising of camels . . .

Beale's reputation as a trustworthy courier and respected leader of men was well known to Secretary Davis. Beale had traveled between Washington and California perhaps more times than anyone, often under conditions of great urgency and peril. Therefore, Davis showed keen interest in Beale's opinion and welcomed his support.

Actually, Beale knew little about camels and had no practical experience with the beasts. But let it not be said that Edward Beale ever failed to respond to a stimulating idea. He had seen camels during naval tours to the Mediterranean, and had read Abbe Evariste Huc's 1852 publication, *Recollections of a Journey Through Tartary, Thibet and China,* in which Huc expounded at length on the value of camels for desert travel.

Beale agreed with Wayne about the geologic and climatic similarities of the American Southwest to the great deserts of Asia and Africa. What worked there would work equally well here. They were right, as it turned out, and Beale proved it.

Beale was in Washington answering charges against his stewardship of Indian affairs when Congress passed the camel bill. He recommended to Secretary Davis that his cousin, Lieutenant David Dixon Porter Jr., of the United States Navy, be appointed to command an expedition to purchase the camels. He also recommended that Porter's brother-in-law, Gwynne Harris Heap, Beale's trailmate on the 1853 expedition, be included. They were logical choices. Both had spent time in the Near East, Porter when his father served as United States Consul at Constantinople and Heap when his father was Consul at Tunis. And Heap, from his prior adventure with Beale, knew very well what the American desert looked like.

Wayne accepted responsibility for the purchase and care of the camels, while Lieutenant Porter commanded the store-ship USS *Supply* to bring them back. Wayne studied camels at the London Zoological Gardens in June, 1855. "Camel," he learned, applied without discrimination to both the one-humped dromedary or Arabian riding camel, and the two-humped bactrian, used primarily as a pack animal. Porter visited the estate of the Grand Duke of Tuscany and found "250 camels doing the work of a thousand horses." Wayne rejoined Porter and the *Supply* in Italy, from where they proceeded to Tunis. The Bey presented Wayne with two camels and Wayne purchased one other.

They next stopped at Balaklava, where the Crimean War was in progress. The British employed camels to pack 600 pounds each over a distance of twenty-five to thirty miles per day. Nine of the animals were purchased at Alexandria in December and twenty-four at Smyrna in February, 1956.

The *Supply* arrived at Indianola (later called Port Lavaca), Texas, with its exotic cargo of thirty-four camels, one more than boarded the ship at Smyrna. Wayne first stabled his charges at Major Howard's ranch on the Medina River near San Antonio. He later moved them to Camp Verde army post in Green Valley, some sixty miles from San Antonio. Porter sailed again and brought back forty-four of the beasts in February, 1857.

Wayne built stables for his seventy-eight camels and watched them contentedly munch their daily rations of government grain, an unaccustomed rich diet for which they performed no useful service. Unsure what to do with his herd of *genus camelus* now that he had them, Wayne wrote to Secretary Davis for instructions. Perhaps, he suggested, they should be used primarily for breeding until a large herd had accumulated.

Jeff Davis wasn't interested in breeding camels. He wanted to test their fitness for military purposes. Wayne said it would take time and training before "men may be mounted upon them to accompany scouting parties." Camp Verde did not have the funds, authority or instructors to carry out such training. Porter opined that "with such training a corps of mounted dromedaries would soon drive every hostile Indian out of the country." These are the only indications that such a "camel corps" was ever contemplated, and none ever existed — although books have been written about a mythical "U. S. Camel Corps." At no time were the camels ever officially ridden or used for anything but supplements to, and in conjunction with, pack-mules for carrying supplies.

President James Buchanan took office in March of 1857. John B. Floyd replaced Jefferson Davis as Secretary of War. A tense situation in Utah took their minds off the camels for awhile. Brigham Young, Governor of Utah Territory, proposed to set up his own government and secede from the Union. The hostility of the Mormons and their Ute Indian allies greatly restricted emigrant travel over certain routes to California, and the often-proposed southern transcontinental wagon road became even more important. In addition, a revolution in Nicaragua led by William Walker had interrupted steamship connections between the coasts. Land routes were the only solution to increasing problems of communication.

The Beales spent January of 1857 in Chester and fortunately missed the "Fort Tejon Earthquake" along 250 miles of the San Andreas Fault. They read newspaper accounts of the ground opening in a wide rent for thirty or forty miles, of large trees uprooted and of cattle rolling down hillsides. Immense landslides blocked the road between Fort Tejon and Los Angeles.

The tremor reached its maximum intensity at Fort Tejon, where the buildings suffered severe damage. "Not a structure at the fort was left standing intact," according to Don Benito Wilson.

In early spring of 1857, Secretary Floyd ordered a survey for a wagon road along the 35th Parallel from Fort Defiance, New Mexico (now Arizona), to the Colorado River. He directed that some of the camels languishing at Camp Verde accompany the expedition to test their adaptability for military service in the Southwest.

Beale had remained in Washington after the inauguration of his old friend and benefactor, James Buchanan. Once more he stood at hand when opportunity knocked. Buchanan would hear of no other than Edward Beale to command the expedition. He notified Beale on April 22: "You are hereby appointed superintendent of the wagon road authorized by the last session of Congress, from Fort Defiance to the mouth of the Mojave River." (The Mojave River actually sinks into the California desert of the same name, but many maps of that day show it flowing into the Colorado River.)

He received three pages of instructions into which Secretary Floyd had cranked every possible contingency. Beale was to recruit a working party of not less than twenty-five nor more than thirty-five men, and take along a number of strong wagons to demonstrate that the route he would select could be negotiated by wheeled conveyances.

The survey, for which Congress appropriated $50,000, would be preliminary to an actual construction project. Expenses were in no event to exceed the appropriation. Vouchers were to be taken for all disbursements, with accounts rendered quarterly. At the termination of his services Beale was to submit a general report. He would go to Texas and take delivery of "as many camels as you may deem necessary, not to exceed twenty-five, to test their usefulness, endurance and economy."

At Fort Defiance he would be furnished an escort of twenty-five soldiers plus a sergeant and two corporals to see him safely through the hostile Indian country. At Fort Defiance he would "start construction of the road which he would make passable for loaded wagons throughout." From the Colorado he would "proceed to Fort Tejon along the route best adapted to the passage of troops." His instructions called for a return from Fort Tejon over the same route and submission of estimates for constructing bridges where they would cut down time and distance of travel.

Beale prepared estimates for the $50,000 appropriation. Salaries included his own of $3000, a chief assistant at $2500, seventeen assorted teamsters and mechanics at $2 per day, and three cooks and twenty-five Mexican laborers at $1 per day. He needed ten wagons, 120 mules, and harness and saddles at a cost of $15,000; provisions worth $6125; and such other items as arms and ammunition, camp and cooking equipment, India-rubber boats, blankets and other presents for Indians, and numerous miscellaneous articles. His total estimate reached $49,462. This figure, and Beale's bond, were approved by Floyd on April 23.

Beale also requested fifty dragoon saddles, bridles, pairs of spurs and ten tents from Army stores. Floyd approved that, too, but required they be paid for out of the appropriation. Beale thus started his journey with obligations already exceeding the amount of the appropriation, a deficit condition to which he was thoroughly accustomed.

Beale ordered his supplies and recruited the nucleus of his party at Chester and Washington. He enlisted Gwynne Harris Heap as his chief assistant; Lieutenant Charles E. Thorburn of the Navy; geologist Lewis W. Williams; and a wagon-master named Alex H. Smith. Floyd instructed that, "In the event of your death, Mr. G. W. [sic] Heap, your first assistant, will continue the duty you have been sent to perform and will be recognized as your successor in command of the expedition."

There were also three teen-agers in the party, May Humphreys Stacey, J. Hampton Porter and Joseph Bell. Beale called them "my boys, May, Ham and Joe."

According to the journal of May Humphreys Stacey, the only record that covers the expedition from Chester to San Antonio, horses and mules were purchased at New Orleans. Beale engaged teamsters, laborers and cooks at San Antonio. A light ambulance wagon carried surveying instruments, medicine chest, camera and chemicals for developing photographic glass plates.

They departed from Chester on May 12, 1857. The party traveled by train from Philadelphia to Pittsburgh, thence by packet boat to Cincinnati. There Beale bought a 350-pound Little Giant corn cracker, expected to be of great service in grinding corn into meal. Beale found time at Cincinnati to write to Secretary Floyd asking to be relieved of the quarterly reports as required by his instructions from the War Department.

The party took passage on the stern-wheeler *Queen of The West* down the Ohio and Mississippi rivers to New Orleans. They spent a week there buying supplies, five horses and forty-six mules. Beale purchased for his own use a "very nice blooded little mare." At the St. Charles Hotel, Stacey saw some of William Walker's unfortunate "American Phalanx" just back from Nicaragua. "They were about as hard a set as one is likely to see in a month's journey," he wrote. "Walker himself is staying at the hotel but keeps himself very close, and I have not seen him." Beale's path came close to the legendary filibuster who created at least part of the need for the transcontinental wagon road. This was the same William Walker, a former San Francisco newspaper man, who had acted as Beale's agent in the purchase of Rancho la Liebre. So Beale knew him, but apparently made no effort in New Orleans to contact the controversial figure.

The party boarded the transport USS *Fashion* and landed at Indianola, Texas, on June 4. "The mules were harnessed up to the wagons for the purpose of trying out how they would go," Stacey explained, "and considering it was the first time, they went to our satisfaction."

On the day of their arrival at Indianola occurred an incident we would be ignorant of but for a bill of sale found years later among Beale's personal papers:

> On June 4, 1857, in Calhoun County, State of Texas, Joseph W. Baldridge, Daniel P. Sparks and Joseph H. Baldridge have this day sold and conveyed to Edward F. Beale our negro man named Jourdan, of yellow copper color, for and in consideration of the sum of $1500 paid by said Edward F. Beale, the receipt of which is now acknowledged. The boy, supposed to be from twenty-five to thirty years of age, is healthy, sensible and a slave.

On the back of the document, yellowed with age, there is recorded in Beale's own hand, "I bought the slave referred to within and gave him his freedom. E.F.B." Beale's aversion to the "peculiar institution" — despite the fact that his own family had been slave owners — would incline him toward the Republican Party in 1860.

Teamsters and packers were added to the party. Jesse Chisholm, the man who later gave his name to a famous cattle trail, hired on as guide to San Antonio. Two incidents gave the expedition an inauspicious start. A drunken teamster fell under a wagon wheel the first day out, badly injuring his leg. Beale sent him back to Indianola.

A few days later, Beale left the party to round up stray mules. He ordered Heap to stay put with the wagon train until all wagons had crossed a stream. Heap elected not to wait. He went on with the first eight wagons, expecting the others could easily follow. Beale came up later with the last two teams and had a terrible time getting them across. According to Stacey, Beale arrived at camp "most damnably disgusted. He dressed down Heap in a very harsh and ungentlemanly manner for abandoning the two wagons and continued to castigate him in the strongest terms." Heap cut him short with, "Sir, I will not submit to this." Heap resigned and returned next day to Indianola. Beale's occasionally volatile temper had cost him the friendship of a kinsman and fellow explorer, as well as the services of his chief assistant. Heap later said his resignation stemmed more from his weariness of world travel than his altercation with Beale.

The group made camp on Major Howard's ranch while Beale went on to Camp Verde. He presented an order to Captain J. N. Palmer, Quartermaster of the Second Cavalry, for eight dromedaries and seventeen bactrians, "to be selected by Mr. Beale himself, with all the accoutrements and men who accompanied them from the Mediterranean." By what criteria Beale selected his camels is a mystery. The order added that foals would be allowed to accompany their mothers.

Stacey, busy in camp with his laundry on the Twenty-first, heard the jingling of bells. There presently hove into view a large dromedary named Seid, led by a Turk. High in the saddle rode Beale, grinning like a schoolboy. A second camel lumbered into camp, then a third and fourth, and soon the entire string of twenty-five had assembled.

"Our mules and horses were very much frightened at their approach," wrote Stacey. "They dashed around the corral, snorting in wild alarm."

All the animals quieted down in a few hours and soon became accustomed to each other. But if the animals weren't a problem, the mule-packers were. The men didn't like the big teeth and unpredictable temper of the camels, nor their odor and spitting. And it took awhile to become accustomed to the moaning and grunting as the camels knelt to receive their loads.

Actually, the men had far more trouble with the mules than with the camels. Stacey noted, "There was much difficulty in gearing some wild mules and much time lost in preparing them for the teams."

But Beale knew his mules as well as any man did and soon had the situation under control. The wagons and mules were finally loaded. Packs of corn which had been run through the Little Giant were lashed to the camel's backs. Beale gave the order to mount on June 23, 1857, and the journey got underway. Only two cameleers could be persuaded to go along. None of them had received so much as a day's wages since January and neither the Army nor Beale had funds to make up their back pay. The two who did elect to remain with the animals on the journey achieved a permanent niche in Western history and are regarded with affection in every story told about the camels. One was a Turk named Hadji Ali, dubbed "Hi-Jolly," the other a Greek named George Caralamba, never for the rest of his days called anything but "Greek George."

Beale wanted a photograph of the caravan as it started out but Stacey, with collateral duties of photographer, confessed he had no opportunity to master the camera. Beale delayed their departure while he sent to San Antonio for a professional photographer. Research fails to reveal any pictorial record of this historic occasion, and Stacey never did master the art. "The photographic apparatus proved a failure," was the way he put it.

Beale began his official account when the party left San Antonio. They covered sixteen miles the first day, bringing them to the Spring of San Lucas where Beale's first entry noted:

> The camels carried each, including pack saddles, over 500 pounds. This being the first day, they seemed tired on arriving at camp, but I hope as we proceed and they harden in flesh, to find them carrying their burdens more easily.

Stacey seemed less optimistic. "The camels travel so very slow that they cannot keep up with even a six-mule team, not generally very fast. It is my decided opinion that these camels prove a failure."

Beale found four men already camped at the spring. One of them, Samuel McLenegham, had crossed the country by every overland trail and said he much preferred the Beale-Heap route through Colorado and Utah.

It took the expedition a month to cover the 500 miles to El Paso. Beale recorded the distance between each campsite, adding altitude, longitude and latitude, morning and evening temperatures, descriptions of the country and presence or absence of water and grass. A bugle raised the camp each morning at three o'clock. The party started down the road at four.

Beale's appreciation of the camels increased daily, as he reported in his records:

> I would rather undertake the management of twenty camels than five mules. The camel gives no trouble whatsoever. Contrast the lassoing, blindfolding, saddling and adjusting the pack of a mule flying around in all directions with the patience of the camel kneeling for his load. They seek bushes for food instead of grass, which certainly indicates their ability to subsist easier than horses and mules in countries where forage is scarce.

Beale said he only regretted that he didn't have double the number of camels.

> The camel's foot, like gutta percha, yields without wearing off, enabling him to travel continuously in a country where no other barefooted beast would last. The camels are . . . worthy the pen of a great artist . . . Old Mahomet with the long line of his grave and patient followers, winding cautiously their way down the road, is a very interesting and beautiful scene.

So wrote the sailor on horseback, reviewing his ships of the desert.

The road from San Antonio to El Paso, called the Old Comanche Trail, was heavily traveled and comparatively safe. A few years earlier, however, every mile had its horror tale. Graves still marked the sites of Indian massacres. Scattered along the way were several infantry posts, which Beale remarked were ". . . very useful in protecting this portion of Indian territory. Foot soldiers are especially well adapted to the pursuit of tribes always mounted on the best horseflesh to be stolen in Texas and Mexico."

"While not even the track of an Indian is visible," Stacey confided to his journal, "I am confident that some red devil was observing all our movements from a neighboring elevation." Tongue in cheek, Beale entered in his own notes:

> This evening many of our party have seen Indians but for me, sinner that I am, I was not permitted to witness such a sight. I encourage the young men, however, in the belief that deer, bushes,

etc., which they have mistaken for Indians are all veritable Comanches, as it makes them watchful on guard at night.

The caravan visited Fort Clark and Fort Davis. At Fort Lancaster, on the Pecos River, Beale paraded his camels for the entertainment of the troops. He relaxed discipline there and allowed his men to fraternize with the soldiers while he and his leaders were entertained by the officers. Stacey described the latter as:

> . . . very clever young men who drank their grog without winking! The whole party after dark got very funny. This morning I observed some of our gentlemen coming into camp with a gait that denoted a slight indulgence in alcoholic stimulants.

Beale well knew of the propensity for strong drink shared by teamsters, packers and soldiers. Having allowed his men a good party at Fort Lancaster, he ordered that Fort Bliss be bypassed.

At Fort Fillmore, on the Rio Grande River in New Mexico, they heard alarming accounts of the Apaches and Navajos on the warpath. "Our route lies right through the country of both these savage tribes," Stacey wrote with some trepidation:

> It is likely that we shall have a brush with them. We have only twenty-five men out of forty that are reliable, while the Navajos can turn out at least 2000 warriors well armed and equipped. I came on this expedition prepared for the worst and if it comes I shall not be disappointed, although very sorry we cannot get along peaceably and quietly.

Beale seemed more concerned with the performance of his camels. "Since leaving San Antonio," he boasted, "I have never heard of one stumbling." They passed through squalid villages of Mexicans and Indians where crowds came out to visit the camp under the impression it was some sort of traveling wild animal show.

The party reached Albuquerque on August 5 without incident. Beale received Secretary Floyd's denial of his request to be excused from the quarterly reports. He scribbled off a hasty note to President Buchanan:

> A law of Congress obliges all disbursing officers to submit their returns quarterly and only yourself can relieve one of the necessity of compliance with the law. I, therefore, request you will use your authority to excuse me from the requirements of this law which, however proper under ordinary circumstances, was never intended to apply in such cases as mine.

The President forwarded the note to Secretary Floyd without comment. Floyd, unaware that Beale's case and circumstances were anything but ordinary, simply ignored it.

While the party rested, Beale went to Santa Fe to arrange for the military escort he intended to pick up at Fort Defiance. The Santa Fe *Weekly Gazette* for August 15 made but brief notice of his visit: "Lieutenant Bealle [*sic*] arrived Monday from Texas, in charge of a company which brought camels across the great southern plains, but has returned to Albuquerque."

The party set up camp a few miles outside Albuquerque at Hatch's Ranch. Wagons were loaded with provisions for the sixty days calculated to take them to California. One hundred sheep were to be driven along for fresh mutton. Superfluous articles were disposed of, including the photographic apparatus which Stacey never mastered. The Little Giant wouldn't grind corn fine enough to make corn bread, as advertised, but only coarse stock feed. It was also jettisoned.

Brigadier General John Garland, commander of the Department of New Mexico at Santa Fe, issued these orders:

> A detail of one sergeant, three corporals and thirty-five picked men from the post of Fort Defiance, provisioned for sixty days and supplied with ammunition (will) report to E. F. Beale, Esq., superintendent of the wagon road from Fort Defiance to the Mojave River. The most intelligent and trustworthy sergeant will be selected. Two mountain howitzers with ammunition will be turned over to Mr. Beale upon his requisition. As soon as Mr. Beale can dispense with the services of this party, it will return to its station.

Cannons weren't notably effective against Indians in the West and usually caused more trouble than they were worth, so Beale didn't take the howitzers. Instead, he sold five of his wagons to General Garland to carry supplies for the escort he was to pick up at Fort Defiance. He thus, at one stroke, relieved himself of the upkeep of thirty mules and five teamsters, their expense to be defrayed by the Army.

During Beale's absence in Santa Fe, teamsters Joe McFeeley and John Hoyne got liquored up at a Mexican fandango and according to Stacey:

> Hoyne became crazy and kicked up Old Harry, calling a Mexican woman some very hard names. He was armed with two revolvers and a knife and, in McFeeley's struggle to disarm him and get him away from the Mexicans, he managed to get off two shots, one of which hit McFeeley in the left hand. Hampton Porter dressed the wound.

On Beale's return the next day, he discharged both Hoyne and McFeeley.

The party got underway again on August 13, heading west toward the old Indian village of Zuni. The camels had gained weight and strength, and were loaded with packs of 700 pounds. Beale remained in Albuquerque an extra two days to complete his affairs and engage a guide, then rejoined the train on the Seventeenth. His socializing in town required more formal attire and upon returning to camp was pleased to "get back to flannel shirt, big boots and greasy buckskins once more." In an oblique reference to the shooting incident, he expressed satisfaction over,

> . . . getting the men out of Albuquerque, as the fandangos and other pleasures had rendered them rather troublesome. I was obliged to administer a copious supply of oil of the boot to several, especially my Turk [Hi-Jolly] who had not found the positive prohibition of the Prophet a sufficient reason for temperance but was as drunk as any Christian in the train. To move a stubborn, half-drunken Turk, give me a good tough piece of wagon spoke, aimed tolerably high!

On the first day out the man hired to replace John Hoyne

became drunk and soon found himself on the way back to Albuquerque. Learning that Colonel William Wing Loring, commander at Fort Defiance, followed some miles back on the trail, Beale mounted Seid and rode to escort him into camp. This round trip of thirty miles took only five hours and he gloated about it afterward:

> Seid seemed not the least bit tired. It was as much as I could do to hold him in. The best mule or horse in our camp could not have performed the same journey in twice the time, although they have been fed on corn while Seid was grazed entirely on grass.

The expedition crossed the Continental Divide over a wooded ridge in the high, rocky plateau country some 100 miles west of Albuquerque. Stacey climbed a rocky formation at El Morro, west of the divide and about a day's march from Zuni. He inspected ancient stone ruins there and, as many a traveler did before and after him, carved his name on the cliff at a point called Inscription Rock.

Beale established camp some fifteen miles from Zuni and rode with Colonel Loring to pick up the military escort at Fort Defiance, a day's ride north of their trail on the 35th Parallel. They were met on the way to the fort by Captain Josiah H. Carlisle of the Second Artillery. Beale recalled a pleasant surprise:

> As we stood in the warm sun of August, it was most refreshing to see the Captain's servant throw off the folds of a blanket from a tub in the bottom of the wagon, and expose several large and glistening blocks of ice, while at the same time the Captain produced a delicate flask of red-eye.

Where the Captain managed to obtain ice that time of year in New Mexico, Beale neglected to mention.

At the fort he selected but twenty of the thirty-five soldiers authorized — all from Companies "B" and "H" of the Third Infanty — and arrived with them back at camp on August 29.

The pueblo of Zuni had a population of some 2000 Indians

living in mud-splattered adobes. The roofs of these buildings, Beale noted, were reached by ladders and were used more than any other part of the house:

> Like all Indians with a fixed abode, they are quiet and inoffensive. A knowledge of this fact induced me to establish the same system in California but the government did not appreciate the fact as I did, and it was not carried out.

Zuni, one of Coronado's fabled Seven Cities of Cibola, it situated virtually on the Thirty-fifth Parallel about twelve miles from the present Arizona border. Beale reported in his papers the existence of "an old Jesuit church in ruins" where he "found a painting over the altar done in 1701." The route of their survey extended due west of Zuni in trackless desert. All hands turned to shucking corn purchased from the Indians. On the eve of their departure from Zuni, Beale wrote:

> No one who has not commanded an expedition of this kind where everything is dim, uncertain and unknown, except the dangers, can imagine the anxiety with which I start this journey. Not only responsible for the lives of my men, but my reputation and the highest wrought expectations of my enemies, all dependent on the next sixty days good or evil fortune. Let us see what I shall say in this journal, if I live to say anything, on the day of my return here.

This moment of introspection is not entirely characteristic of Beale. He preferred to keep his own counsel. Neither a prolific writer of letters nor keeper of journals — beyond minimal documentation required by the government — Beale rarely expressed personal feelings. That simply wasn't his style. Though drawn to the sea in his younger days, he later found his place among men of the land, strong men of the frontier in many cases. He fit in with them because he seemed to be cut from the same cloth. Toughness, intelligence and a high degree of resourcefulness were prime requisites for survival in the West. Beale had these qualities in abundance and, in addition, a strong sense of rightness and justice, and an intense loyalty toward his friends and loved ones.

The historical record cannot show us Beale's thoughts, of course, but from it we have learned that when his journal expresses anxiety for the lives of his men, we can believe that he felt it deeply.

Beale carried maps of the southwest, but none of them were in any sense accurate. Geographical features often had several names applied by previous explorers, or no names at all. The only prior expedition to leave any kind of visible track for Beale to follow was that of Amiel Weeks Whipple in 1853, and his was only the faintest trace. Other expeditions headed by Lorenzo Sitgreaves in 1851 and Francois Xavier Aubry in 1852-54 left no trace at all. Even earlier, Ewing Young and eighteen trappers, including a boyish Kit Carson, had traveled part of this route from Santa Fe to California. The year was 1829, and of course not a sign of that trail remained either. The blowing desert sands west of Zuni seemed eternally capable of claiming their own.

Beale, the navigator, followed the stars along the 35th Parallel and made his own map as he went. And the wheels of his wagons made a road that is still in use today. He named landmarks for friends and members of his party, just as all explorers do, and many of those names remain on the Arizona land. This was the *tierra del ningun provecho,* the worthless land described by the earliest Spanish explorers. From Zuni west, as the buzzard flies, J. R. Bartlett's map from the 1850-53 expedition shows not a single road, not a trail or village, not one sign of habitation. Through this country Beale headed his wagons and camels.

Some of northern Arizona is not uninhabitable wasteland at all, which Beale learned once he got into it. The Indians had known it for centuries. But much of it, including the first leg of his trek west of Zuni, is largely nonproductive. The caravan moved into the pastel wonderland of *el desierto pintado,* the vast painted desert noted by Spanish explorers in 1540. Beale and his men wound their way among the fallen stone giants of the petrified forest, striking the Little Colorado

River near present day Holbrook. They stayed with the river
to the mouth of Walnut Canyon. There they headed directly
westward toward the majestic 12,000-foot San Francisco
Mountains.

One of the Fort Defiance soldiers wandered off from camp
and failed to return. After two days of searching, the party
resumed its journey. Beale noted that it was impossible to
determine "whether he deserted or went off in a fit of mental
aberration." The man eventually found his way back to Fort
Defiance.

Beyond the San Francisco peaks, Beale's guide, Jose Manuel
Saevadra, or "Salvador," confessed he had never been that
far west. He had no idea where the next water could be
found. Beale wrote in some heat:

> We unfortunately have no guide. The wretch I employed at the
> request and advice of everyone at Albuquerque, and at enormous
> wages, is the most ignorant and irresolute ass extant. This obliges us
> to do the double duty of road making and exploring, which is very
> arduous, besides adding infinitely to my anxiety and responsibility.
> Being doubtful of the country ahead, I sent Thorburn and five men
> to look for water.

Leco, another guide, advised that several days travel could
be saved by taking an old Indian trail used by Aubry in
1853. The trail led nowhere and soon petered out. Leco, sent
scouting for water, soon lost himself, causing a delay while
searching parties looked for him. Beale's men found the bewildered Leco two days later and brought him back to camp.

The party probed deeper into western Arizona, searching
constantly for water sources. The camels performed admirably.
Beale's horses and mules suffered repeatedly from a scarcity
of water and forage, but the camels subsisted comfortably
on meager vegetation and infrequent visits to springs. Camels,
in fact, were often put to work carrying kegs of water to
supply the horses and mules. At one dry camp, Beale observed:

> The mules hung around the empty water kegs braying lustily for
> what they were perishing for, the camels viewing the procedure with

great contempt and kept quietly browsing on greasewood bushes, chewing their cuds in cheerful contentment.

Beale went out alone on the trail one day. Darkness fell before he could return to camp. Stacey describes his unconventional arrival:

> Mr. Beale had a narrow escape last night. Not seeing anyone around the fires he thought all hands asleep on watch. He fired his pistol and cried out, "Indians! Indians! Here they are, the damned rascals! Give them hell, boys!" His horse took fright and ran with him seven miles, and at last fell with him, hurting him very much. Mr. Beale was very sick all night, vomiting and in much pain.

Stacey's mule threw him the next day, a mishap which elicited nothing but silence from Beale.

Beale sent the Army's five wagons and twelve of the soldier escort back to Albuquerque. Seven soldiers volunteered to remain until they had seen California. Beale forwarded a report to Secretary Floyd with the returning men:

> I cannot sufficiently express my admiration of that noble brute, the camel, and I look forward confidently to the day when they will be found in use in all parts of the country. The idea that their feet would break down in traveling over rocky ground is an exploded absurdity. Over the roughest possible volcanic rock they have been with us, patiently packing water of which they never drank a drop, and corn of which they never tasted a grain.

Another "exploded absurdity" in Beale's mind was the alleged barrenness of the northern Arizona desert. He had passed through some impressive country and told Floyd about it:

> Up to this point the road is the best in the world and it will prove the greatest emigrant route to California. It is nearly 200 miles shorter than any other, and carries grass, wood and water. It is fertile in all its parts and passes through the finest forests of pine timber possible to conceive.

Beale's enthusiasm seems a little exaggerated. Central Arizona is high altitude, mostly forested and reasonably well watered. But west of there, as the land slopes down toward the Colorado

River through successive basins and ranges, the barrenness returns and water is not so plentiful.

After much exploring in search of water, the entire party reached Alexander Canyon on September 29. Beale named the nearby mountain Floyd's Peak, now the Mount Floyd which rises just northeast of the town of Seligman. They found water at the end of each day's march. For that reason Beale thought they must be near Whipple's old trail, although all traces of it were completely obliterated.

Charles Debrille Poston, out trekking over Arizona for his pioneer Sonora Exploring & Mining Company, records his surprise one day to come upon a camel caravan plodding westward across the desert. Poston wrote in his memoirs, "I have been a warm personal friend of General Beale since the 1850's and camped together with him in Arizona." Beale's wagon road helped to open Arizona to emigration, mining and settlement — and eventually to the Territorial status which Poston and others so energetically advocated.

On October 1, Lieutenant Thorburn failed to return from scouting for water. Beale ordered a search for Thorburn, and a search ahead for water before moving on. Reconnaissances were made for several miles on either side of their present course, searching for Thorburn, water or Whipple's old trail. Supplies ran low. Beale nearly gave up Thorburn when the wanderer showed up and announced discovery of a small stream thirty-five miles ahead. Within two days the train had arrived at the new site. Patches of corn and melons grew among a scattering of crude shelters. The Indian occupants had fled at sight of the camels. Beale ordered his men not to touch the crops, writing: "Poor creatures, their time will come soon enough for extermination when the merits of this road are made known and it becomes, as it most assuredly will, the thoroughfare to the Pacific."

They passed more rancherias, deserted as the party approached. Fires could be seen nightly on nearby hills. Beale doubled the guard, but there were no disturbances. Again

Beale wrote: "Poor creatures. If they had known me they would scarcely have hidden out of sight, or missed the blankets and shirts I would have given them . . ."

The expedition passed Beale's Spring near what is now the city of Kingman, Arizona, and entered the Black Mountains. Beale wrote of the camels again on October 6: "I rarely think of mentioning the camels now. It is so universally acknowleged, even by those who were most opposed to them at first, that they are the salt of the party and the noblest brute alive."

On the same date his journal takes a dig at ex-guide Saevadra:

> This old wretch is a constant source of trouble to everyone, and his entire and incredible ignorance of the country renders him unfit for any service. I keep him moving on all occasions by way of punishment for putting himself upon us as a guide.

Geologist Lewis Williams ventured out to "crack stones" a half mile from camp on October 10. He laid aside his rifle and had become so intent in studying his specimens that he was startled out of his wits to look up and see three Indians standing nearby watching him. He leaped up and raced back to camp, leaving his gun behind. We can picture the good scientist probably running faster than he had in all his life. Beale sent his three boys to retrieve the weapon, then organized a mounted group to join the chase. Two of the Indians were captured. They turned loose the youngest, a boy of fifteen, and brought the elder back to serve as a guide to the Colorado. The third Indian stalked boldly into camp the next day and surrendered Williams' gun. Beale gave both Indians quantities of calico, blankets and handkerchiefs he had carried all the way from Chester.

Emerging from "Boys Pass," so named by Beale because May, Ham and Joe were the first to enter it, the party beheld the shiny surface of the Colorado River in the distance. Beale marked it on his map as John Howell's Pass, for a member of his party. It was later mis-named Sitgreaves Pass, after Lorenzo Sitgreaves, although that explorer never used the route. Beyond the river were the sere desert mountain ranges of California. Beale wrote:

> My heart warmed as I thought of the many friends beyond the distant chain who were looking anxiously for my arrival. We had arrived at the end of a long journey, so far without accident. Only those who have toiled so far, with life, reputation, everything staked upon the result, can imagine the feelings with which I looked down from the heights of this mountain.

Beale described the Mohave Indians of the Colorado River valley as fine looking — fat, merry, barefoot and semi-naked. He said one of the Indians, who had obviously met with whites before, greeted him by exclaiming, "God damn my soul eyes! How-de-do! How-de-do!"

They spent a day trading. "Old clothes, worn out shirts, handkerchiefs or almost anything of ours they fancy" were exchanged for pumpkins, watermelons, cantaloupes and 100 bushels of corn and beans — enough to see them through to the end of their journey.

The party spent two days ferrying wagons across the river and hauling provisions in the India-rubber boats Beale had brought for that purpose. The passage proceeded somewhat nervously, though. The Indians numbered in the hundreds and frequently crowded in on Beale's party. The animals were driven into the water to swim across, but ten mules and two horses were carried away by the swift current. Stacey noted that the Indians recovered the drowned ones and feasted on them.

Beale had been told the camels couldn't swim. They did at first refuse to enter the river until Beale brought old Seid forward. The great white beast unhesitatingly plunged into the stream and swam across. "We tied each one to the saddle of another, five in a gang, and to my delight swam them all over," he wrote to Secretary Floyd. "They not only swam with ease, but with more strength than horses and mules."

They reloaded the wagons and started out along the U. S. Surveyor's trail — later to gain historical renown as the Mojave Road — from the Colorado River to Los Angeles. Beale sent a small party with a couple of camels to Los Angeles to announce his arrival, while he and the main train branched off toward Fort Tejon. The *Alta California* for November 26, 1857, reported the arrival of the camels at Los Angeles:

> They caused a great curiosity and scared all the horses, mules and children. When the docility of the animals was proved, they were all anxious to take a ride on the humps of those awkward locomotives. They remained but two days and then went to join the remainder of the train which had followed up the east side of the mountains to Tejon. The road has been duly surveyed to the Colorado, but it is understood that Mr. Beale intends to terminate it at Tejon, without coming to Los Angeles, and much dissatisfaction is expressed.
>
> Lieutenant Beale has used the national dromedaries to build a road up to his rancho at the Tejon and he alone will benefit by it.

The *Alta California* criticized Beale unjustly. His instructions specifically directed him to proceed from the Colorado to Fort Tejon. Nowhere had Los Angeles been mentioned as the western terminus of his expedition.

The rebuilding of Fort Tejon following the earthquake of January, 1857, was proceeding when Beale got there. The Los Angeles *Star* reported in November that, "All of the buildings are finished and furnished in the best style and the post is generally acknowledged to be one of the finest, if not the best post, on the Pacific Coast."

Beale dispatched Lieutenant Thorburn to Washington with his field notes and then made preparations for the expedition's return to Fort Defiance. He sent some of the camels to a camp in the Sierra Nevada where they lived for two months in snow to determine the animal's ability to withstand cold weather. Beale said they "fattened and thrived wonderfully the while."

Final supplies were drawn at Los Angeles and Beale left that city on January 10, 1858, for the return eastward. He commanded a party of twenty men, including the seven soldiers from Fort Defiance. Major George Alexander Blake — whom Beale had befriended at Fort Massachusetts, Colorado, in 1853 — commanded a detail of dragoons from Fort Tejon to escort Beale to the Colorado. They reached the river on January 23.

The side-wheel steamer *General Jesup* had been on the lower Colorado since 1854. Under command of its owner, Captain George Alonzo Johnson, the 104-foot boat carried supplies from ships in the Sea of Cortez up to Fort Yuma and other settlements on the river. While Beale re-formed his expedition in California, Johnson had sailed his boat on a free-lance exploration more than 300 miles up the Colorado from Yuma, entering Pyramid Canyon some twenty miles above Beale's Crossing. The steamer, on its way back to Fort Yuma, paused on January 23, 1858, as Beale's eastbound party arrived at the river. The ensuing scene, at once strange and startlingly anachronistic, was not lost on Beale. He described it in a letter to Secretary Floyd:

> I had brought the camels with me, and as they stood on the bank, surrounded by hundreds of wild, unclad savages, mixed with these the dragoons of my escort and the steamer slowly revolving her wheels preparatory to a start, it was a curious and interesting picture.

Camels, mules, horses, soldiers, mountain men, Indians, explorers, boatmen; an awkward and incongruous side-wheeler with steam up and wood smoke pluming from her single stack; a wide, shallow, swift, perverse, canyon-carving, silt-laden river born in Wyoming's Wind River Range and wet-nursed by the glacial peaks of Colorado; an arid and hostile desert stretching for days on end in all directions; and here, at Beale's Crossing, the final two spearheads of the popular "force" that some called Manifest Destiny. A "curious and interesting picture" indeed!

Beale wanted to keep the camels with him on the return journey, but heard a rumor among the dragoons that a company of volunteers might be sent to Utah. It would be an opportunity for the camels to be used for their originally intended "military purpose." He added a postscript to his letter to Floyd:

Due to the threatening appearance of our affairs in Utah, I sent the camels back to Fort Tejon where they may be needed in the spring. Captain Johnson placed his steamer at my disposal and our party was transported with all our baggage to the other side. We then swam the mules over without loss and bid Major Blake goodbye. Captain Johnson was soon steaming down the river toward Fort Yuma and we left the river on our homeward journey.

Beale was pleased to find how clearly the wagons had defined the road. "The Indians have already commenced to follow our broad, well beaten trail, and horse, mule, mocassin and bare-footed tracks are quite plenty on the road." George R. Stewart said about the Humboldt River emigrant route that a trail is a fragile and delicate thing, like some kinds of plants and animals unable to withstand the advances of civilization; "do enough work on a trail and send enough traffic over it, and it necessarily becomes a road." That's what apparently happened to Beale's fresh wheel-marks. By popular use, his trace necessarily became a road.

Day by day the party went back over its trail, camping where they had passed before — sometimes shortening the way and often discovering new springs. But looking for water was no longer the main problem. Warlike Indians followed and watched. On the morning of January 27, the camp came under attack. One mule was killed and another wounded, but none of Beale's men were injured. Two Indians died in the skirmish.

Back at Zuni on Febrary 17, Beale released Sergeant Armstrong and the six other soldiers who had been with him for so many months. "They were excellent men," Beale wrote, "and I parted with them with great regret. I sent them back to Fort Defiance . . ."

Beale reached Albuquerque on the Twenty-first, after an absence of seven months, and brought his journal to a conclusion:

Here my labors ended, a year in the wilderness ended! During this time I have conducted my party from the Gulf of Mexico to the shores of the Pacific and back again to the eastern terminus of the road, through country a great part entirely unknown and inhabited by hostile Indians, without loss of a man. I have tested the value of the camels, marked a new road to the Pacific, and traveled 4000 miles without an accident.

Beale's road today is very close to the route of Interstate 40 and the Atchison, Topeka & Santa Fe Railroad. Others had gone before Beale — Young and Carson, Whipple and Aubry and Sitgreaves — but it remained for Edward Beale to establish a short, straight road which wagons could follow. It was Beale's Road, and that's the name it carried for many years. Beale's name graces several points in Arizona, particularly in and around Kingman. The tiny town of Truxton, despite its misspelling, is named for Beale's son.

Beale's survey was one of the last major explorations to be made into unknown territory in the United States. Its significance is attested to by the major highway and railroad, and at least in a figurative sense by the ranches and towns and cities that occupy the sites where he found sweet water and broke brush for his campfires.

Beale settled accounts and disbanded his expedition at Albuquerque. He rode a stagecoach back to Missouri and addressed his last communication to Secretary Floyd from Kansas City on March 23, 1858:

> I have the honor to report my arrival at this place after a successful and agreeable winter journey over the road which I explored last summer, in obedience to your orders. In a previous letter I informed you that I sent the camels back to Fort Tejon from the Colorado River that they might be used in the campaign against Utah [which they never were]. I parted with these fine brutes with great regret, attached to them with feelings, I think, stronger than one experiences for either the horse or dog. It is to be hoped the government will continue the importation of this valuable animal until sufficient have been procured for the service of the whole army.
>
> I have obeyed your instructions as faithfully as I was able to under the circumstances to do, and hope to find my reward in the approval of the department of what has been done.

Beale headed east and stopped overnight in St. Louis. From the porch of the Planters Hotel, he happened to glance at a passing farm wagon piled high with cordwood. The driver had a familiar look about him. Beale peered at the blue army overcoat, the battered hat and muddy boots. He stared at the stubby beard and the unkempt appearance and then let out a whoop as he recognized Ulysses Grant.

The story goes that Beale asked his old friend Sam Grant quite directly, as was his habit, what in the world he was doing. "Well, Ned," came the reply, "as you can see, I'm hauling wood." They laughed and pounded each other on the back a few more times and then Beale took Grant into the hotel to have dinner with him, despite Grant's protests that he was "not dressed for company."

Over dinner, they related events of the four years since Grant had left the Army in California. He had fallen on hard times and now lived in a log cabin built with the help of neighbors, scratching out a living on a farm he called Hardscrabble. His only source of income, he told Beale, was the sale of cordwood from his lot. It is generally considered that their later intimate and loyal friendship stemmed from this chance meeting in St. Louis.

Beale returned to Washington and found that the War Department approved most highly of his survey. They liked the route so well, in fact, that they wanted Beale and his camels to go back to the desert and finish constructing the wagon road.

14

The Great Wagon Road

Edward Beale's activities in the West created a stir in Congress, as usual, and put him once more in the center of public attention in Washington. Secretary Floyd suggested on March 2, 1858, that "a small appropriation, say fifteen hundred dollars," would be enough to have a report completed and published. Congress approved. On May 10, Floyd advised House Speaker James L. Orr of the delivery of a "report of the exploration of the wagon road from Fort Defiance to the Colorado River in the Territory of New Mexico, made by Edward F. Beale, Esq., and a copy of the map accompanying same."

On May 22, Floyd expressed, with obvious pride, his opinion of Beale's road to M. A. Otero, Congressional delegate from New Mexico Territory:

> The road from Albuquerque to the Colorado River is of very great importance, comparing favorably with any other and in some particulars is superior. In a military point of view, by its construction and the settlements it will superinduce upon its whole length, it will present a line of defense against the Indians. The report which Mr. Beale made demonstrates, in my opinion, that a wise economy would warrant the appropriation of $100,000 toward completion of an enterprise so auspiciously begun.

Speaking as though the road were already completed, Otero told the Santa Fe *Weekly Gazette,* with more than a little optimism, that a large emigration was expected to use the new route "starting at Fort Smith, Arkansas, and passing by Albuquerque to California." It would be perfectly safe, Otero said, for very small parties to undertake the trip. "It is the safest, shortest and best route in every respect for emigrants." Nothing in Beale's report suggested the route to be safe, however, until military posts were established along the way. In fact, Otero's statements were dangerously inaccurate. Hazards existed on all the emigrant trails to California in 1858, but no hazard greater than the Mohave Indians along the Colorado River.

Beale remained at home in Chester with Mary while Congress debated construction of the road. Finally, on August 5, Beale received a letter from Floyd advising him the appropriation had been approved. In addition, Congress awarded another $50,000 for Beale to improve the road from Fort Smith, Arkansas, to Albuquerque. Floyd's instructions of August 5, 11, and 16 were explicit:

> . . . You will proceed to connect the road with the work you were engaged on last year with as much dispatch as possible . . .
>
> All previous instructions, orders and letters from this department will remain in force . . .
>
> For the further trial of camels . . . you will be furnished with such a number of those animals as you may select . . .
>
> . . . Your salary has been increased to $4000 per annum . . .
>
> [You are authorized] to purchase from the Ordnance Department Colt's pistols and such other arms as [you] may require . . .
>
> It is not supposed that the sum appropriated is sufficient to construct a complete road . . .

The last paragraph gave Beale some comfort because the appropriation did not meet the estimates submitted with his report. Past experience taught him appropriations never covered the cost of projects for which they were intended, but somehow the deficits were usually made up.

Beale completed his preparations by the middle of September. Beale's brother-in-law Harry Edwards and Fred Kerlin joined the party, along with Surgeon William P. Floyd, cartographer J. R. Crump and Sindall the artist. Jesse Chisholm again served as guide, and a Shawnee Indian named Little Axe as scout and hunter. Richard Brown, the Delaware Indian who had been with Beale in 1853, also joined the party as a hunter. All were assembled at Fort Smith by the middle of October. A detachment of the Third Infantry under the command of Lieutenant Alexander E. Steen drew the assignment as military escort. Beale ordered twenty-five camels up from Texas.

Major General David E. Twiggs had replaced Colonel Albert Sidney Johnston in command of the Department of Texas. He was an old Army man, a veteran of the War of 1812 and the Mexican War. As a commander of cavalry, he considered the detachment of forty-six camels at Camp Verde to be something less than a military asset. He expressed his opinion to the Adjutant General:

> I have seen these camels and would much prefer mules for packing. As these animals render no service, I trust their expense will not be included in that of this department. According to some reports of the road makers, they never eat nor drink. If such is the fact, they had all better be sent on the roads, as at Camp Verde the full forage ration of grain is issued to them.

It was with certain satisfaction, then, that Twiggs passed on the order to release twenty-five of them from Camp Verde.

Beale sent word to his partner Samuel A. Bishop at Rancho la Liebre. Beale told him to recruit a party of men, obtain supplies and camels from Fort Tejon, and stand by at the Colorado to move eastward on receipt of further instructions. These supplies from California would allow Beale to move westward from Albuquerque with lighter loads.

A message arrived at Fort Smith reporting a Comanche uprising in New Mexico. This news didn't move Beale to postpone the expedition, but he did caution Lieutenant Steen:

> In consequence of the late battle between U. S. troops and the Comanches, making a war with that numerous . . . tribe, through the center of which our route lays, a certain matter, I would suggest that you add to your command at least two pieces of artillery.
>
> I consider this addition [for] the safety of your own men, as well as to the party accompanying me.

The Lieutenant obtained two field pieces from Fort Smith and in the absence of artillery horses took the necessary number from a cavalry regiment at the post. Beale's recommendation for artillery in this case was a considered acknowledgement of two certainties: The Comanches were unsurpassed in their ability to wage war on the western prairies; an infantry escort would be of no use whatever on the plains without the authority of a cannon or two.

Covering this action, Beale advised Secretary Floyd that "Lieutenant Steen acted at my suggestion in accordance with what I believed would have been your views had you been present." He also requisitioned fifty Colt pistols and ammunition. Beale countered the post Quartermaster's request for payment of $1000 with the assurance that he was only borrowing them. He would return them at the end of the expedition, he said, and pay for any that were lost.

Beale's party got underway on November 1, taking two months to grade and improve the road in bad weather from Fort Smith to Albuquerque. Embankments were cut down with pickaxe and shovel. Trees were felled with axe and saw to make bridges. The road followed the general course of the Canadian River for a distance of 780 miles through Indian Territory (now Oklahoma), the Texas Panhandle and into New Mexico.

Lieutenant Steen's military escort proved to be all but worthless to Beale. They lagged far behind the road party, delaying the entire project and providing no protection whatsoever. Beale grew tired of Steen's incompetence and proceeded ahead of the escort, describing the soldiers as "only an embarrassment."

The Fort Smith *Times* announced on November 24 the return of Harry Edwards from Beale's camp. Edwards went to New York on road business, expecting to rejoin the expedition at Albuquerque sometime during the winter.

In his first report to Secretary Floyd on January 3, 1859, Beale advised that the amount appropriated for bridging the many creeks would be totally inadequate. The temporary wooden bridges would last only until others could be built of iron. Beale noted that prairie fires and drunken or hostile Indians were hell on wooden bridges, "and an annual outlay would be necessary to replace that which, built of the proper material, would forever remain indestructible." The department accepted Beale's recommendation. Funds were provided for iron bridges to be made up in sections and shipped from Philadelphia.

Beale could not refrain from describing the admirable character of his route for emigration purposes. Grass, wood and water were abundant. Work oxen killed for food "provided beef fit for the markets of Philadelphia or New York," or so he said.

Although the party reached Hatch's Ranch near Albuquerque without molestation from the Comanches, Beale continued to cite the need for military posts to protect emigrant trains. He had not been instructed to look for a railroad route, but stressed, prophetically, that a rail and emigrant wagon road "might run side by side for the entire distance."

Beale took a few days off and rode from Albuquerque to Taos, some 130 miles northeast, where he purchased 250 sheep from Kit Carson as a supplemental food supply.

Beale found at Albuquerque a sixty-three-year-old Baptist clergyman, John Udell, guiding the J. L. Rose party of Iowa and Missouri emigrants bound for California. Udell had been to California three times before, but had just failed in his fourth attempt. Udell's wagons had followed the 1857 track of Beale's Road across New Mexico and Arizona all the way to the Colorado River. There his party met swift disaster at the hands of the Indians. Beale reported the incident to Floyd:

> They arrived upon the banks of the Colorado with their stock in such a condition as to have insured the most successful and profitable termination to their labors. At this point they were attacked in overwhelming numbers, men and women were murdered indiscriminately by the Indians, and in the first onset eight of their number left dead upon the field . . .
>
> We cannot but desire to see a dreadful retribution promptly meted out to the savages who have wrought this harm.
>
> . . . Both through the press and in my reports to the department,

I cautioned emigrants and others, that until a post should be established upon that river, it would be madness to attempt to pass from this country to California over that road.

During the preceding thirty years, the Mohave Indians had proven to be particularly treacherous and hostile toward travelers attempting to pass through the desert. Beale had recommended in 1857 that a military post be established at the Colorado to protect the road and the river crossing. His reaction to Udell's tragic encounter with the Mohaves clearly indicates that his patience had come to an end. He urged Floyd to employ a force of fifty dragoons and 300 infantry to sweep both banks of the Colorado and "drive the bloodthirsty wretches from their villages." He even offered to lead the raiding party himself.

A punitive expedition was slow in forming, however, and Beale felt determined to push ahead with his road construction. Udell and elements of his emigrant party, numbering twenty in all, accompanied Beale. The travelers did their share of work on the road in return for Beale's protection, but progress through the San Francisco range dragged at a slower pace than anticipated. Not only that, Beale's supplies dwindled at an alarming rate with the extra workers to feed. When it became apparent he would not reach the Colorado by mid-April, as scheduled, he sent word to Bishop to establish a cache of food at Beale's Crossing and send him the extra men he had recruited.

Bishop left Los Angeles on March 1 with forty men, twelve camels and a train of pack-mules. He ran into trouble with the Indians at the river, however, and had to backtrack some twenty miles to Pah-Ute Creek to cache Beale's supplies. Bishop then proceeded to cross the river further upstream. After another fight with Indians, he joined Beale's party in the San Francisco Mountains. There, as Floyd had anticipated, winter caught up with the expedition. They suffered days on end of miserable rain and snow, but the work went on. Beale's spirit

and optimism never wavered, at least not in his reports to
Floyd:

> The work prosecuted during the entire winter of 1858-59 affords
> a striking and gratifying proof of what I have stated before of the
> route on which I have been employed, that winter offers no obstacle
> on that parallel to the passage of men and wagons, or travel of any
> description . . .

Beale worried about his reputation and felt that any failure
of the road, due even to bad weather, would be a direct reflection on his abilities.

Beale determined to push on ahead as rapidly as possible
to get the emigrants to California, then pick up the supplies
Bishop had cached at Pah-Ute Creek. The remaining food in
camp would suffice until his return. The cached goods would
be enough to get the entire work party to California.

Bishop came through with a small advance party and told
Beale of his troubles with the Indians at the river. He said
the Army had sent out a punitive expedition from Fort Tejon
to destroy the Mohave villages. The troops were then to camp
at Beale's Crossing to protect his transit of the river. So
Beale's work party, including the emigrants and Bishop's men,
pushed on toward the river. The Mohaves attacked on the
night of April 27. They killed one mule and ran off another.

That was the final straw for Beale. He moved his party
down the trail in the dark, leaving a small detachment of men
hidden in the rocks. It was an old ruse he had learned from
Kit Carson, one which the more sophisticated plains tribes
would not have fallen for. At daylight, the Indians came into
the abandoned campsite for the dead mule and were set upon
by Beale's men. Four Indians were killed in the skirmish.

Beale's party reached the crest of the rough and broken
Black Mountains on April 30, within sight of the Colorado
River. They saw no sign of the troops supposed to be there.
Beale prepared for a fight. He described a plan in his journal,
in which he would ". . . take with me thirty-five men and three

days provisions on three camels. The men will go on foot so that we shall not be encumbered with mules to guard while we are fighting . . ."

A forced march of twenty-five miles in six hours took them to the river. A band of Indians had been observed waiting for them at the crossing but they scattered into the brush as Beale's men approached. Some of the men "started out to get a shot," as Beale put it, when three white men appeared. They belonged to a detachment of troops camped a few miles down the river.

Beale learned that Lieutenant Colonel William J. Hoffman of the Sixth Infantry had indeed commanded an expedition against the Mohaves. But instead of destroying the villages Hoffman simply made a hasty treaty with the Indians, who promised to behave. Hoffman then returned to his headquarters at Los Angeles. Beale and his men were intensely disgusted. Beale wrote that the Indians should have been severely punished before any peace treaty was discussed. He said that within twenty steps of the place where Hoffman made his treaty, "we saw sticking to the rough bark of the trees the golden hair of a child whose brains the bloody savages had knocked out . . ."

Beale's anger reached another peak when he found that the soldiers had opened Bishop's cache at Pah-Ute Creek and stolen virtually all the provisions. He fired off an angry letter to Colonel Hoffman:

> I visited the caches a few days after the last [of your] companies passed and found them entirely empty, with the exception of four sides of bacon . . . no one can view the amount of labor necessary to open caches so securely made without seeing that a very large number of men must have been industriously employed for some time at the work. It required two full days labor of forty men constantly employed to render them secure as was thought from molestation.
> . . . It is perhaps unnecessary I should detail the annoyance to me and distress to my men occasioned by this occurrence, but . . . an

important public work is greatly delayed, and the appropriation of Congress for its completion seriously diminished . . .

The theft was no idle prank. The list of provision secured in the cache by Bishop included more than a ton of flour, 1,700 pounds of bacon, 600 pounds of beans, 400 pounds of sugar, 200 pounds of coffee, and large quantities of rice, dried beef, tobacco, soap and spices. Incredibly, everything had vanished except the four sides of bacon.

Colonel Hoffman responded with a vigorous denial that his men had taken the stores:

> They could not have kept the act secret from their officers, nor had they any means of transporting such quantities.
> . . . Two trains of public mules preceeded [my] command, and may have discovered the cache . . .

Hoffman said he would instruct his subordinate, Captain R. B. Garnett, to make inquiry. If anything had been taken by the two companies under him, a full report would be made to Beale. He refrained from mentioning that the "two trains of public mules" were quartermaster stores brought along to supply his command at the river. The only "citizens" were his packers.

In the usual Army way of doing things, Captain Garnett passed the buck to his subordinate, First Lieutenant Clark, who handed it to Second Lieutenant Sawtelle, and he in turn queried Corporal Anderson, who obtained a full report from Privates Knapp and Boyers. The official correspondence in this chain of command from Colonel to Private and back up to Colonel is tedious and not worth repeating.

Beale, still fuming, reported the theft to Secretary Floyd. Accusations, evasions, inquiries, and eventually a token court-martial went on for a period of many months, resolving nothing. Floyd demanded the Army punish those responsible. Investigations and charges and arguments continued interminably. The months stretched into years. It has not been determined in the voluminous paperwork generated by the incident whether Beale ever received payment for the stolen supplies.

While Beale engaged himself in this futile campaign of words with the Army, he and Bishop took the emigrants on to Los Angeles. There he purchased new supplies for his main party, which remained on the east bank of the Colorado at Beale's Crossing.

Beale's men had to defend themselves in repeated skirmishes with the Indians. Major Lewis Addison Armistead, commanding the small detachment at the river, experienced difficulty in coping with these attacks and provided practically no protection for the road crew. Whatever the terms of Hoffman's "treaty" with the Indians, the pact had little effect. It would be years before peace finally settled on the desert.

Beale struggled to get his mind back on the task at hand. A supply train loaded with 6000 pounds of corn made its way from Los Angeles across the Colorado and on to the San Francisco Mountains. Beale addressed Floyd from there on July 16:

> . . . The road is now two-thirds completed and the most formidable obstacle to its success entirely removed — I refer to the rugged Colorado mountains [the San Francisco Mountains] — over this chain a road has been constructed of such a grade that teams or stage coaches may pass with the most perfect ease, with loads of any weight, without doubling the teams [or] locking to go down.
>
> Important springs . . . have also been discovered and the alterations to include them on the direct line of the road has shortened it in every instance . . . I am more than ever disposed from this year's exploration to believe it the best, shortest, and most easily traveled of any thoroughfare leading from the Eastern states to the Pacific.

Once again, Beale couldn't refrain from expressing his respect and affection for the camels:

> I have lately tried effectually the comparative value of mules and camels as pack animals — the experiment leaving the palm with the camels . . . The mules [carrying] a burthen of 200 pounds, the camels packed with 400, besides a rider armed with his rifle, revolver,

and ammunition, and his bedding laid over the pack to set on. [Beale spoke hypothetically. The camels, with rare and unofficial exceptions, were used only as pack animals.] The young are great pets in camp but very mischievous, poking their noses into every . . . pot and pan about the campfires; their great end and aim in life at present seems to ape the manners and habits of their sires . . .

A story published in the Kansas City *Journal of Commerce* for August 25, 1859, gives an informative summation:

> No matter on what route the government may send out its explorers over the plains . . . when they return home we always meet them in Kansas City. Thus . . . yesterday we had the pleasure of greeting Lieutenant Beale on his return from his . . . expedition to the 35th Parallel.
>
> He . . . arrived at this city . . . having traveled with mules that have . . . seen a year's service drawing heavy wagons a distance of 1800 miles – a feat never before performed with a like equipment on the continent . . .
>
> This energetic and efficient officer has now traversed the plains thirteen times . . .

Following his usual custom on completing an expedition, Beale rejoined his family at Chester for several months of rest. During that time he prepared his final report and settled his accounts. Beale's road drew criticism from some quarters but generally met with enthusiastic approval among men familiar with the difficulties of travel in the West. The August 25 *Journal of Commerce* also said that Beale had "done more of the practical character to develop and open up the overland travel on the continent than any other man who has preceded him."

The Philadelphia *Press* published a version of Beale's expedition on October 15 seen through the eyes of its correspondent, "Wanderer." The writer's closing remarks about Beale are of more than passing interest:

> If Edward F. Beale had been a Massachusetts man, his services to his country would have teemed the papers with his exploits, his

daring and his usefulness. Still the people are neglectful of the courage, hardihood and suffering of the man who traversed this continent amid every conceivable danger from disease, the elements, and bands of ruthless savages to prepare a way for new cities and states and greater power and influence for our Republic.

Secretary Floyd approved Beale's accounts in January of 1860. In compliance with a resolution of the House of Representatives on March 8, Floyd provided a copy of Beale's final report to Speaker of the House William Pennington.

Beale now found himself the father of a second daughter, Emily. He intended moving Mary and the children to California and devoting himself to management of the ranch. Meanwhile, there were still a few wooden bridges to be replaced with iron. These he proposed to take care of with a small construction party. He left Chester in June of 1860, accompanied by Fred Kerlin, with an appropriation of $10,000 to complete his work.

He heard the alarming rumor at Westport that Fort Mohave on the Colorado River faced abandonment by the Army. He wrote Floyd that his small party would soon be at the river without escort. He depended on the Fort Mohave garrison to protect his river crossing. Floyd's reply reached him at Albuquerque on July 26. The message assured Beale the War Department would continue to man the fort with two companies of the Sixth Infantry.

The Los Angeles *Star* for September 29 heralded Beale's arrival once again at the Colorado River:

> . . . Lieutenant Beale arrived at Fort Mohave, his party all well. The Indians were hostile all through the route and he was strongly advised not to make the experiment, but he came through without loss of man or animal . . .
>
> He brings the startling intelligence that the Navajos attacked the sutler's store at Fort Defiance and held possession of the post for six hours in the face of four companies of soldiers. Mr. Beale reports the road to be in first rate condition but from the hostility of the

Indians would not encourage emigrants to come that way as their stock would be in danger . . .

To commemorate establishment of Beale's Road across Arizona, a pyramidal monument of stones topped with figures of a camel caravan has been erected in Kingman, Arizona. It bears a bronze tablet inscribed:

EDWARD FITZGERALD BEALE

1822   1893

PIONEER IN THE PATH OF EMPIRE

HERO IN THE WAR WITH MEXICO

LIEUTENANT IN THE UNITED STATES NAVY

APPOINTED GENERAL BY THE GOVERNOR OF CALIFORNIA

COMMANDED EXPLORATION OF WAGON ROUTE TO THE

COLORADO RIVER WITH THE ONLY CAMEL TRAIN

IN AMERICAN HISTORY, 1857-1858

Beale's exploring days came to an end with completion of the wagon road, but not his days of service to his country. The impending war between the states would bring him another call to duty, but not the call that Beale wanted to hear.

15

Surveyor General of California

While Edward Beale occupied himself with road grading and bridge building in the remote Southwest, the nation's complex political structure weakened and became vulnerable to stresses that would nearly destroy it.

James Buchanan's long career of public service ended with his one term as President. John C. Fremont dissuaded those who wanted to put his name up again for President. Fremont announced his support in 1860 to any Republican who favored a Pacific railroad. The Republican National Convention adopted virtually the same platform it had in 1856, calling for a transcontinental railroad and final suppression of the slave trade. The party nominated Abraham Lincoln. Beale pledged his support.

Meanwhile, Beale saw to his affairs and investments in Chester when his road work was finished. After that he took his family to California and turned his attentions to the livestock business at Rancho la Liebre.

Removal of the Tejon Indians to the Tulare River reserve reduced the importance of Fort Tejon. The War Department proposed abandoning the post. Beale protested by dispatching an urgent petition signed by himself, Fred Kerlin, Samuel Bishop and scores of others to General Albert Sidney Johnston on February 28, 1861:

> We, the subscribers, having heard the removal of Fort Tejon is in contemplation, desire to enter our earnest protest against the intention. People are settling and developing the resources of a new country, with the implied assurance from the location of Fort Tejon, of protection for their lives and property. If this protection is to be withdrawn, those who have under its promises made their homes in the wilderness will be left to the mercy of the ruthless savages . . .

We feel justified in remonstrating in the strongest manner against the removal of Fort Tejon.

Before any response to this appeal, news came in April of the assault on Fort Sumter which marked the beginning of the Civil War. The entire garrison of Fort Tejon left on June 15, 1861. Supplies, stock and wagons, including the camels, were sent to Drum Barracks at Wilmington, south of Los Angeles. Fort Tejon remained unoccupied until taken over by the California Volunteers on August 17, 1863. They stayed until September 11, 1864, when the post was abandoned for good.

Shortly after Lincoln's inauguration, Beale received an appointment to the office of United States Surveyor General for California. He had been strongly recommended for the job by Representatives John Hickman and John W. Forney of Pennsylvania, and Secretary of War Simon Cameron.

Beale went to San Francisco, where the survey office was located, and learned from Jessie Fremont that her husband had gone abroad to secure additional financing for the Mariposa mines. She said Lincoln had commissioned Fremont a Major General and that Fremont was on his way back to the States. Jessie and the Fremont children left San Francisco by steamer on May 21. Beale leased their San Francisco cottage at Black Point from Jessie and moved his family up from the ranch.

Beale signed his bond on May 22, 1861. He took up his new job at the Surveyor General's office on the third floor of Henry Wager Halleck's Washington Block (later to be known as the Montgomery Block, or more popularly the "Monkey Block") at the corner of Washington and Montgomery streets. Beale found the staff of ten too small for the demands of the office. Wartime austerity would soon descend upon the General Land Office in Washington, however, and Beale would feel an even tighter pinch in San Francisco. One of Beale's first communications from Commissioner James M. Edmunds instructed him to reduce expenses.

Beale's duties called for him to certify all registrar's reports for sales and locations of properties, complete sketches for private and public land surveys, post bonds for deputy surveyors to be hired under contract, check field notes and prepare maps of townships, keep the early Spanish archives and files of the United States Land Commission, render accounts, and submit quarterly and annual reports.

One of the new clerks hired — despite Edmunds' warning — was a young writer named Francis Bret Harte, a friend of the Fremonts and frequent visitor to Black Point. The Beales "inherited" Harte along with the cottage, and Mary encouraged her husband to find a job for the writer in the Surveyor General's office. Beale also hired Fred Kerlin as a clerk.

There had been several Surveyors General since the California Land Act of 1851. The offices showed the wear and tear of eight years occupancy since completion of the building in 1853. Carpets lay tattered and torn, furniture creaked and sagged, dust and grime covered everything. Neither the rent nor the employees had been paid in six months. Beale found other federal offices in the same sorry state. Many department heads still awaited appointment under the new administration. Everyone seemed to be waiting for something to happen — and nothing happened. Beale seemed to be the right man to start things going.

He found more suitable offices with greater space at a lower cost in a building at the corner of California and Montgomery streets. Beale moved with what he must have regarded as great efficiency as he sold the old furniture and purchased new, paid up the back rent and his staff's salaries, and submitted vouchers to the Washington office for all of these expenditures.

Beale justified all this by advising Commissioner Edmunds that moving the office saved $300 per year in rent. He requested appropriations to be made in advance to pay his staff monthly, and on time. "I feel quite sure," he wrote, "that the officers in Washington are paid regularly."

He noted that a standard fee per lineal mile, regardless of

terrain, had been paid to deputy surveyors for establishing township lines. The contract surveyors consequently chose the flat desert areas and valley areas, easily surveyed but often of no value and little interest to settlers. On the other hand, Beale knew there were hundreds of fine locations between the central valleys and the Pacific Ocean which could be quickly disposed of when properly surveyed and subdivided. "They are well timbered with a good supply of water," he advised Edmunds, "and although somewhat mountainous, they contain many valleys eagerly sought for by the settlers as homesteads."

Beale asked for $150,000 to provide larger fees for surveyors, two additional clerks, and permission to devote two-thirds of his budget to public lands and one-third to private land claims. Beale signed off trusting his requests "would merit the Commissioner's approval."

They did not.

Edmunds wrote back in some pique. He ignored Beale's request for increased budget and staff and zeroed in on the change in office location, "which should not have been done without application being first made for permission to do so." He also issued additional orders:

> Obtain oaths of allegiance from all deputy surveyors, making sure no contracts were given to Knights of the Golden Circle [who supported the Confederacy]; prepare sketches of the country surveyed noting growth of timber, character of diversified products and value of the public domain; and transmit to Washington samples of precious metals, interesting fossils or petrified organic remains.

In addition to a survey executive and administrator, he was now expected to be an inquisitor, artist, timber cruiser, agricultural agent, land appraiser, geologist, archaeologist and paleontologist.

But the bureaucratic frustration wasn't all that chafed Beale. There was a war going on right in his own country, his heartland, and it didn't rest well with a man of Beale's character to remain glued to a government desk while it all happened. He wrote to the President on July 10, 1861:

A short time ago you did me the honor to appoint me to a most important and responsible position for which I beg you to accept my grateful acknowledgement. Under any other condition of public affairs, you have left me nothing to desire; but to the flag under which my father and grandfather fought for the honor and glory of the country, I think I owe something more in this hour of trial than a mere performance of duty in a position of ease and quiet . . .

From fourteen to twenty-five, my life was passed at sea, and for the past fifteen years principally on the great plains and in the Rocky Mountains. I served during the Mexican War, and at its close I resigned and have been engaged in many expeditions of some importance since. I know that I am resolute and active, and if I had no courage my love of country would supply the want of it in such a time as this. Devoted to my country, and owing it everything I have in the world, I write to offer my services to you in any capacity you may wish to use them until the present rebellion is crushed out of the land . . .

President Lincoln's response was not what Beale wanted to hear. With the unsettled situation in California, the President could not afford to have every loyal man leave the state. He urged Beale to continue as Surveyor General. Reluctantly, Beale set about doing the President's bidding. Years later, Beale wrote of the incident:

I wrote to him . . . [to] send me an appointment of any rank whatever in the Union Army. All my relations being in the Confederate service and belonging to slave-holding families, my request was not granted. My appointment as Surveyor General had not so much to do with rods and chains, but the metes and bounds of the nation.

Mary received a letter from her brother, Harry Edwards, who wrote that he was "off to save the Union as captain of the Chester Blues." They also learned that May Humphreys Stacey had been commissioned a First Lieutenant in the Twelfth Infanty Regiment. Some of Beale's Virginia kin signed with the Rebels. Indeed, all their friends and relatives, it seemed, answered the call to serve one cause or the other.

Their minds were taken from the war when tragedy of a

different kind struck in their own home. Their youngest child, Samuel Edwards Beale, died on August 11, 1861, at the tender age of two.

The Army's Department of the Pacific had been under the command of Beale's friend from Fort Tejon, Colonel Benjamin Lloyd Beall, who was soon relieved by Brigadier General Albert Sidney Johnston. When Johnston left San Francisco to join the Confederate forces he was replaced by Brigadier General Edwin Vose Sumner who, upon his arrival, found California in a perilous political situation. Southern Democrats controlled the state government. Army resignations poured in, with one-third of the officers defecting from the Sixth Regiment alone. Sumner received orders to send all the regular troops east as rapidly as they could be replaced by local volunteers. By the end of 1861, all the regulars were gone except small garrisons at Benicia Arsenal and Fort Point. San Francisco businessmen, alarmed at the withdrawal of the regulars, wrote to Secretary of War Cameron:

> A majority of our present state officials are avowed secessionists and three-fifths of our citizens are natives of slave-holding states. There are about 16,000 Knights of the Golden Circle organized in our most loyal districts and the powerful native Mexican population has been won over to the secession side.

Aware of the respect Californios held for their *personas de razon*, Beale solicited an expression of loyalty from the most influential of them, the Pico brothers. Pio Pico had voted for Lincoln, but Andres was a registered Democrat. Beale addressed a letter to Andres Pico on June 6, 1861:

> The high respect I entertain for you induces me to write this letter, and I trust you will receive it as a proof of friendship on my part. I desire to know if you are in favor of maintaining the present federal government of the United States at all hazards, or if you favor under any circumstances a Pacific republic and the secession of the state. Your social position and the influence of a powerful family connection make your reply of substantial importance, and I trust will be such as to give those who have already had occasion to admire

your gallantry in the field of battle additional reason to desire your esteem.

You cannot but be aware that any attempt of the few disaffected men of the southern portion of the state to create a rebellion against the government would lead to scenes of violence and bloodshed dreadful to contemplate. Permit me to ask that you will also submit this letter to your distinguished brother, Señor Don Pio Pico, and also that he will join in your reply.

Beale was gratified to receive an almost immediate reply from Andres Pico:

> My distinguished friend, I hasten to reply to your favor, thanking you for the opinion you entertain of me. On the acquisition of California by the United States of America, I elected to become a member of the confederation, adopting the citizenship of the same, of which I am proud. Although my political opinions have differed from those of the Republican Party, these considerations cease in the face of the attack made against the federal government. Unconditionally, at all hazards, I am for the constitution and the Union entire, to maintain which I would cheerfully offer as a soldier my sword, and as a citizen my fortune.

Andres had become so Americanized that he signed his letter, "Andrew." Pio Pico also wrote to Beale:

> My brother, Don Andres, has shown me your letter. My acts, and my vote placed in the ballot box in favor of the worthy President ... are faithful testimonials of my political opinions. Although I lament the disturbance occasioned by the southern states, I approve the energetic measures adopted by the government for the preservation at all costs of the constitution and the Union entire.

Both letters received wide publication. The *Daily Alta California* of June 8, 1861, commented, "It is very satisfactory to know that the Picos are sound on the Union question." As Beale had anticipated, the numerous friends and relatives of the Picos were favorably influenced by these expressions of loyalty.

Beale joined the Home League in San Francisco, an association promoting enlistments and supporting the administration in Washington. But California Adjutant General William Kibbe notified General Halleck that 20,000 to 30,000 California men had joined secret organizations for the overthrow of the government. They intended to "carry the state out of the Union."

Beale became convinced that should the Conscription Act be imposed in California the result would be open warfare. The state would surely fall to the Rebels. He transmitted this message to President Lincoln, who responded, "The draft is suspended in California until General Beale shall indicate that the times are more auspicious." The times never became more auspicious. California remained the only Union state which did not enforce compulsory conscription.

Meanwhile, Beale's headaches at the survey office originated not only with the Washington bureaucracy. Land ownership in California had been incredibly confused. It was the duty of the Surveyor General to help untangle the maze of Spanish, Mexican and American property claims. Most of the survey work in connection with these claims had been completed by others, but Beale inherited many residual problems connected with claims still in litigation.

At one point Edmunds castigated Beale for including Rancho la Liebre in a survey, although Beale's instructions from Edmunds specifically gave priority to mapping private grants.

As a further complication of his duties, Beale had to maintain a crew of men in the mountains of California keeping pace with Theodore Judah's surveyors on the Central Pacific Railroad. On January 8, 1863, Governor Leland Stanford turned the first shovelful of dirt at the Sacramento River levee symbolizing the start of construction. A large crowd assembled and responded to Charles Crocker's call for nine rousing cheers. A band blared, causing nervous ripples through nearby teams of mules and horses. Oratory commenced, and sometime later it ended. The Central Pacific was on its way. A mural depicting the ceremonial scene shows Judah near the speaker's platform. Beale probably attended too, but neither he nor Judah were listed among the speakers.

Meanwhile, the livestock business at Rancho la Liebre prospered. Thanks to Beale's considerate treatment of the California Indians in 1855, and afterward, a large supply of self-supporting laborers were permantly settled on the ranch and growing their own food. Indians made up the work force of herders, shearers and vaqueros, while the squaws provided a reservoir of domestic servants.

To add to the ranch's water supply Beale purchased eighty acres encompassing Willow Springs in Antelope Valley for $100, and an additional forty acres for $50. Both parcels were public lands sold at the going rate of $1.25 per acre. He subsequently became involved in a number of real estate transactions throughout the state, apparently using his office from time to time to further his personal interests.

Beale is listed as one of five trustees who incorporated the Soledad Gold, Silver and Copper Mining Company in Soledad Canyon north of Los Angeles. The company planned to set up a $780,000 reduction mill to process ore mined in Santa Barbara and Los Angeles counties. The Los Angeles *Southern News* reported on June 20, 1862, that the company was importing heavy machinery.

The San Francisco *Daily Alta California* noted in 1863 that Beale had expanded his mining interests by buying into the New Antrim Gold and Silver Mining Company, capitalized at $617,000. The firm owned claims in the Slate Range of Southern California, near the Panamint Mountains and Death Valley.

Beale took on added official responsibilities in 1863 when he was made Surveyor General of Nevada Territory as well as California.

Beale found his budget trimmed again in 1863 as a war economy from $17,300 for salaries to $15,000. His own salary dwindled from $4500 to $3000. Forced to cut down his staff, he found employment for Bret Harte in the San Francisco branch of the U. S. Mint. There the young writer found his clerical duties less demanding and had more time for his literary efforts.

With reduced staff and increased responsibilities, Beale found it impossible to keep up with the work load. Nor could he operate within his reduced budget. He and Edmunds constantly butted heads over expenses. Complaints filtered through the Washington office about tardy reports and accounts, and delays in fulfilling surveying contracts. Criticism arose over his lack of technical qualifications and administrative experience. While not a professional engineer, Beale's practical experience gained as a navigator in the Navy and during three years on the wagon road served him well. But no matter, the hounds bayed close at his heels.

Further economies were pressed on his office. His expenses underwent frequent review and the cost of such things as tracing paper and the laundering of towels were not considered too insignificant to be brought to his attention by clerks in the Washington office. "Stricter economies will be required in these matters in the future" became a frequent admonition.

Beale's reports, although tardy, were accurate and complete and he was never charged with negligence in that regard. He felt he had more important things to do than worry about the cost of laundering towels. He continued to do the best he could, but Beale's position in government seemed once again to be on shaky ground.

The Beales had to vacate Fremont's cottage in 1863. Fremont learned that his land "encroached" on property which in 1850 had been declared a military reservation. Fremont protested this seizure in the courts but never received compensation for the loss. The Army evicted Beale and tore down the Black Point cottage. Ironically, the post became Fort Mason, named for Colonel Richard Barnes Mason, former Military Governor of California. Fremont had challenged him to a duel in 1847. The duel never came off but Mason, it seems, now had the final satisfaction.

The Beales moved to living quarters at 821 Bush Street on the warm southern slope of Nob Hill.

For the fiscal year 1863-64, Beale's budget remained at

$15,000 with an additional $10,000 for his work in Nevada. His duties east of the Sierra consisted of mapping only those areas "over which township lines have heretofore been extended."

He was admonished to devote as much of his funds as possible to surveys along the route of the railroad, which he did. Thanks to the Homestead Act, the coming of the railroad, and Beale's insistence on surveying the most desirable public lands, more property went into private ownership during the years of his tenure in the Surveyor General's office than in any similar period since the conquest.

Toward the end of 1863 he received a letter of bitter incrimination from Joseph S. Wilson, Acting Commissioner of the General Land Office, complaining about his office expenses. Along with Wilson's letter came instructions to submit all subsequent contracts for deputy surveyors to Washington before the work could be authorized. Beale had been relegated to the rank of clerk.

Beale's insistence on doing things his own way and largely according to his own personal schedule and budget — right or wrong — kept him perpetually at odds with his superiors. Beale could not easily bend to accommodate the bureaucracy, and it is chiseled in stone that the bureaucracy bends to accommodate no man. The stultifying density of the federal system perhaps no longer dismayed Beale, but the steady erosion factor eventually wore him down. Beale himself must share responsibility for his debacle, however. He had devoted a great deal of his time to personal affairs and had used the weight of his position for his own benefit. The practice was universal in those days, but Beale's speedy decline as Surveyor General must be attributed largely to his own actions.

By the end of 1863 Beale's duties had become so onerous and his relationship with his superiors so strained that he requested U. S. Senator John Conness to intercede with the President. He asked again that he be relieved of his office and given a military command. Senator Conness transmitted the request, without recommendation, to President Lincoln on February 6, 1864, along with a copy of Beale's earlier petition of July 10, 1861.

No response came from the White House. Beale never did receive a commission in the Army. Meanwhile Edmunds, at the end of his patience, determined to have Beale removed from office. Three weeks later a formal letter arrived from the Land Office advising simply that Beale's official duties would terminate on the day preceding the arrival of his successor. He was replaced by Lauren Upson on April 19, 1864.

With a great sigh of relief — a sigh heard perhaps in Washington as well as San Francisco — Beale settled the affairs of his office. He gathered up his family in San Francisco and took off for the peace and quiet of Rancho la Liebre.

His "retirement" didn't last long, however. While America remained preoccupied with the Civil War, France, England and Spain each sought to overthrow the Republic of Mexico. Edward Beale had been quietly trying to do something about it.

16

California Ranchero

Mexico, occupied with a Civil War of its own from 1855 to 1861, found itself in a state of financial ruin. Its debts, acknowledged by President Pablo Benito Juarez to be some $82 million, were owed to Britain, Spain and France. These nations claimed the only way to collect was by force of arms, but the real interests of Spain and France were not financial. Both countries had territorial ambitions in North America. France's invasion had little to do with the money Mexico owed her.

Outbreak of the American Civil War in 1861 weakened the United States at a time when Mexico needed support against these European powers — although Mexico understandably feared the political strings which would surely be attached to U. S. assistance. Certain Mexican conservatives and monarchists sought a European Prince to come to Mexico and "stabilize" the nation. Spain and Napoleon III of France decided to take this responsibility upon themselves. England went along with the plan for awhile, interested primarily in collecting her debt. The three nations invaded Mexico in the winter of 1861-62.

Napoleon III decided that Ferdinand Maximilian Josef, the "sailor Prince," younger brother of Emperor Franz Josef I of Austria, should be the ruler of Mexico. Napoleon made it clear that France, with the help of Mexican conservative factions, would be the dominant power in Mexico. Spain and Britain, perhaps seeing how the wind blew, decided to withdraw. Juarez took a beating from the French at Puebla. He retreated with his 6000 troops to northern Mexico.

Edward Beale followed these developments with intense interest. They revived his earlier concerns with the status of

Lower California and the mouth of the Colorado River. He wrote to Secretary of the Treasury Salmon P. Chase on August 5, 1863:

> I desire to call your attention to the fact that we have in our power at this time by purchase of Lower California and a very small portion of the opposite coast to possess the mouth of the Colorado. We should then control entirely the navigation of the Colorado which the future will prove the utmost importance to the welfare of the Pacific Coast states.
>
> This cannot have escaped the French sagacity, and if it is not purchased now or taken possession of by us, it may very soon be too late to do so . . . It might easily be accomplished by a purchase from the government [Juarez] party lately expelled from the City of Mexico by the French . . . I offer my services to you in any manner in which I can serve.

Secretary Chase replied by letter to Beale's suggestion on September 5:

> I appreciate as you do the importance of the acquisition you suggest. I fear that the Juarez government is now too entirely broken to warrant negotiations with it, but I will confer with the President and the Secretary of State . . .
>
> What a pity it is that when General Scott took Mexico he did not remain there and establish a protectorate, a policy which would have prevented all our present troubles as far as French domination in Mexico is concerned.

Beale addressed another letter to Chase from San Francisco on November 5:

> I trust you will not think I underrate the hazards of a war with France . . . Since your letter I find Juarez is again at the head of a respectable army, and we will recognize his government, why could not a secret treaty of purchase be made with him and kept secret for the present until we have more time to devote to outside matters?

There was no response from Chase on this fanciful plan — only one of many land-grabbing schemes concerning Mexico — and it proceeded no further. All such ideas for U. S. interference, in fact, were doomed to failure from the start. Mexico had long since acquired for her northern neighbor a distrust so monumental that its traces are still clearly visible in the closing decades of the twentieth century.

In his communications Beale did not mention to Chase that General Placido Vega, commander of the Juarez Sinaloa Brigade, had come to San Francisco soliciting support for the Mexican Republic cause. Beale and others pledged themselves to render what assistance they could. Vega responded by including Beale in a lucrative salt mining lease arranged with the Juarez government.

In a series of meetings with Sam Brannan, George Green, Harry Lake and General Vega, Beale agreed to act as Vega's agent in shipping to Juarez a supply of Austrian arms consigned to San Francisco from Canada. In addition, San Brannan agreed to finance, outfit, arm and transport a company of 100 volunteers to a prearranged Mexican port. Brannan kept his word and expended $16,000 to outfit the "Brannan Contingent" that sailed from San Francisco in the spring of 1864, thus violating the country's neutrality laws and an 1862 Presidential directive prohibiting arms exports.

The arms intended for Juarez included a shipment of 5000 rifles packed in 208 cases stored in a San Francisco warehouse. Before Beale could smuggle them off to Mexico, however, San Francisco Port Collector Charles James impounded them.

Vega secured assistance from many Americans, working through pro-Mexican societies in Virginia City, Hornitos, Marysville and Sonora as well as larger cities in the West.

Beale wrote to Port Collector James on July 16, 1864, that Lincoln's edict against exporting arms referred only to the Confederacy. Beale's rifles were intended to restore the independence of the friendly Republic of Mexico. James replied on the Nineteenth that Lincoln's directive meant no arms were to be exported to any country for any purpose. The guns remained in their packing cases in the warehouse.

Beale departed for the East with his family, hoping to

get State Department clearance to assist Juarez. The Delaware County *Republican* of Chester reported on October 7 that "General Edward F. Beale and family arrived from California last week."

Beale supported every phase of Lincoln's first administration as an outspoken Unionist. He now found himself recognized as a leading Republican from the West. He strongly urged the reelection of President Lincoln in a patriotic speech at National Hall in Chester, where he likened Lincoln's opponent, the diminutive General George Brinton McClellan, to a bonsai tree, "one of those rare botanical curiosities from far off Japan — a giant pine tree in a flower pot." Beale took the opportunity in this speech to call for support of the Mexican struggle for independence.

Backed by Secretary Chase and General Fremont, Beale urged Lincoln to invoke the Monroe Doctrine. Lincoln refused, as he had in 1861 when Secretary of State William Henry Seward suggested the same thing. Lincoln already had one war too many on his hands. He did not question the right of France to seek redress of her grievances, providing she did not impair the right of the Mexican people to freely choose their own government. The President said:

> Napoleon has taken advantage of our weakness in our time of trouble in utter disregard of the Monroe Doctrine, but my policy must be to attend to one trouble at a time. If we get well out of our present difficulties and restore the Union, I propose to notify Napoleon that it is about time to take his army out of Mexico.

Not put off by the President's caution, Beale, Chase and Fremont had several new planks added to the party's platform. They condemned Napoleon's intervention in Mexico and demanded removal of the French troops. They also proposed a bill whereby this country would guarantee payment of three percent interest to France on the Mexican debts for a five-year period, during which time the two countries might settle their differences by negotiation. Needless to say, this proposal got nowhere in Congress.

Beale returned to the West Coast soon after the election. The Sacramento *Union* for December 24, 1864, reported Beale and General H. M. Naglee as passengers on the *Constitution*.

France began to realize by March of 1865 that war with the United States loomed as a distinct possibility. Not only that, France worried more and more that Prussian Chancellor Otto von Bismarck had designs on France. Napoleon began to respond to the growing Prussian-German threat by bringing home his scattered troops — including those in Mexico.

The end of the American Civil War brought repeal of Lincoln's directive prohibiting the exportation of arms. General Grant ordered Major General Philip H. Sheridan to the Rio Grande in a letter dated May 17, 1865. Sheridan was not only to receive the surrender of Confederate forces under Major General Edmund Kirby Smith of Texas, but reinforce the Rio Grande as well and place himself in a position to assist Juarez against Maximilian.

Consequently, several thousand of the Army's new repeating rifles, superior to anything the French had, found their way across the Rio Grande to the Juarez headquarters in Chihuahua. And, finally, Beale's 5000 Austrian rifles were shipped off to Acapulco.

Napoleon advised Maximilian that he could not support troops in Mexico after April of 1866. Bismarck had become too great a threat to France. Grant itched to go after the French in Mexico but Napoleon finally debarked his troops from Vera Cruz early in 1867. As the tricolor came down for the last time, the scattered forces of Benito Juarez gathered together, shouldered the arms sent to them by Sheridan and Beale, and marched on Maximilian.

Their meeting at Queretaro was a climactic episode in Mexican history. Juarez lay siege to the city. Maximilian surrendered after two months. A military tribunal condemned him to death and he died on the "Hill of The Bells" in front of a firing squad on June 19, 1867. President Juarez once again raised the standard of the Republic of Mexico over the National Palace.

In his declining years, Sam Brannan petitioned the Mexican government for relief in consideration of the $16,000 spent on the "Brannan Contingent" and received a large parcel of land in Sonora.

Beale's influence as a friend of Mexico was also not forgotten. He chaired a meeting in 1884 of the Union League in New York with Mexican President Porfirio Diaz as the principal speaker. Diaz singled out Beale as "a friend of Mexico in her hour of trial, and one who contributed mightily to the restoration of her liberties." We can assume Diaz spoke of Beale's "contribution" of the rifles for Juarez rather than Beale's plans for gaining more Mexican territory for the United States.

While Beale involved himself in running guns to Juarez, he also worked to expand his land holdings in California. He purchased 97,000-acre Rancho El Tejon from John Temple and Ignacio del Valle on February 9, 1865, for $21,000 in gold. On May 1, 1865, he bought the 35,000 acres of Rancho Los Alamos y Agua Caliente from Agustin Olvera for $1,700. Both of these parcels adjoined his Rancho la Liebre.

Bonsal states in his biography that "General Beale purchased all of his land in California long before he became Surveyor General." It has also been claimed, sarcastically, that President Lincoln felt reluctant to appoint Beale to the post because "Beale became monarch of all he surveyed." Neither statement is true. Except for Rancho la Liebre, purchased in 1855, and the two small parcels at Willow Springs, Beale bought all of his land in 1865 and 1866, after Lincoln's death and a year or more after Beale left the survey office. There seems little doubt, however, that Beale took steps during his term as Surveyor General to investigate these properties and pave the way for their eventual purchase.

On May 3, 1865, Beale wrote from the ranch to Mary and the children at Chester:

> The past few days have been of excessive labor. On the first of
> May I rode from noon until six o'clock, forty-five miles, working hard

on the *rodeo* with from 5000 to 7000 head of cattle, parting out 500 for market. The country is in a very disturbed condition. Robbers swarm over it and only today some fifty soldiers stopped here looking for a large party of thieves who had stolen from my rancho a large herd of one of my neighbor's horses, who had just collected them to gather his cattle with . . . So far they have not robbed me but my turn may come, and when it does I shall defend my property as long as I have life. Our house is well provided with arms and my people are faithful and attached so that I feel prepared and secure.

Beale joined his family back at Chester toward the end of 1865 for a visit that became an annual custom. The Beale family never broke its ties with the East, but spent much time in the healthful climate of California.

Beale had long since become a person of some consequence in Chester, where he often found himself in demand as a public speaker. The Delaware County *Republican* reported two such occasions during this visit. On November 5, he spoke in the County Courthouse at Media to the organizational meeting of the Ladies Monday Association. On the Seventeenth, he delivered an address in Chester on "The Enfranchisement of the Colored Race."

The Beales returned to the Tejon in the spring of 1866. In their absence, Kern County had been carved out of portions of Tulare and Los Angeles counties. Beale's holdings were mostly in Kern County, named after topographer Edward Kern. The Beales' residence on Rancho la Liebre, however, established them as taxpayers in Los Angeles County.

Beale had performed considerable work at his own expense on the road between Fort Tejon and Los Angeles for the purpose of operating it as a toll road. "Beale's Cut" through the steep hills north of Mission San Fernando required deep excavation and heavy grading over a period of several years before the Los Angeles County Board of Supervisors gave the project its final approval. Beale operated the toll road franchise under a twenty-year contract with the county. Toll collector O. P. Robbins became a familiar figure to travelers as he manned the gate at the foot of the grade.

Beale also invested heavily in speculative oil lands in Southern California and profited modestly from the early success of petroleum development. Beale is listed as the number one taxpayer in Los Angeles County for 1866.

West of Beale's Rancho Los Alamos y Agua Caliente lay Rancho Castac where Fort Tejon had been established in 1854. Alfred Packard had bought the ranch the year previously from original grantee Jose Maria Covarubbias. Beale's first partner, Samuel Bishop, ran cattle on Rancho Castac while at the same time managing Rancho la Liebre for Beale until 1861, when they ended their partnership. Bishop bought out Packard on October 22, 1860, for $9000 and by 1866 the property and livestock had appreciated in value so much that he sold it to Colonel Robert S. Baker for $65,000. Beale and Baker posted a notice at Fort Tejon:

> The undersigned desire to notify the public that they have associated themselves for the greater convenience of sheep raising, but have formed no partnership, neither party being responsible for the debts contracted by the other.

Under this arrangement, their combined flocks grazed at either ranch, wherever the grass grew most abundantly.

Baker sold Rancho Castac to Beale on October 13, 1866, for the same consideration of $65,000 he had paid Bishop. The transaction gave Beale the adobe buildings of Fort Tejon, which had been abandoned in 1864. Beale converted the old fort buildings to ranch offices and quarters for his herders and vaqueros, although he continued to maintain his own residence and headquarters at Rancho la Liebre.

Twenty years had elapsed since Beale came ashore as a young Midshipman at Monterey, years during which he experienced enough adventures for several lifetimes. Yet, he was only forty-four years old in 1866 when he combined the four ranches under the name Ranchos El Tejon. His property totaled more than 200,000 acres and became nationally known as one of the country's largest sheep ranches. It remained in the Beale family for more than fifty years.

Rancho San Emigdio (also called Emidio) dated back to 1806 when Franciscan Padre Jose Maria Zalvidea explored the valley with a party of Spanish soldiers and named it for St. Emigdius, patron saint of earthquakes. (The San Andreas earthquake fault runs through the property.) Rancho San Emigdio was granted to Jose Antonio Dominguez in 1842. He died two years later. John C. Fremont bought half interest in the 18,000 acres from Francisco Dominguez in 1851 for $2000. Fremont hired Alex Godey to run cattle on the property.

To help Fremont with his tangled finances in 1869, Beale bought out his interest in San Emigdio. Two years later Beale sold his portion to James Ben Ali Haggin, who ultimately joined with his brother-in-law Lloyd Tevis and used the rancho as a nucleus to form the giant Kern County Land Company.

Beale, Baker & Company marketed 175,000 pounds of wool in 1872. They grazed 125,000 sheep and 25,000 head of cattle. Spanish and Mexican law required branding of cattle to distinguish ownership. A California statute of 1851 required cattle brands to be registered with the County Recorder in the Book of Marks and Brands. Beale, Baker & Company registered the cross and crescent brand in Los Angeles County in 1865 and in Kern County in 1868. Beale designed the brand from his family coat of arms which carries three Maltese crosses.

Beale's total land acquisition at Ranchos El Tejon:

Purchase	Date of deed	Acres	Price per acre	Total price
Rancho la Liebre	August 8, 1855	48,825	$ .03	$ 1,500
Willow Springs	December 10, 1862	80	1.25	100
Section 32	June 8, 1863	40	1.25	50
Rancho El Tejon	February 9, 1865	97,617	.21	21,000
Rancho Los Alamos	May 1, 1865	34,560	.05	1,700
Rancho Castac	October 13, 1866	22,195	2.93	65,000
Total		203,317		$89,350

That Edward Beale could pay out $89,350 in cash over an eleven-year period indicates his success. The acreage seems enormous, but considering the dry seasons in the Tejon, the size and steepness of the mountain portions and the remoteness of the entire area, a large parcel was necessary to be economically productive.

Beale's nearest base of supplies was Los Angeles, a 200-mile round trip. Son Truxtun recollected, as one of his earliest experiences, "driving with my father from Tejon to Los Angeles in a sulky behind a tandem of camels." Beale had the Army's permission to use the camels before the animals left Fort Tejon in 1861. Trux, five years old at that time, was not too young to remember such an exciting occasion.

The camels worked out of Drum Barracks for awhile after leaving Fort Tejon, but roads had been so well graded that large freight wagons proved more economical. Teamsters still objected to camels because the beasts continued to frighten their horses and mules. The Army no longer wanted to keep them in fodder, and they suffered from neglect. Beale asked that they be turned back to him for use in hauling his own supplies, but the request was denied by Secretary of War Stanton. Instead, Stanton ordered Quartermaster E. B. Babbit to sell the animals at auction. Although Bonsal indicates that Beale bought the camels himself, nothing in Beale's writings or personal records indicate that he did. Furthermore, when Charles Nordhoff wrote about his pleasant days at Tejon in 1872, he filled many pages with descriptions of the life, people, manners and customs at Ranchos El Tejon. The writer made no mention of a single camel.

Actually, all thirty-six camels were driven by Captain Dempfill from Drum Barracks to Benicia Arsenal, north of San Francisco Bay, in December of 1863. There they were stabled in two stone warehouses, forever after known as "the camel barns." They were bought at public auction by Sonoma County rancher Samuel McLenegham, one of the four men Beale had encountered at the Spring of San Lucas, Texas, in 1857. McLenegham intended starting a camel freighting service from Sacramento to Nevada, but when he got them to the Comstock mines he found an eager buyer and his freighting project never materialized. These are probably the camels Dan DeQuille (William Wright) speaks of in his book *Big Bonanza* being used for "packing salt from the desert, carrying wood, hay and freight of all kinds." Later, other camels were imported for the same purpose.

Greek George Caralamba, who had remained with the Army's camels all those years, settled in Los Angeles, changed his name to George Allen and became an American citizen in 1867. He is buried at Mt. Olive Cemetery in Whittier.

The other faithful camel driver, Hi-Jolly, lived out his days in Arizona as a miner, scout and packer. He died at Quartzite, Arizona, in 1903 and is buried there under a pyramidal stone monument built by State Highway Department maintenance foreman Jim Edwards.

At age eleven, Truxtun was old enough in 1867 for formal education, but before entering him in school Beale decided to give his family a European vacation. The Beales traveled with Charles Poston and his family, perhaps through a chance meeting on board ship. Beale left no evidence of this journey, but an entry in Poston's diary gives reference to the Beales: "We crossed the Atlantic together in 1867 and enjoyed the luxuries of London and Paris in various ways." Beale entered Trux in Pennsylvania Military Academy on their return.

Beale became involved in other land deals. Thompson & West's *History of Santa Barbara and Ventura Counties* lists Edward F. Beale as one of four investors purchasing 48,822 acres of the old Mission San Buenaventura lands. His associates in this transaction were Stephen J. Field, Justice of the U. S. Supreme Court; Timothy G. Phelps, U. S. Congressman from 1861 to 1863; and Jeremiah Sullivan Black, U. S. Attorney General from 1857 to 1860. In the East, Beale occupied himself with a project that eventually resulted in the development of a large part of the business section of Chester. The Delaware County *Republican* reported on November 22, 1867, "General E. F. Beale plans to build a four-story hotel building on the corner of Sixth Street and Edgemont Avenue."

Beale might be excused by this time if he felt that his life had begun settling into a rather monotonous pattern of success and respectability, but a startling bit of news reached him in 1868 that surely gained all his attention. An old comrade was going to run for President, and Edward Beale promised his full support.

17

In Washington

Edward Beale first met Ulysses S. Grant in San Francisco some fifteen years before the 1868 Presidential election. Grant, a thirty-year-old infantry Lieutenant at the time, followed the habit of treating his homesickness with alcohol. His forced resignation from the Army at Fort Humboldt in 1854 seemed to end his prospects for a military career. Beale remembered their chance meeting in St. Louis in 1858 when the impoverished Grant was barely scratching out a living on his Hardscrabble wood lot. Grant's meteoric rise to prominence during the Civil War needn't be detailed here, but Beale and Grant remained friends during good times and bad.

Beale campaigned vigorously for Grant, providing strong support with public addresses in various Pennsylvania towns. Grant won the Republican Party nomination on the first ballot. President Andrew Johnson's Reconstruction problems after the war and his near impeachment in the U. S. Senate weakened his chances for reelection. The general election never seemed in doubt. Grant, the hero of Appomattox, won decisively.

President Grant depended on Beale for advice on Western affairs. In 1871, Beale placed operations at Ranchos El Tejon under the supervision of the dependable Jose Jesus Lopez, a seventh generation Californio, and sought a permanent residence convenient to Washington, D.C. He discovered that Decatur House, only a block from the White House, might be available.

Buildings around Lafayette Square had been commandeered by the War Department. U. S. Commissary General Amos Beebe Eaton maintained offices in Decatur House at a monthly rental of $650. Beale asked the owners, the John Gadsby (also called Gatesby) estate, if they would sell the house. On May 25, 1871, Gadsby's agent Walter S. Cox sent an advisory to

General Eaton: "I sold to Edward F. Beale, in trust for his wife, Mrs. Mary E. Beale, the house lately belonging to the Gatesby heirs. All rent accruing is payable to Mrs. Beale, the sale having been confirmed by the court."

Mary Beale paid the purchase price of $60,000 in installments out of "her own separate estate" and received a deed to the property on July 10, 1871. Beale wrote Grant's Secretary of War, William W. Belknap, on August 14:

> Being desirous to repossess the premises at the corner of H Street and Jackson Place, you are therefore required to remove from, quit and yield up same at the expiration of the tenancy of the United States which will expire on the first day of March, next ensuing.

General Eaton asked that the lease be extended until September, 1872, and the Beales agreed.

The house stood in a poor state of repair after the Army's eleven-year occupancy. The Beales commenced restoration of the old mansion to its former elegance, and introduced a number of modern conveniences in the heavy Victorian style then popular. In the main second floor drawing room, Beale had the parquetry of the new flooring inlaid with twenty-two different species of California woods depicting the great seal of that state as it was adopted at the 1849 constitutional convention in Monterey.

The house, designed by Benjamin Latrobe and built for Commodore Stephan Decatur, was the first private residence on Lafayette Square. Decatur's widow leased it to a succession of notable persons — the French Minister to the United States, the Russian Minister for four years, Secretary of State Henry Clay, and to Martin Van Buren. It later became the residence of British Minister Sir Charles Vaughan. In 1835 slave dealer John Gadsby purchased the house. He owned the National Hotel and Gadsby's Tavern in Washington and Gadsby's Tavern in Alexandria, Virginia. Subsequent tenants included Vice President George M. Dallas, Secretary of the Treasury Howell Cobb and U. S. Senator Judah P. Benjamin.

Mary Beale happily involved herself in refurbishing the

old place. She selected Victorian furniture to be mixed with earlier Beale and Edwards pieces, draperies and naperies, wall coverings, and a profusion of pictures and paintings. Beale's mother helped with several family heirlooms that included the silver-chased, urn-shaped cup presented to Grandfather Truxtun by Lloyd's Coffee House, the silver medal that Congress awarded to Beale's father, and two portraits of Beale himself — one as a Midshipman and the other in his Mexican disguise of 1848. Mary also found room for his Indian and Mexican collections from Ranchos El Tejon. Beale seemed perfectly content, as most men are, to leave the decorating and furnishing chores to his wife.

Mary had been a gracious hostess at the ranch but found the rough life there more suitable to younger people. She quite readily agreed to leave it behind her and enjoy her status as *chatelaine* of Decatur House. There she could prime her two daughters, Emily and Mary, for their debuts in the social life of Washington. The family had been accustomed to spending most of the year in California with a month or two at Chester. That routine was reversed now. For the rest of his life, Edward Beale spent most of his time in Washington and Chester, traveling West for only a month or two each year to check on his interests. With Baker watching the business and the faithful Lopez running the ranch, Beale had little to worry about.

Decatur House soon became a major social center of the nation's capital. The Beales were on the White House special invitation list for dinners, receptions, musicals and official functions. The three younger Grant children were frequent guests of the Beale teen-agers, as were other neighboring children on both sides of Lafayette Square.

Other property owners around the square followed Beale's lead and repossessed their homes from the government. The Beales found themselves in a neighborhood as socially and politically distinguished as it had been in Decatur's day. Next door on Jackson Place lived James G. Blaine, U. S. Senator from Maine. His youngest daughter, Harriet, became the first wife of Beale's son, Truxtun. Vice President Schuyler Colfax lived a few doors further down. Next to the corner resided U. S. Supreme Court Justice John McLean whose grandson John Roll McLean, publisher of the Washington *Post,* married Beale's daughter, Emily. Around the corner on Pennsylvania Avenue sat the old home of Thomas Ewing, later occupied by Francis P. Blair and his son, Montgomery Blair, Postmaster under Lincoln. Diagonally across from Decatur House on Connecticut Avenue stood the mansion of philanthopist William Corcoran, and down the block on H Street were the homes of former Senator John Slidell, Henry Adams and poet-historian John Hay.

Beale was not too preoccupied with Decatur House renovations to be unconcerned with current events. In 1871, *Harper's Weekly* published "Song of the Sierras," a collection of poems by Indiana-born Cincinnatus Heiner Miller under his pen name "Joaquin Miller." One of the poems, "Kit Carson's Ride," portrayed Beale's old friend more rogue than hero in an unsavory adventure in which Carson never participated. Incensed at the insult to the memory of Carson, who had died at Fort Lyon, Colorado, in 1868, Beale fired off an angry protest to the publisher:

> It is rarely that the license allowed poets has been more thoroughly abused than in these ill-written lines. As a rule in poetry, when fact is departed from, it has always been to exaggerate the virtues of a departed hero, but never to slander him. As we recall the modest, earnest refined simplicity of Carson and compare it with the frenzied and licentious buffoon presented in the poem we cannot but regret that the scalp of Joaquin Miller had not been counted among the "coups" of that redoubted knight of the prairie and mountains. Carson was a man cleanly of mind, body and speech, and by no manner of means a border ruffian. He had great dignity and was not given to the least vulgarity of thought or expression. What an abuse of common sense is such stuff.

Bayard Taylor, by now internationally recognized as a man of letters, read Beale's scathing reprisal and hastened to add his own. He addressed Beale from Kennett Square on August 27, 1871:

> Thank you heartily for writing your defense of Kit Carson, and scarification of that vulgar fraud, Joaquin Miller! I am very glad to have my own immediate impression confirmed that the fellow really knows nothing about the life he undertakes to describe. We authors have really fallen on evil days when such stuff passes for poetry!

Beale himself had been moved in 1870 to express himself about his late friend in more lasting phrases: "Dear old Kit . . . Oh wise of counsel, strong of arm, brave of heart and gentle of nature . . ."

The Modoc Indian War along the California-Oregon border captured the nation's attention in 1873. Following alternate periods of war, peace, confinement, and a string of broken promises and treaties, the Modocs fled to their ancestral lands and vowed to defy the Army. They did so during a protracted period of warfare until the Army sent Brigadier General Edward Richard Sprigg Canby, one of its most distinguished officers. Canby arranged a truce and peace council, secretly planning to capture the Modoc leaders during the talks. Fighting broke out right at the council. Captain Jack, the Modoc leader, pulled a pistol with which he shot and killed the General.

The death of Canby, the first General of the U. S. Army killed by an Indian, aroused the nation. There were demands for extermination of the entire Modoc tribe. Only one voice of dissent rose above the clamor. In a letter of April 25, 1873, to the Chester *Republican* and copied by every major paper in the country, Edward Beale braved public opinion by writing:

> In the heat of a great public excitement, caused by the loss of a most useful exemplary officer, it is very doubtful if a fair judgement can be had in relation to the cause which have produced the event we all deplore. General Canby served his country with such efficient zeal in two great wars that the intelligence of his death was received as a shock by the whole people of the United States. There was not in the army a man whose public and private character stood so high, and the manner of his death has added a sentiment of bitterness toward

the Indians which nothing but their extermination will satisfy. The press of the country is eagerly demanding blood for blood.

Beale pleaded for rational consideration rather than a commitment to a policy he considered more savage and remorseless than any act committed by the Indians. Beale continued his letter by pleading to the American people to,

> . . . ask ourselves if the treachery to which the gallant Canby fell a victim is not the repetition of the lesson which we have taught these apt scholars, the Indians? If we are correctly informed, the act of council was to make Captain Jack and the others prisoners. The Modoc Indians were fighting for a right to live where God created them, and we have exasperated them by insisting on our right, which they do not see, to remove them to a distant and unknown country. Having been taught by us a violation of flags of truce, they have followed our example, and unhappily a noble victim to our teaching of falsehood and crime is the result, whereupon there goes out a cry of extermination throughout the land.
>
> We enter our protest against this course, and we ask for justice and a calmer consideration by the public of the Indian affairs of our country. We cannot restore the good men who have been killed by an indiscriminate slaughter of all the tribe of Modocs, and it does not become a Christian people to hunt to death the poor remnant of those from whom we have already taken the broad acres of thirty-seven states of this Union.

Beale's voice cried alone in the wilderness, however, and the letter cost him the friendship of many old comrades in the Army. Despite his plea for calmness and reason, the Modocs were hunted down. Captain Jack and three of his men were tried and executed. What was left of the Modoc tribe scattered to the four winds.

Beale and Baker suffered a major setback at the ranch. They shipped 175,000 pounds of wool from San Francisco and the entire consignment burned in the great Boston fire of that year. Their insurance company failed, leaving Beale and Baker to face the total loss. Most of Baker's capital was tied up in Los Angeles building ventures. In one of these, which never got past the promotional stage, Beale planned to participate with Baker in a railroad from Los Angeles to the vicinity of San Pedro, where they wanted to build a town called "Truxtun."

Truxtun Beale completed the curriculum at Pennsylvania Military Academy in 1874. As Beale's only son, he would eventually inherit management of the family's estate. Beale decided a sound legal background would best prepare Trux for his future responsibilities. Trux agreed, and entered Columbia University Law School. He was graduated in 1878 and gained admittance to the Pennsylvania Bar.

President Grant frequently crossed Lafayette Square for a quiet talk with Beale and respite from pressures at the White House. Beale often took the President to visit with his mother at Bloomingdale. Beale's brother Truxtun had died in 1870, but the brother's son — Beale's nephew and namesake, Edward Fitzgerald Beale — recalled how impressed Grant had been with the charm and poise of Emily Truxtun Beale. As sixteen-year-old Edward put it, "She was always at home with royalty or woodchopper."

Beale maintained stables adjoining Decatur House on H Street where he kept horses and carriages. But he missed the wide-open spaces of the Tejon and decided to look around for a country place where he and his family could escape the capital's oppressive summer heat, and where he could indulge his abiding preoccupation with horse breeding. He found exactly what he sought less than ten miles from Decatur House, near Hyattsville in Prince Georges County, Maryland. There on a high wooded ridge in the center of an estate of 427 acres rose a commodious two-story brick mansion. A high columned porch shaded the entire front facade. The owner and builder, Robert Thomas Clark, had purchased the old plantation from George Calvert in 1836. He erected the house in 1840 and now wished to sell it. Beale presented Mary with the deed on April 27, 1875.

Calvert had called the place Hitching Post Hill. That name appeared in his deed of 1836 to Robert Clark, and Clark's

deed to Beale. The Beales saw no reason to give it any other
name. The house was then, as it is now, one of Maryland's
historic landmarks. There the Beale family spent many of
its happiest days.

Beale erected several large stables for his brood mares.
He also constructed a ring and track for showing and racing
horses. He invited President Grant to stable his own horses
there. After a hard day at the White House, Grant and Beale
would race their buggies to the farm.

Beale had become accustomed to the wild riding habits of
his California vaqueros, who never rode at less than a full
gallop. Grant wasn't satisfied either unless his horses were
stretched out. The good folks of Hyattsville became resigned
to leaping for the sidewalks when the rigs of Grant and
Beale came tearing through town. On one occasion, President
Grant was actually arrested by the town constable for reckless driving. Grant spent whatever time he could take from
his official duties with Beale at the farm. It is no idle as-
sumption that he passed the most carefree hours of his Presidency at Hitching Post Hill.

Buffalo Bill Cody once complained to Beale about the lack
of good winter facilities for his famous Wild West Show.
At Beale's invitation, Cody wintered his buffalo and other
animals at Hitching Post Hill.

Los Angeles investments began to take all of Baker's time
and he dissolved his sheep-raising affiliation with Beale. The
firm of Hill, Rivers & Company tendered an offer to lease
grazing rights at Ranchos El Tejon, and Beale accepted it.
At fifty-four years of age, Beale had earned a leisurely retirement and could be expected to take advantage of it. But
such was not to be, for one more bright star glowed on
Edward Beale's horizon.

18

The Nation's Servant

Relations between the United States government and Austria's House of Hapsburg in Vienna had been cold and strictly formal since the execution in Mexico of Maximilian, brother of Austrian Emperor Franz Josef. President Grant told Edward Beale in the spring of 1876 that he wanted him to be U. S. Minister to Vienna replacing Godlove S. Orth. Beale doubted he would be acceptable to the Hapsburg Court. Besides, he had no experience in international affairs and his direct manner little qualified him to be a diplomat. Yet, Beale had achieved stature in the United States as a highly regarded man of strength, character and integrity. He told Grant he would be honored to serve, if the Hapsburg Court would accept him.

Grant formally appointed Beale Envoy Extraordinary and Minister Plenipotentiary to Austria-Hungary. Secretary of State Hamilton Fish submitted Beale's name to the Austro-Hungarian Minister of Foreign Affairs, Count Julius Andrassy.

The Count, fully aware of Beale's complicity in the failure of Maximilian's empire in Mexico, recommended Beale's acceptance anyway, with reservations. They would see how it worked out. On that basis, Emperor Franz Josef accepted Edward Beale as the American Minister.

Beale decided Truxtun's graduation from Columbia Law School could be postponed in favor of the European experience. He took his son along as secretary. Mary and the girls were, of course, ecstatic.

Beale's selection created a measure of provincial satisfaction in California. The San Francisco *News Letter* said, "The news of Ned Beale's appointment to be Minister to Austria is as refreshing as a shower of rain, for if there ever was a typical and representative Californian, Ned Beale is he."

The Beales arrived in Vienna late in July of 1876. The court received Mary Edwards Beale with warmth and affection. She had, since girlhood, been familiar with the upper strata of American society and politics. She had entertained many of the foreign legation members at Decatur House and now found several old friends serving as attaches at the Austrian court. Mary excelled as a pianist, and that endeared her to the music loving Viennese. She was a faithful patroness of the opera and the concert halls, diversions which had little appeal for Beale but afforded her the pleasure of appreciating at first hand the music of Haydn, Mozart, Brahms, Beethoven, Schubert and the Strausses. Mary possessed a ready command of French and Spanish. Her natural poise and charm established her very quickly as a favorite of the court.

Beale, frank and open in speech if not particularly polished, let his accomplishments and the stature of his country speak for themselves. By nature courteous and considerate, he was accepted at all diplomatic levels in Vienna. The fame of his Western exploits had preceded him. He gained ready acceptance as a comrade-in-arms by the Austro-Hungarian nobility, all of whom by birth and training were military men who had seen action in Austria's wars. Beale retained his interest in all things nautical and had the privilege of inspecting the Austrian Naval Base at Trieste, a creation of Maximilian before he departed on his ill-fated Mexican adventure. Beale proved to be an accomplished and respected envoy, a valuable aid to his government and a credit to his country.

The Beale daughters, Emily and Mary, enjoyed the endless round of parties, levees and balls. They were eagerly sought as partners by young officers and attaches of the diplomatic corps. It soon became apparent that young Mary bestowed most of her favors on George Bahkmeteff, Secretary to the Russian Embassy.

Crown Prince Rudolf, two years younger than Trux, found much in common with the American. They both loved sports and were more at home in the field together with dogs and guns than in the pomp and ceremony of the court. Rudolf devoted most of his time to Army life in garrison with his regiment, and Trux accompanied him on annual maneuvers.

All the Beales were excellent riders from their long hours in the saddle at the Tejon and at Hitching Post Hill. They were afforded the courtesy of the Imperial Stables, where they had their choice of the Emperor's thoroughbreds. They received frequent invitations to join riding parties or, dressed to the nines, accompany the Emperor's coach in his daily drives. On these rides the ladies wore their smartest habits and the officers their most resplendent dress uniforms ablaze with decorations. An escort of hussars trotted along with flashing sabres. All the horses were groomed to perfection and pranced accordingly. The royal coach sparkled with gilt and varnish, adding proper focus to the brilliant cavalcade.

On occasion, Empress Elizabeth, generally acknowledged as the most beautiful woman of the era, invited Beale to be her escort at the hunts. Beale, with a wink at Trux, always assumed an air of reluctant compliance.

It was a glamorous and enjoyable year for the Beales. But the time soon came to return to America. While his duties were largely ceremonial, Beale had done what he could to improve relations between the United States and Austria-Hungary. He yearned to get back to his own concerns at home. Trux had a year of college to make up. Mary and the girls went about packing for the voyage home, but it soon became obvious that one of them had no intention of leaving Vienna.

A page at the American Embassy announced a visitor to see General Beale. George Bahkmeteff, flustered and stammering, asked Beale for the hand of his daughter Mary in marriage. Beale recognized the young man as one frequently in attendance on his daughter. He expressed amazement to learn matters had progressed that far. He refused to even discuss such a possibility and stormed from his office in search of his daughter, leaving the young swain in a state of shock.

Tears flowed freely when Mary met with her father. How could she consider such a thing, Beale wanted to know. A Russian! And the young fop even sported a monacle! Mary had reached an age not requiring her father's consent and proved to be as stubborn as he. The rest of the family could go home, she said. With or without their blessing, she resolved to stay in Vienna as the Russian's bride.

Mary Edwards, perceptive as most mothers are, had watched the budding romance develop. Protective, too, she made it her business to learn all she could about George Bahkmeteff. He descended from a distinguished St. Petersburg family. The Russian Minister to Vienna told Mary that a brilliant career lay ahead for George in the diplomatic corps. Mother saw behind the monacle and fancy uniforms. The young Russian's manners were impeccable, his conversation intelligent, his devotion to young Mary total and undeniable. Surely his family would be as much aghast at his marrying an American as Beale was about his daughter falling in love with a Russian.

Trux and Emily sided with their mother and sister. With the whole family beating down his objections, Beale reluctantly gave in.

The Beales delayed their departure for home while Mary took instructions in the Russian Orthdox religion and became a convert to that faith. The marriage took place in Vienna, a marriage which over the years Beale never had cause to regret. So many doting mothers brought their debutante daughters to Europe in search of a title, not always with salutary results, that Senator Simon Cameron said Mary was "one of the few smart American girls who did not marry a fool."

Edward Beale had not yet returned from Europe when President Grant delivered his last annual message to Congress in December of 1876. Grant said something in that speech that no President had ever uttered before. He declared that he had been politically unqualified for the Presidency and had learned little from his eight years in office.

Shortly after departing the White House, Grant sailed with

his wife and daughter for a tour of Europe. Accorded a wildly enthusiastic reception everywhere they went, greeted by cheering crowds and given lavish official welcomes, the Grants decided they rather liked being tourists. Their journey extended from weeks into months.

Grant maintained a steady correspondence with Beale. He wrote on September 9, 1877, from Inverness, Scotland, where he had been entertained by the Earl of Sheffield at Castle Grant, ancestral home of the Grants: "I will feel more at home back in Washington than anyplace else, and no place would I rather be than visiting your farm with you."

From Paris he wrote, "We have now been here nearly two weeks and are getting ready to go to Spain, Portugal and a little of Africa." Another letter said:

I found Vienna one of the most beautiful cities in Europe, but everyone retires so horribly early! After ten at night the streets are as silent as the grave. We have not yet met Mrs. Bahkmeteff [Beale's daughter]. I hope your diplomacy will prove successful in bringing over the Arabian steeds. I would like to be with you visiting the farm, out looking at the colts!

The Arabian steeds were two stallions given to Grant by the Sultan of Turkey. Beale managed through his Navy connections to have both horses brought back to the States. They were eventually taken to Hitching Post Hill.

The Beales joined the Grants in Paris in the spring of 1878 and, according to Julia Grant's memoirs, they enjoyed "many happy excursions together."

Grant returned to Paris after visiting Egypt and the Holy Land. He wrote to Beale on January 17, 1879: "We start in the morning for Alexandria, thence by rail to Suez, thence the P. O. Line to Bombay." The Grants embarked on a cruise that became a voyage around the world, taking in India, Siam, China and Japan.

The summer of 1879 was excessively dry. Beale went to Ranchos El Tejon from where he penned a note to Colonel Baker: "I am black as an Indian having been constantly at the cattle camps." Forage became scarce in the severe drought. They decided to move their sheep to the free, open range of Montana. The drive, although considered a legend in Kern County, ended tragically. Of the 17,600 head starting, only 8500 survived the desert crossing. Beale rode out into Nevada to survey the flock and wrote to Baker in September from Eureka:

> The great disaster to our sheep will have reached you through the papers. My feeling after two days of hard riding through dust to find' this little remnant of what might have been a fortune has not put me in a frame of mind to enjoy very much this filthy little mining town.

The fifty-seven-year-old Beale spent the entire summer in the saddle. While he and his herders pushed the sheep northeastward, Lopez drove 7000 head of cattle, divided into bands of 1000, over the Fort Tejon road to Los Angeles. The drive stands as the largest cattle movement ever made from the Tejon and is also a Kern County legend. All seven herds reached Los Angeles in good condition. Beale concentrated on cattle raising from then on and kept his sheep flocks relatively small. He organized the firm of Shoobert & Beale, commission merchants for the sale of wool, sheep and all kinds of livestock. The four partners in the company were himself, Truxtun, J. E. Shoobert and H. H. Woodward.

Cattle drives were no longer necessary after the Southern Pacific Railroad completed a line across the edge of Beale's property on its route over Tehachapi Pass. Loading chutes were constructed at "Bealville," right on the ranch, and cattle shipped from there.

General Grant's touring party disembarked at San Francisco from the Orient on September 20, 1879. They traveled by train to Washington, terminating a journey of two and a half years after leaving Philadelphia for what had originally been intended as a few months in Europe.

Beale, learning that Grant neared home, returned to Decatur House to prepare for the ex-President's reception. The Grants found what seemed to be the entire city present to welcome them when their train pulled into Washington. They rode in an open carriage up flag-lined Pennsylvania Avenue in a procession led by an escort of cavalry. The cheering throngs nearly equalled the turnout for the Grand Army review in 1865.

The Grants repaired from Lafayette Square to Decatur House where the Beales hosted a reception later described in the press:

> The beautiful drawing rooms were the scene of a brilliant company. General Beale stood within the gold embroidered portieres of the main drawing room greeting the guests with Mrs. Beale and Miss Emily Beale. General and Mrs. Grant stood at the other side of the room, the center of a large group of guests. A handsome supper was served in the dining room during the evening.

The Grants remained as overnight guests. After attending services at St. John's Church the next day Grant and Beale drove out to Hitching Post Hill, where they watched the Arabian stallions, Linden Tree and Leopard, go through their paces.

Grant agreed to support Garfield in the general election of 1880 if Garfield would appoint Beale Secretary of the Navy. There could be no more logical choice than Beale, and Garfield agreed. Once in the saddle, however, Garfield reneged on the promise and appointed William Hunt to the post.

Beale again turned to his business investments. The Chester *Republican Steam Press* carried this report in 1881:

> General Beale has sold many valuable lots in the business part of the city on easy terms, and supplied money to those wishing to build thereon. This has greatly improved Edgement Avenue and has resulted in the erection of many imposing dwellings and stores.

Not the least of these projects was Beale's office building, still standing and known by the inscription on its main facade — the Beale Block.

Beale also became involved in a gigantic promotion to build a transcontinental canal through Nicaragua. But construction progressed on the Panama Canal and eventually the Nicaragua project was abandoned.

A happy event occurred in October of 1884 when Beale's popular daughter Emily married John R. McLean, publisher of the Cincinnati *Enquirer,* and later the Washington *Post.* The wedding took place at Decatur House with a small group of family and friends in attendance.

Grant, failing rapidly under the ravages of cancer, was moved in June of 1885 to a cottage at Mount McGregor, near Saratoga. He spent his few remaining weeks there writing out the last lines of his memoirs. Grant's memoirs end with the Grand Army review of 1865 and do not cover the last twenty years of his life when his friendship with Beale became most intimate. Unfortunately, Grant's many biographers have overlooked his close friendship with Beale.

Among Grant's final visitors was Beale's son Truxtun, who later wrote:

> I saw General Grant a few days before he died. He had been on terms of intimate friendship with my father, and during many years our house had been his accustomed home whenever he was in Washington. I looked upon him with awe as the greatest of military heroes . . . Though suffering intense pain, and indeed well nigh in the last agony of death, instead of speaking of his own distress, he first saw that I was comfortable and asked about my father . . .

Beale and his family were in mourning for the passing of his mother when they attended the funeral of General Grant in New York, along with a host of national and foreign dignitaries.

Beale's mother, Emily Truxtun Beale, died at Bloomingdale on May 1, 1885. In settling her estate, Bloomingdale was sold to Senator John Sherman. Its site is now occupied by Truxtun Circle.

Grant's death had a lasting impact on Beale. They were the closest of friends. After his death Beale's many interests and personal energies seemed to wane. As Grant's trusted confidante, Beale had reached his pinnacle of respect and political influence. He had become a true pillar of the Republican Party, and his family enjoyed high status in Washington society.

Beale gave a brief autobiographical sketch to Hubert Howe Bancroft in 1886, the original of which is in the Bancroft Library at Berkeley. Beale, in his mid-sixties, was none too accurate in his recollections: "The Beales came to this country from the West Indies." The first Beale in America, Colonel Thomas Beale of Kent, came directly to Virginia from England in 1640 and did not establish his West Indies plantation until after 1651. The year of his father's death Beale gave as "about 1842," but the date was actually April 4, 1835. In like manner, Beale gave the year of his own birth as 1820, but his true birthdate was February 4, 1822.

On a visit west in 1888, a group of Bakersfield's most prominent citizens feted Beale at a lavish banquet which Beale said lasted until 4 o'clock in the morning. Speakers recalled his arrival in the territory in 1846 and all his many contributions to the growth and prosperity of California and the West. Beale had become a polished speaker. He held the crowd's rapt attention in a talk about California and about General Grant.

That same year Beale's name appeared in nomination for a Congressional seat, but he declined for personal reasons — the press of business and perhaps his declining health. Beale also received brief support from influential members of the National Republican League and several Eastern newspapers as a possible Presidential candidate. One paper said, "If we could have our way, Washington should furnish a President of the United States, and his name would be Edward Fitzgerald Beale." Again Beale declined, choosing to work for the election of Benjamin Harrison.

Author Mary Austin moved with her parents onto the Tejon Ranch in the late 1880s. Beale befriended her and soon became aware of her talent as a writer. The Tejon is generally regarded as the setting and inspiration for several of Austin's works — *Land of Little Rain, The Flock, The Ford, Isidro* and *Arrowmaker*. Jose Jesus Lopez is described in *The Flock*. Beale inspired *Isidro* and *The Arrowmaker*.

A newspaper account of 1889 described Beale:

> [He is] of short, sinewy stature, of a very dark complexion, with a closely-cut mustache and hair almost white. He has a nervous energy in his actions and movements which indicates the high spirit and gallantry which he has shown in all walks of life, whether in the peaceful pursuits of Indian Administration, as pathfinder across the continent, as diplomat at the Court of the House of Hapsburg, or in the management of his vast land possessions.

White hair was not the only indication of Beale's advanced age. Periods of illness occurred more frequent and he stayed close to home at Decatur House.

The last appraisal of Ranchos El Tejon in 1891 contained this description of Beale's holdings:

> Extending forty-two miles from north to south, and thirty miles from east to west, the finest body of agricultural land still undeveloped in the State of California, with 25,000 head of cattle, 7,500 sheep, 350 horses and mules, 200 miles of barbed wire fencing, forty-five acres of alfalfa, twenty acres of oranges, twenty acres of figs, a fifteen-acre vineyard, 35,000 acres of wooded land that would yield 3.5 million cords of railroad ties, and 90,000 acres suitable for irrigation.

Beale considered selling the property and estimated its value to be $3.5 million. His friend, writer Charles Nordhoff, called it the most valuable property in America owned by an individual. No transaction developed. The ranch remained in the Beale family for many more years.

Star Oil Company, in which Beale and Baker owned nearly a half interest, grew to become Standard Oil Company of California, one of the giants of the industry. With extensive real estate investments, business ventures, and the ranching and oil properties, Beale had become a millionnaire several times over.

Beale walked across Lafayette Square to the White House on March 4, 1893, to help out on the reception committee for the inaugural ball of President Grover Cleveland's second term. He returned home that night completely exhausted. He took to his bed, never again to leave Decatur House. He lay ill with jaundice for six weeks, comforted at his bedside by friends and family — all except Truxtun, who anxiously hurried home from Europe. Fearing he would not see his son again, Beale dictated a letter to him:

> Dear Trux: I wish you to live with your mother and take care of her and cherish her — remember the devotion she has always shown you. You have done all that I have asked of you and have acquired a well earned high reputation. Enjoy the rest of your life. I do not wish you to go to the ranch. It is a wearing life and Pogson is quite competent to conduct it, and moreover, I want you near your mother, who will need all your assistance. Go to California occasionally and look into our affairs. That is all that is necessary.
>
> Goodbye my dear boy. I have always loved you and been very proud of you. Your affectionate father . . .

Most of Beale's oldest and closest friends were already gone —Carson, Taylor, Kerlin, Edwards, Grant. May Humphreys Stacey died in 1886. Sam Brannan and Alex Godey both died in obscurity in 1889. Fremont died in 1890.

A man will make assessments of his life at such times. Beale might have considered that he compared favorably and in detail with two of his closest friends, for he possessed strong characteristics of each.

He had Kit Carson's strength, courage and endurance. Beale was a quick study. He learned in a short time mastery of the frontier environment and the art of survival nearly as well as a mountain man. He learned Indian fighting from Carson, and perhaps from him too he gained his great understanding and sympathy for the Indians. Both were men of immense energy and industry and native wisdom; men of action and quick perception, competent and invincible.

But in many ways Beale more resembled John Fremont. He married well, as Fremont did, accepting and utilizing the influence of a powerful political family. Beale was perhaps a little smarter than Fremont, for he played the political game and profited while Fremont became a perpetual loser. Beale apparently felt no compunction in thus satisfying his ambitions. He made huge gains throughout his lifetime from political connections. It appears that Beale had a bit of Fremont's ego too, as well as his flare for press-agentry and his eternal image-consciousness. Both men displayed a talent for leadership growing out of a mildly authoritarian personality. Both were literate, eminently civilized, articulate and family-oriented. Unlike Fremont, Beale had a quick and lively sense of humor, a genuine sociability and a far more realistic outlook on life. Beale always had his feet solidly on the ground, even if the ground beneath him proved to be unstable at times.

Unlike either Carson or Fremont, Beale possessed a volatile temper. He showed a capability for dressing a man down in rich Naval expletives. If provoked, stubborn pugnacity and a natural boxing skill were sometimes employed to emphasize his point.

He was a sharp, shrewd, enterprising businessman — an empire builder, literally. His aptitude for success combined with a vivid personality — a colorful eccentric personality at times — kept him always in the limelight, always among friends, always on the leading edge of things.

Beale, Carson and Fremont all showed a propensity for being where events of historical magniture unfolded. During his lifetime, Beale saw the nation develop from a shaky confederation of twenty-four states along the Atlantic seaboard to a sprawling giant of forty-five states, spanning the continent and all atremble with an unnamed potential for greatness. It isn't possible to measure and label the contributions of a single man, no matter how great or small. Let it be enough to say that Edward Beale was there and deserves to stand for posterity among his contemporaries — a position which our fickle memories have long denied him.

In his declining days, Beale drew strength and comfort from his family and his friends — and his memories. He had only

to look around him at Decatur House to see the gold sword
and epaulettes given him by fellow officers of the Pacific Squadron after the Battle of San Pasqual; the set of silver service
presented for his tenure as Superintendent of Indian Affairs;
the dagger with the golden bear on the handle for his service
under two Governors as Brigadier General in the California
State Militia; the framed sketches of the Beale-Heap Expedition of 1853; the noted Narjot paintings of the camels on the
1857 wagon road survey; a framed and signed photograph
presented to him by the Empress Elizabeth; a framed and
signed photograph of Kit Carson; and Kit's own rifle, which
he had given to Beale.

What memories to keep! Meeting Old Hickory on the White
House lawn; navigating all the way across the Atlantic and
back to deliver a message to President Polk; riding the long
Pacific swell into Monterey Bay on the USS *Congress* to the
sound of booming cannons; training his "leather-ass dragoons"
to go out and conquer California; facing the deadly lances of
San Pasqual and making a good account of himself; slipping
through the enemy lines with Kit Carson and the Delaware
Indian to bring help to General Kearny; riding with Carson
on the overland dash to Washington; rushing east again on his
wild ride across Mexico with the first gold samples from California; hair-raising adventures with the Ute Indians; mule-
skinning on the Mother Lode; helping the doomed and battered
Indians of California; serving as sheriff of San Francisco; building a wagon road with a string of camels; surveying the wilderness into farms and homes; ranching on a grand scale;
entertaining the most illustrious figures of the day at his stately
Washington home; and proudly representing his country in the
storied Hapsburg Court at Vienna.

And what comrades to cherish! Robert Field Stockton, who
recognized a good man when he saw one; gruff old Alexis
Godey; straight-backed John C. Fremont, whom no one ever
called "Jack"; Archibald Gillespie; irrepressible Sam Brannan,
the tarnished Saint; Gwynne Harris Heap; Don Benito Wilson;

Thomas Hart Benton; James Buchanan, who also recognized a good man when he saw one; Bret Harte; Theodore Dehone Judah; Sam Grant, as comfortable as an old boot; trapper White Elliott; Simon Cameron; Lawrence Graham; Greek George; Samuel Bishop; gentle Bayard Taylor; Jesse Chisholm; J. Ross Browne; Andrew Sublette; Fred Kerlin; Hi-Jolly; May Humphreys Stacey; Jose Jesus Lopez; Richard Brown, the proud Delaware Indian; Harry Edwards; Charles E. Thorburn; Baptiste Perrot; Robert S. Baker; Charles Nordhoff; and dear old Kit Carson in his greasy buckskins.

On April 22, 1893, with members of his beloved family gathered around him, America's sailor on horseback, Edward Fitzgerald Beale, quietly departed this life to join his old comrades.

Epilogue

Edward Beale left instructions that his remains be cremated. Funeral services were delayed for six days, however, until Truxtun returned home on the *Teutonic* from his post as United States Minister to Greece. Services conducted at Decatur House by the Reverend Dr. Aspinwall of Calvary Episcopal Church "were of the simplest character, but very impressive," according to a report in the Washington *Post:*

> The plain black coffin, hidden beneath a mass of roses, occupied the center of the great reception room on the second floor, and the gathering which filled the darkened room was as distinguished as many that had filled the same apartment in the old and gayer days when the house was one of the city's brightest social centers. There were many members of both army and navy, some of them old fellow officers who had served with General Beale on the *Congress.*

After the service the casket was carried out to the waiting hearse. The Washington *Post* listed the honorary pallbearers:

> . . . Vice President Levi P. Morton, Justice Stephen J. Field, Senator Henry Cabot Lodge, Judge Bancroft Davis, Admiral Daniel Ammen, John A. King, Colonel Haywood and Mr. Becker. The remains were carried to the Loudon Park Crematory outside Baltimore, and final interment was at Chester, Pennsylvania, the place named by General Beale before his death.

Edward Beale's cremated remains were buried in the Edwards family plot at Chester Rural Cemetery. A granite monument over the grave bears this simple legend:

EDWARD FITZGERALD BEALE
AN EXPLORER OF THE WEST
A FOUNDER OF CALIFORNIA
A HERO OF THE MEXICAN WAR
BORN FEBRUARY 4, 1822
DIED APRIL 22, 1893

Beale's son Truxtun had received his law degree from Columbia University in 1878, after serving a year as his father's secretary in Vienna. He toured China and Japan in 1879, then returned home to assume management of Ranchos El Tejon — performing this function mostly in absentia. He maintained his residence in San Francisco, at Decatur House with his mother, and frequently at Washington's Metropolitan Club.

In 1891, at the age of thirty-five, Truxtun Beale accepted a year's appointment from President Benjamin Harrison as U. S. Minister to Persia, in Teheran. He left Robert M. Pogson in charge of the ranch.

In 1892, Trux served as U. S. Minister simultaneously to Greece, Rumania and Serbia. But two years abroad proved to be enough for the young American. He returned home in time to attend his father's funeral.

Trux lacked his father's passion for horses and prevailed upon his mother to dispose of Hitching Post Hill. Colonel Haywood, who had been one of his father's pallbearers, and a Colonel Ainsworth bought and subdivided the property in 1895. They sold all but twenty acres to Davis Brothers, a Washington real estate firm. The remainder, including the house, became the residence of Rear Admiral Chauncey Thomas.

Trux carried out his father's wishes by living with his mother, but he possessed the same nervous energy which propelled his father through his eventful life. Trux spent little time sitting around Decatur House. He made frequent trips to the bright lights of New York and the social climate of Newport, Bar Harbor and Palm Beach. In Washington he renewed acquaintance with the James G. Blaine family, his neighbors on Jackson Place.

Blaine, a major Republican Party figure, had died in 1893, the same year as Edward Beale. Trux paid his respects and extended his sympathy to daughter Harriett, whom he had known since she wore pigtails. He soon began squiring the young lady to social affairs and on April 30, 1894, the two were married. She bore him a son in 1896, whom Trux wished

to name for his father but Harriett held out for Walker Blaine
Beale. The marriage ended that same year in divorce. Harriett
retained custody of the child. Upon her father's death, she
inherited the Blaine House in Augusta and there she raised
her son.

Both of Edward Beale's daughters married well. Mary to
George Bahkmeteff and Emily to John Roll McLean. Mary
and George left Vienna soon after their wedding and took up
residence in St. Petersburg where George served as diplomatic
advisor to the Czar. McLean owned both the Cincinnati *Enquirer*
and the Washington *Post*. He and Emily divided their time
between mansions in Washington and at Bar Harbor. As a
leading society matron, Emily entertained lavishly and well
at both places. She gave birth to a son, Edward Beale McLean,
in 1886.

During the Civil War when the Beales lived at Fremont's
Black Point cottage in San Francisco, they spent their summers
in San Rafael, on the north shore of San Francisco Bay. Young
Trux became familiar with the Marin County hills and redwood
forests. Trux first met Marie Chase Oge there, the daughter
of prominent San Francisco attorney William L. Oge. She
was a relative of Salmon P. Chase, former Senator and Governor of Ohio, Lincoln's Secretary of the Treasury, and a Chief
Justice of the United States Supreme Court.

In 1900, Trux and his mother gave the city of Bakersfield,
California, a library building as a memorial to Edward Beale.
Trux spoke at the dedication on March 27 and received a silver
plaque reading, "Testimonial from the citizens of Bakersfield,
Kern County, California, to Mrs. Mary E. Beale and her son
Truxton Beale." On the reverse side it said:

> To Mary E. Beale and Truxton Beale: In presenting this testi-
> monial, the citizens of Bakersfield desire to express their appreciation
> and gratitude for the munificent gift of a Memorial Library building.
> It will remain a monument, keeping warm in their hearts the memory
> of their tried and true friend, Gen. E. F. Beale.

Trux made a speech of acceptance and sent the plaque, with
his name misspelled on both sides, to his mother at Decatur

House. In addition to the library, Trux subsequently gave the city an adjoining clock tower and an outdoor Greek Theater.

Trux returned to Washington in 1902 to attend his mother's sickbed. Mary Edwards Beale died on April 6. Every major newspaper noted her passing. The doors of Decatur House were closed for a year after her death while Trux went back to San Francisco to settle his affairs.

The doors swung open again in 1903 when Decatur House became the new Washington residence of Truxtun and Marie Chase Oge Beale of San Rafael. Forsaking his bachelor status, forty-seven-year-old Trux married twenty-three-year-old Marie in New York on April 23, 1903.

The Truxtun Beales traveled frequently abroad and made annual visits to the Tejon. And they always made a point of being in Washington for the President's reception each year, after which the entire diplomatic corps repaired to Decatur House for a supper which became an institution in Washington society. Splendid uniforms ablaze with gold trim and decorations mingled with the sober black formal garb worn by members of Congress, Cabinet and Supreme Court. Ladies in dazzling silks, satins, and sparkling jewels gave the old drawing rooms the brilliance they had known under Truxtun's parents.

In her *Adventures of a Novelist,* Gertrude Atherton related that she was a friend of Trux and Marie, and Marie was one of the handsomest and most popular women in Washington.

The Beales were frequent guests at Friendship House, the home of Truxtun's niece, Evalyn Walsh McLean. They were often entertained at 1747 Drode Island Avenue, too, at the house which a grateful nation presented to Admiral George Dewey, hero of the Spanish-American War. The Admiral was a brother-in-law of Truxtun's sister, Emily Beale McLean.

On the night of June 25, 1906, Truxtun and Marie were dinner guests of fellow socialite Harry Kendall Thaw and his actress wife, Evalyn Nesbit, "The Girl on the Red Velvet Swing." The party took place on the roof terrace of recently completed Madison Square Garden in New York, a project of socially prominent architect Stanford White. Thaw suspected

White of having an affair with Evalyn Nesbit. When the architect put in an appearance, Harry excused himself from the
table. A shot rang out. Thaw returned to the table with a
smoking pistol in his hand and requested Trux to "please
see Evalyn home. I've just shot Stanford White."

The police took Harry Thaw into custody. To seek counsel
for his defense, Trux left at once for San Francisco where
he engaged Delphin Michael Delmas, "the Napoleon of the
bar," foremost criminal lawyer in the nation. The trial proved
a sensation. The murder of Stanford White had been deliberate, committed before many witnesses, yet Delmas so swayed
the jury that it brought in a verdict of not guilty by reason
of insanity. The court committed Thaw to Mattewan Sanitarium. Evalyn Walsh McLean wrote, "Uncle Trux never came
back across the Rockies until the trial was over and the Pitts-
burg playboy, Harry Thaw, was safely in an asylum."

Edward Beale (Ned) McLean, the spoiled and pampered
scion of a tremendously wealthy family, aped his Uncle Trux
as a *bon vivant*. At age twenty-three, in 1909, he married
Evalyn Walsh, daughter of Colorado mining tycoon Thomas
F. Walsh. As wedding gifts each family presented the newly-
weds with $100,000 and, incredible as it seems, the couple
managed to spend the entire $200,000 on their European
honeymoon.

A visitor arrived at the Tejon Ranch in 1911. The conversation that took place on the grapevine-covered patio of the
old Beale adobe marked a turning point in Truxtun's life.
The visitor, Harry Chandler, expressed interest in acquiring
Ranchos El Tejon. He caught Trux in a receptive mood.
Chandler represented a group of Los Angeles businessmen
which included his father-in-law, General Harrison Gray Otis,
co-founder of the *Los Angeles Times*. Negotiations led to a
purchase price of $3 million for 270,000 acres and 15,000
head of cattle. Trux accepted $1.5 million in gold and assumed
a mortgage for the balance. Thus ended more than half a
century ownership of Ranchos El Tejon by the Beale family.

For a time Truxtun occupied himself assembling his father's

papers for an "official" biography, engaging writer Stephen Bonsal of Bedford, New York, to prepare the text. The book, *Edward Fitzgerald Beale, A Pioneer in the Path of Empire,* published in 1912, is largely a loose compilation of accessible government reports, published stories and certain correspondence. Bonsal, apparently not hired to do more than edit material handed to him by Trux, reveals little about Edward Beale beyond the provided resources.

When Truxtun's son, Walker Blaine Beale became twenty-one in 1917, his mother made him a gift of Blaine House in Augusta, Maine. He didn't live to enjoy its possession, however. In September of 1918 Evalyn Walsh McLean received a cablegram signed by General John J. Pershing and forwarded by Secretary of War Newton Baker stating:

> ... on September 18, 1918, Lieutenant Walker Blaine Beale, Company "I," 310th Infantry, died of wounds received in action on that date and was buried in the military cemetery of Commune Euvezin, Department Meurthe-et-Moselle.

"Mine was a ghastly job," Evalyn remembered. "I had to break the news to Uncle Truxtun and Aunt Harriett."

Edward Beale's camels were paid final tribute in 1935 "to commemorate a strange experiment Uncle Sam made just before the Civil War." The Los Angeles *Evening Herald and Express* for November 4 carried the story:

> In 1857 the Camel Mail between Fort Tejon and the little settlement of Los Angeles was a regular thing. A weird procession of camels supplied by Hollywood movie studios started today from Fort Tejon. over the modern roads that have replaced the old winding trail surveyed by Lieutenant Beale, the Camel Mail swung along. Tomorrow the Arabic beasts of burden are to deliver their cargo to Postmaster H. B. R. Briggs at Hollywood . . .

On June 2, 1936, the Reverend W. A. R. Goodwin of Old Bruton Parish Church in Williamsburg, Virginia, received a wire: "Truxtun Beale died today." Truxtun's last resting place in the old churchyard is marked by a large, flat stone bearing the Beale coat of arms and an inscription:

TRUXTUN BEALE
BORN MARCH 6, 1856 DIED JUNE 2, 1936
A DIRECT DESCENDANT OF LT. COL.
THE HONORABLE THOMAS BEALE
EMIGRANT FROM ENGLAND 1640
MEMBER OF THE COUNCIL OF VIRGINIA 1662
VESTRYMAN OF BRUTON PARISH 1684

The *non sequitur* epitaph remembers Truxtun Beale only as a remote descendant of Vestryman Thomas Beale, but one must understand that in Virginia that sort of thing often outweighs other considerations.

In 1936 Ranchos El Tejon became the Tejon Ranch Company, incorporated at a value of $20 million — land for which Edward Beale had originally paid less than $90,000.

An earthquake destroyed the Beale Memorial Library in Bakersfield in 1955. Now there is a new Kern County Library with one section named the Beale Memorial Wing. In its vault rests the memorial plaque, returned to the library for safe keeping after Truxtun's death. On public display in the wing is a bronze bust of Edward Beale, the work of sculptor Robert Hinckley. An identical likeness reposes in Headquarters Building 2400 at Beale Air Force Base near Marysville, California.

The World War II years saw heightened activity at Decatur House, where Marie Chase Oge Beale sponsored relief campaigns for England, France, Italy and Greece. She donated a "Truxtun Unit" to the British-American Ambulance Corps and headed a benefit for the Royal Air Force. She subsequently became involved in many similar activities.

Many buildings that once surrounded Lafayette Square were gone. St. John's remained as the city's principal, if not its largest, church. Dolly Madison's residence had been made into a clubhouse. Gone were the residence of James G. Blaine, Corcoran's mansion, and the double structure of Henry Adams and John Hay. The Blair house remained, just off the square, as the official hostel for distinguished guests of the government.

Marie wrote that Decatur House belonged to history. It

QUARTERDECK AND SADDLEHORN

had been the very first private residence on Lafayette Square and would now become the last. She said she inherited the responsibility of bringing its historic career to a graceful close.

Congress passed the Historic Sites Act in 1935, declaring a national policy to preserve historic sites and buildings. The Department of the Interior began a survey of such places to determine their importance. Decatur House was included in the Historic American Buildings Survey and deemed "worthy of most careful preservation for the benefit of future generations."

Marie undertook the restoration of portions of the exterior and interior furnishings to early 19th century designs. She leased the carriage house to the Naval Historical Foundation for one dollar per year, and the Truxtun-Decatur Naval Museum opened its doors in that building on May 12, 1950.

Marie died in Zurich, Switzerland, while traveling to Greece on June 11, 1956, and her cremated remains were interred next to Truxtun in Old Bruton Parish Churchyard. Having no immediate descendants, Marie had bequeathed Decatur House, and a trust fund for its maintenance, to the National Trust for Historic Preservation in 1954. The headquarters for the National Trust are located on the third floor of Decatur House. She wrote at that time, "I have bequeathed Decatur House to future generations as a national monument."

Edward Beale once wrote to his wife from the wilds of northern Arizona in the dead of winter expressing a strong and rather poignant hope that his deeds would count for something, that he would be remembered in the history of the vast Western country he knew so well after his alloted time on this earth had expired.

Beale, as it turned out, left a more lasting legacy in a greater number of places than he dreamed at the time. But his symbolic mark on this land is perhaps nowhere more indelibly exemplified than in the foursquare structure of his home — sturdy, dignified, timeless Decatur House.

Bibliography

Albright, George Leslie. *Official Exploration for Pacific Railroads, 1853-55*. Berkeley: Univ. of Calif. Press, 1921.

Alward, Dennis M., and Rolle, Andrew F. "Surveyor General Edward F. Beale's Administration of California Lands." Los Angeles: *Southern Calif. Qtly.*, June 1971.

Austrian National Archives. E. F. Beale file. Vienna.

Bailey, Paul. *Sam Brannan and the California Mormons*. Los Angeles: Westernlore Press, 1953.

Bain, Naomi E. *The Story of Colonel Thomas Baker and the Founding of Bakersfield*. Bakersfield: Kern Co. Hist. Soc., 1944.

Barry, T. A., and Patten, B. A. *Men and Memories of San Francisco in the Spring of '50*. San Francisco: A. L. Bancroft & Co., 1873.

Beale, Edward Fitzgerald. "Report of Survey of the Wagon Road from Fort Defiance to the Colorado." House Ex. Doc. 124, May 10, 1858.

———. "The Wagon Road from Fort Smith to the Colorado." House Ex. Doc. 42, Dec. 4, 1860.

———. "Exporting Arms to Mexico." Bancroft Library, 1864.

———. "Autobiographical Sketch." Bancroft Library, 1885.

Beale, Marie Chase Oge. *Decatur House and Its Inhabitants*. Washington, D.C: National Trust for Hist. Preservation, 1954.

Beale, Mary Edwards. "Autobiographical Sketch." Bancroft Lby., 1885.

Benton, Thomas Hart. Papers and Speeches in the Senate, 1849-1853.

Bieber, Ralph P. "Early News of the Gold Discovery." *Southern Trails to California in 1849*. Glendale: Arthur H. Clark Co., 1937.

Blair, Gist. *Lafayette Square*. Washington, D.C: Columbia Hist. Soc., 1936.

Bonsal, Stephen. *Edward Fitzgerald Beale, A Pioneer in the Path of Empire*. New York: G. P. Putnam's Sons, 1912.

Bowman, Eldon G., and Smith, Jack. *Beale's Road Through Arizona*. Flagstaff: The Westerners, 1979.

Brack, Gene M. *Mexico Views Manifest Destiny, 1821-1846*. Albuquerque: Univ. of N.M. Press, 1975.

Browne, J. Ross. *A Western Panorama, 1849-1875.* Glendale: Arthur H. Clark Co., 1966.

Browne, Lina Fergusson. *J. Ross Browne, His Letters, Journals and Writings.* Albuquerque: Univ. of N.M. Press, 1969.

Buchanan, James. Letter to Colonel Samuel C. Stanbaugh, 1836. Catalog 72, Kenneth W. Rendall, Inc., Somerville, Massachusetts.

Burdett, Charles. *The Life of Kit Carson.* New York: A. L. Burt Co., 1902.

Cagle, Malcolm W. "Lieutenant David Dixon Porter and His Camels." U. S. Naval Inst. Proc: Dec. 1957.

California Division of Mines. Geologic Guidebooks: "The Mother Lode Country." San Francisco, 1948. "San Francisco Bay Counties." San Francisco, 1951.

California Historical Society. Articles in *Quarterly* issues. "Edward F. Beale"; "Battle of San Pasqual"; "Camels and Rancho El Tejon"; "Gillespie and the Conquest of California"; "The International Boundary Survey, 1849-50"; and others.

California State Archives. Official E. F. Beale Documents: Indian Wars File; California State Land Commission Records. Sacramento.

Camp, Charles L. *Kit Carson in California.* San Francisco: California Historical Society, 1936.

Carter, Harvey Lewis. *Dear Old Kit, The Historical Christopher Carson.* Norman: Univ. of Okla. Press, 1968.

Casebier, Dennis G. *Carleton's Pah-Ute Campaign; Fort Pah-Ute, California; The Mojave Road.* Norco: Tales of the Mojave Road Pub. Co., 1972-75.

Chaput, Donald. *Francois X. Aubry: Trader, Trailmaker, and Voyageur in the Southwest, 1846-1854.* Glendale: Arthur H. Clark Co., 1975.

Clark, C. Raymond. *Quarterdecks and Spanish Grants.* Felton: Glenwood Pubs., 1971.

Clarke, Dwight L. *The Original Journals of Henry Smith Turner.* Norman: Univ. of Okla. Press, 1966.

———. *Stephen Watts Kearny, Soldier of the West.* Norman: Univ. of Okla. Press, 1966.

Cleland, Robert Glass. *From Wilderness to Empire.* New York: Alfred Knopf, 1944.

———. *California In Our Time.* New York: Alfred Knopf, 1947.

———. *This Reckless Breed of Men.* New York: Alfred Knopf, 1950.

Colton, Walter. *Deck and Port: Or, Incidents of a Cruise in the United States Frigate Congress to California.* New York: A. S. Barnes and Burr, 1860.

———. *My Three Years In California*. New York: A. S. Barnes & Co., 1851.

Couts, Cave Johnson. *Hepah, California! From Monterrey, Mexico, to Los Angeles, 1848-49*. Tucson: Arizona Pioneer Hist. Soc., 1961.

Craven, Tunis Augustus MacDonough. *A Naval Campaign in the Californias, 1846-49*. San Francisco: The Book Club of Calif., 1973.

Crouter, Richard E., and Rolle, Andrew F. "Edward Fitzgerald Beale and the Indian Peace Commissioners in California, 1851-54." Hist. Soc. of So. Calif. *Qtly.*, 1960.

Crowe, Earl. *General Beale's Sheep Odyssey*. Bakersfield: Kern Co. Hist. Soc., 1960.

———. *Men of El Tejon, Empire in the Tehachapis*. Los Angeles: Ward Ritchie Press, 1947.

Cullimore, Clarence. *Old Adobes of Forgotten Fort Tejon*. Bakersfield: Kern Co. Hist. Soc., 1941.

Dana, Richard Henry. *Two Years Before the Mast*. Los Angeles: Ward Ritchie Press, 1964.

Davis, William Heath. *Seventy-Five Years in California*. San Francisco: John Howell, 1929.

Delaware Co. Hist. Soc., Chester, Penn. Beale file.

Dillon, Richard. *J. Ross Browne: Confidential Agent in Old California*. Norman: Univ. of Okla. Press, 1965.

———. *Burnt-Out Fires. California Modoc Indian War*. New York: Prentice-Hall, 1973.

Downey, Joseph T. *The Cruise of the Portsmouth, 1845-47*. New Haven: Yale Univ. Press, 1958.

———. *Filings From An Old Saw*. San Francisco: John Howell, 1956.

Duvall, Marius. *A Navy Surgeon in California, 1846-47*. San Francisco: John Howell, 1957.

Dwinelle, John W. *The Colonial History of the City of San Francisco*. San Francisco: Towne and Bacon, 1866.

Egan, Ferol. *The El Dorado Trail*. New York: McGraw-Hill Book Co., 1970.

———. *Fremont, Explorer for a Restless Nation*. New York: Garden City, 1977.

Ellison, Joseph. *Sentiment for a Pacific Republic*. Los Angeles: McBride Pntg. Co., 1929.

Emmett, Chris. *Texas Camel Tales*. Texas: Steck-Vaughn Co., 1969.

Emory, William Hemsley. "A Military Reconnaissance From Fort Leavenworth to San Diego, 1846-47." House Ex. Doc. 41, 30th Cong.

Farquhar, Francis P. "Camels in the Sketches of Edward Vischer." San Francisco: Calif. Hist. Soc. *Qtly.*, 1930.

Faulk, Odie P. *The U. S. Camel Corps: An Army Experiment.* New York: Oxford Univ. Press, 1976.

Floyd, William P. "Diary of a Journey with Beale's Wagon Road Expedition, 1858-59." Orig. ms. Huntington Lby., San Marino.

Foreman, Grant. *A Pathfinder in the Southwest.* Norman: Univ. of Okla. Press, 1941.

———. *Marcy & The Goldseekers.* Norman: Univ. of Okla. Press, 1939.

Fowler, Harlan D. *Camels to California.* Stanford: Stanford Univ. Press, 1950.

———. *Three Caravans to Yuma.* Glendale: Arthur H. Clark Co., 1980.

Fremont, Elizabeth Benton. *Recollections by Daughter of the Pathfinder.* New York: Frederick H. Hitchcock, 1912.

Fremont, Jessie Benton. *A Year of American Travel; A Narrative of Personal Experience.* San Francisco: Book Club of Calif., 1960.

———. "Kit Carson: An Interview With Jessie Benton Fremont." *The Land of Sunshine.* Vol. 6. No. 3. Los Angeles: Feb., 1897.

Fremont, John Charles. *Memoirs of My Life.* New York: Belford Clark & Co., 1887.

———. *Narratives of Exploration and Adventure.* New York: Longmans, Green & Co., 1956.

———. *Defense of Lt. Col. J. C. Fremont.* Washington: Jan., 1848.

Fremont Court-Martial. "Proceedings of the Court-Martial." Washington: April 7, 1848.

Gates, Paul W. "The California Land Act of 1851." San Francisco: Calif. Hist. Soc. *Qtly.*, Dec. 1971.

Ghent, W. J. "Kit Carson." *Dictionary of American Biography.* Vol. III. New York, 1939.

Gideon, J. and G. S. *General Regulations for the Navy and Marine Corps.* Washington: 1841.

Giffin, Helen S., and Woodward, Arthur. *The Story of El Tejon.* Los Angeles: 1942.

Goetzman, William H. *Army Exploration in the American West, 1803-1863.* New Haven: Yale Univ. Press, 1959.

Grant, Blanche C. *Kit Carson's Own Story of His Life.* Taos: 1926.

Grant, Ulysses S. *Personal Memoirs.* New York: Charles L. Webster Co., 1885.

Gray, Arthur A. "Camels in California." San Francisco: Calif. Hist. Soc. *Qtly.*, Dec. 1930.

Greenly, A. H. "More Light on the Original Bear Flag of California." North American Vexillological Assoc., Winchester, Mass: 1953.

Griffin, John S. *A Doctor Comes to California*. San Francisco: Calif. Hist. Soc., 1943.

Grimshaw, William R. *Grimshaw's Narrative*. Sacramento: Sacramento Book Club, 1964.

Hall, Frederic. *The Laws of Mexico*. San Francisco: 1885.

Halleck, Henry Wager. *The Mexican War in Baja California, 1846-1848*. Ed. by Doyce B. Nunnis, Jr. Los Angeles: Dawson's Book Shop, 1977.

Hamilton, Andrew. "Beale: He Won The Gold Dust Derby." U. S. Naval Inst. Proc: Sept. 1949.

Hamlin, Teunis S. *Historic Houses of Washington*. 1893.

Harding, Bertita. *Maximilian and Carlota*. Mexico: 1960.

Harlow, Alvin F. *Old Waybills; The Romance of the Express Companies*. New York: D. Appleton-Century Co., 1934.

Hasse, Adelaide R. *Index to the Documents of the State of California, 1849-1904*. Washington: Carnegie Inst., 1908.

Hayes, Benjamin. *Diaries, 1849-1875*. Los Angeles, 1929.

Heap, Gwinn Harris. *Central Route to the Pacific. Journal of the Expedition of E. F. Beale, 1853*. Phila: Lippincott, Grambo & Co., 1854.

Heitman, Francis C. *Historical Register and Dictionary of the U. S. Army*. Washington: G.P.O., 1903.

Henry, Robert Selph. *The Story of the Mexican War*. New York: Frederick Ungar Pub. Co., 1950.

Hodges, Frances Beal Smith. *The Genealogy of the Beale Family, 1399-1956*. Ann Arbor: Edwards Brothers, 1956.

Hunt, Aurora. *The Army of the Pacific, 1860-66*. Glendale: Arthur H. Clark Co., 1951.

Hunt, Rockwell D. *California and Californians*. New York: Lewis Pub. Co., 1926.

Hunter, J. Marvin. *Old Camp Verde, The Home of the Camels*. Bandera, Texas: Frontier Times, 1936.

Ingersoll, Ernest. *Crest of the Continent*. Chicago: R. R. Donnelley & Sons, 1885.

Jackson, Donald, and Spence, Mary Lee. *The Expeditions of John Charles Fremont*. Urbana: Univ. of Ill. Press, 1971.

Jackson, W. Turrentine. *Wagon Roads West*. New Haven: Yale Univ. Press, 1952.

Johnson, Kenneth M. *K-344, Or The Indians of California Vs. the United States*. Los Angeles: Dawson's Book Shop, 1966.

Jones, William Carey. "Land Titles in California." Ex. Doc. 18. Washington, D.C., 1851.

Kappler, Charles J. *Indian Affairs; Laws and Treaties.* Washington, D.C: 1929.

Kemble, John Haskell. *The Genesis of the Pacific Mail Steamship Company.* Berkeley: Univ. of Calif. Press, 1934.

———. *The Panama Route.* Berkeley: Univ. of Calif. Press, 1943.

Knox, Dudley W. *Naval Sketches of the War in California.* New York: Random House, 1939.

Latta, Frank F. *Saga of Rancho El Tejon.* Santa Cruz: Bear State Books, 1976.

Lavender, David. *The Rockies.* New York: Harper & Row, 1968.

Lesley, Lewis Burt. *Uncle Sam's Camels. The Journal of May Humphreys Stacey and Report of Edward Fitzgerald Beale, 1857-58.* Cambridge: Harvard Univ. Press, 1929.

Lewis, Oscar. *Sea Routes to the Gold Fields.* New York: Alfred Knopf, 1949.

———. *The War in the West.* New York: Doubleday & Co., 1916.

Lingenfelter, Richard E. *Steamboats on the Colorado River, 1852-1916.* Tucson: Univ. of Ariz. Press, 1978.

Lovette, Leland P. "Naval Customs, Traditions and Usage." U. S. Naval Inst. Proc., 1939.

Luce, Stephen B. "U. S. Navy Training Ships." *United States Mag.,* U. S. Hist. Foun: Washington, D.C.

MacKensie, A. S. *Life of Stephen Decatur.* Boston: Charles C. Little and James Brown, 1846.

Marsh, George P. *The Camel.* Boston: Gould and Lincoln, 1856.

Mason, Jack, with Park, Helen Van Cleve. *Early Marin.* Petaluma: House of Printing, 1971.

McLane, Louis. *The Private Journal of Louis McLane.* Los Angeles: Dawson's Book Shop, 1971.

McLean, Evalyn Walsh. *Father Struck it Rich.* Boston: Little, Brown & Company, 1936.

Miner, H. Craig. *The St. Louis-San Francisco Transcontinental Railroad.* Lawrence: Univ. of Kan. Press, 1972.

National Archives, and Records Service, General Services Administration. Nine microfilm reels of Beale Documents and "The Decatur House Papers." Washington, D.C.

Nevins, Allan. *Fremont, Pathmarker of the West.* New York: D. Appleton-Century Co., 1939.

Nordhoff, Charles. *California*. New York: Harper & Brothers, 1872.

Nunis, Doyce B. *The San Francisco Vigilance Committee of 1856*. Los Angeles: Westerners, 1971.

O'Meara, James. *The Vigilance Committee of 1856*. San Francisco: James H. Barry, 1887.

Paul, Rodman W. *California Gold: The Beginning of Mining in the Far West*. (New edition.) Lincoln: Univ. of Neb. Press, 1965.

Peters, Dewitt C. *Kit Carson's Life and Adventures*. San Francisco: Frances Dewing & Co., 1874.

Pitt, Leonard. *The Decline of the Californios*. Berkeley: Univ. of Calif. Press, 1966.

Polk, James Knox. *The Diary of James K. Polk During His Presidency, 1845-49*. Ed. by Milo M. Quaife. Chicago: A. C. McClurg, 1910.

Porter, David Dixon. *Memoirs of Commodore David Dixon Porter*. 1875.

Rather, Lois. *Jessie Fremont at Black Point*. Oakland: The Rather Press, 1974.

Rensch, Hero Eugene, and Hoover, Mildred Brooks. *Historic Spots in California*. Stanford: Stanford Univ. Press, 1966.

Revere, Joseph Warren. *A Tour of Duty in California*. New York: C. S. Francis & Co., 1849.

————. *Keel and Saddle*. Boston: James R. Osgood and Co., 1872.

Robbins, Millie. *Dromedaries? In Benicia?* San Francisco: San Francisco Chronicle Books, 1967.

Robinson, W. W. *Land in California*. Berkeley: Univ. of Calif. Press, 1948.

Sacks, B. *Be It Enacted: The Creation of the Territory of Arizona*. Phoenix: Ariz. Hist. Foun., 1964.

Schultz, John Ritchie. *The Unpublished Letters of Bayard Taylor*. San Marino: Huntington Lby., 1937.

Scott, Reva. *Sam Brannan and the Golden Fleece*. New York: Macmillan Co., 1946.

Secretary of the Navy. Report of Commodore Stockton's Dispatches. Washington, D.C: Feb. 16, 1849.

Secretary of War. Report Respecting the Purchase of Camels for the Purpose of Military Transportation. Ex. Doc. 62. Washington, D.C: 1857.

Sherman, Edwin A. *Life of Rear Admiral John Drake Sloat*. Oakland: Carruth & Carruth, 1902.

Sitgreaves, Lorenzo. "Report of an Expedition Down the Zuñi and Colorado Rivers." 32nd Congress. Sen. Ex. Doc. 59. Washington, D.C: 1853.

Smythe, William E. *History of San Diego*. San Diego: The History Co., 1908.

Soule, Frank. *The Annals of San Francisco*. New York: D. Appleton & Co., 1855.

State Printer. "The Use of Camels on The Plains." Sacramento: Sen. Doc. 24: 1855.

Stellman, Louis John. *Sam Brannan, Builder of San Francisco*. New York: Exposition Press, 1954.

Stewart, George R. *Committee of Vigilance; Revolution in San Francisco, 1851*. Boston: Houghton Mifflin, 1964.

Stockton, Robert Field. *Defense of Col. J. C. Fremont. Speeches in the Senate*. New York: Derby & Jackson, 1856.

Stull, John C. "The Last Pathfinder; General Edward F. Beale." U. S. Naval Inst. Proc., Feb. 1966.

Summerhayes, Martha. *Vanished Arizona. Recollections of My Army Life*. New York: J. B. Lippincott, 1963.

Sutter, John A., Jr. *Statement Regarding Early California Experiences*. Sacramento: Sacramento Book Coll. Club, 1943.

Taylor, Bayard. *Eldorado. Adventures in the Path of Empire*. New York: George F. Putnam, 1850.

Terrell, John Upton. *The Six Turnings. Major Changes in the American West*. Glendale: Arthur H. Clark Co., 1968.

Thompson, Gerald Eugene. "The Public Career of Edward Fitzgerald Beale, 1845-1893." Ph.D. diss: Univ. of Ariz., 1978.

Thompson, Erwin N. *Modoc War*. Sacramento: Argus Books, 1971.

Turner, Henry Smith. *Letters of Captain Henry S. Turner*. Los Angeles: Cole-Holmquist Press, 1958.

Upham, Charles Wentworth. *Life of John Charles Fremont*. Boston: Ticknor & Fields, 1856.

Wadsworth, W. *The National Wagon Road Guide*. San Francisco: Whitten, Towne & Co., 1858.

Wagner, Henry R., and Camp, Charles L. *The Plains and The Rockies, A Bibliography of Original Narratives of Travel, Exploration and Adventure, 1800-1865*. (Fourth ed. ms., author's library.)

Wagoner, Jay J. *Early Arizona, Prehistory to Civil War*. Tucson: Univ. of Ariz. Press, 1975.

Wallace, Edward S. *The Great Reconnaissance*. Boston: Little, Brown and Co., 1955.

Walpole, Frederick. *Four Years in the Pacific*. London: R. Bentley, 1849.

Wells, Evalyn. *Champagne Days of San Francisco*. New York: Doubleday & Co., 1947.

Wells Fargo History Room. Louis McLane Collection. San Francisco.

Wheat, Carl I. *Mapping The Trans-Mississippi West, 1540-1861*. San Francisco: Inst. of Hist. Cartography, 1963.

————. *The Shirley Letters from the California Mines, 1851-1852*. New York: Alfred Knopf, 1949.

Willey, Samuel Hopkins. *California's Transition Period; 1846-1850*. San Francisco: Whitaker & Ray Co., 1901.

Wilstach, Paul. *Tidewater Virginia*. New York: Baker & Scribner, 1849.

Wiltsee, Ernest A. *The Pioneer Miner and the Pack-Mule Express*. San Francisco: Calif. Hist. Soc., 1936.

Wise, Henry Augustus. *Los Gringos*. New York: Baker & Scribner, 1849.

Wood, William Maxwell. *Wandering Sketches of People and Things*. Philadelphia, 1849.

Woodward, Arthur. *Feud on The Colorado*. Los Angeles: Westernlore Press, 1955.

————. *Lances at San Pasqual*. San Francisco: Calif. Hist. Soc., 1945.

Wright, George W. "History, Life and Indian Affairs of the San Joaquin Valley in the Early '50s." Ms., Calif. Hist. Soc., 1852.

Index

Little Axe (Pawnee Indian) : 216
Little Salt Lake Valley (UT) : 150
Livingston, Lt. John W: 70
Lloyd's Coffee House: 255
Lodge, Henry Cabot (Sen.) : 275
Loeser, Lt. Lucien: 96-97
Lopez, Francisco: 170
Lopez, Jose Jesus: 253, 255, 266, 270, 274
Lorenzo Castle (Panama) : 23
Loring, Col. William W: 201
Los Angeles: 31, 35, 37; under siege by
  Flores, 42-45; 47, 55, 58, 64-65, 69-70;
  Americans enter, 75-76; US Navy
  leaves, 78-80; 151-52, 156-58, 165, 171,
  190; camels arrive, 208-09; 258-60,
  266, 280
Los Angeles Co: 182, 237, 247-49
Los Angeles newspapers: *Evening Her-
  ald,* 280; *Star,* 209-26; *Southern News,*
  236; *Times,* 279
Loudon Park Cemetery (MD) : 275
Lower California: *see* Baja California
Lugo, Jose del Carmen: 118

McClellan, Capt. George B: 187, 244
McClelland: 136, 139
McDougal, John: 127-29, 161
McFeely, Joe: 200
McKee, Redick: 127-29, 136, 162
McKenzie, David: 169
McLane, Louis: 31, 49
McLean, Emily Beale: 277-78
McLean, Evalyn Walsh: 278-80
McLean, John (Justice) : 256
McLean, John Roll: 256, 268, 277
McLenegham, Samuel: 196, 250
HMS *Macedonian:* 28
Machado, Rafael: 51, 54-55, 65
Madison Co. (KY) : 43
Madison, Dolly: 281
Madrid, Gregorio: 140
Mansfield, Gen. Joseph K. F: 171
Manypenny, George W: 155-56, 158-64,
  166-68
Mare Isl. (CA) : 46
Maria (brig) : 19, 21, 24
Marin Co. (CA) : 134, 277
Mariposa Battalion: 129
Mariposa Co. (CA) : 129
Mariposa Indians: 122
Mariposa Ranch ("Las Mariposas") : 11-
  12; mining activity, 118-21; 160, 230
Marshall, James W: 88
Martinez (CA) : 133
Maryland: 117, 243
Mason, John Y: 28, 85
Mason, Col. Richard B: 96-97, 99, 238
Massachusetts: 225
Matamoros: 27

Mattewan Sanitarium: 279
Maximilian, Emperor: 241, 245, 261-62
Maxwell, Dr. Charles D: 64
Mazatlan: 23, 28-30, 37, 92, 110, 118
Media (PA) : 247
Merced River (CA) : 112, 127
Mervine, Capt. William: 30, 37, 46-50,
  70
Mesa, Ramon: 133
Mexican land grant: 160, 163, 169-70,
  236
Mexican bandits: 94-95
Mexico: 12, 18, 21, 22-23, 27, 44; occu-
  pation duty, 91-93; 109, 112, 114, 119,
  125, 197, 240-45, 261
Mexico City: 37, 89, 94-96
Micheltorena: 169
Miller, "Joaquin" (poet) : 256-57
Minnesota: 22
Minor, Lt. George: 71
Misroon, Lt: 63
Missions: San Buenaventura, 251; San
  Diego de Alcala, 54, 71; San Fernan-
  do, 78, 247; San Gabriel Archangel,
  71; San Jose de Guadalupe, 112; San
  Juan Capistrano, 71-72; San Luis Rey
  de Francia, 71-72
Mississippi: 187
Mississippi River: 96, 155, 193
Missouri: 22, 128, 155, 212, 219
Missouri River: 22, 98, 139
Mobile (AL) : 96-97
Modoc Indians: 257-58
Mohave Indians: 208, 216, 219-24
Mojave Desert: 99, 151
Mojave River (CA) : 151, 191, 199
Mojave Road: 208
Mokelumne River (CA) : 113-14
Monroe, James: 17
Monroe Doctrine: 244
Montana: 266
Montebello (CA) : 72
Monterey: 11-12, 23; flag raised at, 29-
  37; 39, 41, 44, 49, 79-80, 91, 110-12;
  constitutional convention, 116; 118,
  248, 254, 273
Monterrey (Mexico) : 112
Montgomery, Cmdr. John Barrien: 30-
  32, 34-35, 62
Moore, Capt. Benjamin D: 49, 56-58, 60,
  65
Moore, Risdon: 86
Moreno, Capt. Juan B: 57
Morgan, Henry: 23-24
Mormons: Migration, 21-22; at Hono-
  lulu, 27; 143-44, 149-50, 190
Mormon Battalion: 28, 65, 70, 72
Mormon Militia: 150
Morton, Levi P: 275